# Genius

# Genius

## How to Take Smart Ideas Global

Bruce Whitfield

MACMILLAN

First published in 2022
by Pan Macmillan South Africa
Private Bag x19
Northlands
Johannesburg
2116
www.panmacmillan.co.za

ISBN 978-1-77010-756-4
e-ISBN 978-1-77010-757-1

Editing by Sally Hines
Proofreading by Wesley Thompson
Design and typesetting by Triple M Design, Johannesburg
Cover design by publicide
Author photograph by Abigail Javier

Printed by **novus print**, a division of Novus Holdings

*For Catherine,*
*this book would not have happened without you.*

# Contents

# Contents

# Setting the Scene

*We are a scintillating success waiting to happen.*
— Desmond Tutu

There was a time when South Africa was a critical cog in the complex machinery of global commerce. By virtue of its location on the southern tip of Africa, its geography gifted the country with a role in a system of trade that shaped the modern world. The Cape of Good Hope was a strategic, life-saving, stop-off point between Europe and Asia that not only enabled global trade but also played a critical role in leapfrogging global commerce and human development.

It is hard to imagine now that South Africa ever played that role. For about 200 years, it was the halfway point to almost everywhere, thanks to its location on the most valuable trade route in the world. Europe's insatiable quest for spices drove commerce along its shores for hundreds of years. There was a time when spices were among the most valuable commodities on earth. Nutmeg, now a mere dusty sprinkle atop a rice pudding, was once worth more than its equivalent weight in gold.

The same goes for cinnamon, one of the first spices traded in the ancient world when Indonesian rafts transported it to East Africa from Sri Lanka, from where local traders then carried it north to the Roman market.

It was first the Portuguese, then the Dutch, who used the Cape of Good Hope as a stopping-off point and monopolised spice distribution for centuries. As technology improved and the world became faster and more impatient, shipping moved from sail power to steam. Journey times shortened and advancements in technologies, such as onboard refrigeration, meant what had once been an obligatory stop at the southern tip of Africa was no longer required. When the Suez Canal opened for business in 1869, South Africa lost its global relevance.

The world's interest might have ended there had it not been for the discovery of minerals. Within less than two decades, South Africa was once again the centre of global attention with the diamond rush to the northern Cape in 1870 and the discovery of the world's richest single gold deposit on the Witwatersrand in 1886. The country became a magnet for a wide range of fortune hunters, opportunists, rogues and warmongers. Those discoveries led to the creation of the most advanced economy in Africa. While they generated extraordinary wealth, they also laid the groundwork for conflict, bloodshed and a system of violent political repression.

South Africa remains the favoured entry point to the sub-Saharan region for multinationals looking to exploit the multitude of business opportunities that are presented by the continent's young, upwardly mobile and rapidly growing population. The region provides one of the most exciting consumer opportunities on the planet, and South Africa could once again become a vital link for global opportunity and expansion. But that role is by no means guaranteed as an accident-prone nation struggles to define itself in a highly competitive global environment.

The swagger South Africa demonstrated on the global stage in the first fifteen years of its young democracy, starting in 1994, is all but gone. A decade of widespread, private-sector-aided state corruption emptied the national coffers and pushed an already strained economy deeper into debt than at any other point in its long history. Tax collection plummeted amid falling business and consumer confidence. While foreign investment flows stalled, South African citizens who could afford it focused on offshoring as much of their wealth as possible, worried about the future value of the currency and wary that government might seek to nationalise private wealth.

Despite the real and legitimate worries about the future of South Africa, the country has a strong legacy of creative problem solving. In most cases, it has been country-specific, and not all ideas transcend borders. But some do, and their creators are among the finest business builders anywhere.

Ideas, like plans, are worthless without effective execution.

How often have you seen a product or come across a service and berated yourself for not developing your own similar concept?

It is much harder to execute and deliver on an idea than simply dream one up. It is one of the greatest failings in the thinking

3

around what makes entrepreneurs. The difference between them and the rest of us is that they deliver their big idea rather than waiting for the right time, the right place, the right partner or the economic climate to improve before launching.

Some of South Africa's most successful entrepreneurial ventures emerged from its darkest days: Bidvest and Nando's from 1987 as South Africa defaulted on its debt and P.W. Botha clung to power and his intransigence over entering negotiations with the then banned African National Congress (ANC) and its jailed leader, Nelson Mandela; and Discovery in 1992, around the time of South Africa teetering on the brink of civil war and a year before the assassination of South African Communist Party leader Chris Hani. The storming success of Capitec emanates from a time when a small-banks crisis took hold in the early 2000s, leading to a collapse in a vulnerable sector; its single survivor now has the biggest retail footprint of any domestic bank and its growth is outstripping that of its rivals.

Growing a business domestically is hard enough in a tough regulatory environment that is hostile to business success. Globalising that business is considerably more difficult and takes a particular kind of genius.

The reality is that the South African domestic economy provides plenty of opportunity for start-ups looking to solve the myriad problems the country faces, from basic issues, such as water and electricity provision, to security, healthcare and education. Some of these businesses are transcending the domestic environment in new and ingenious ways.

Not all succeed, but many do. There is a new generation of

young business leaders cutting their teeth on solving problems locally, whether it be creating the perfect coffee experience, finding sustainable models for health insurance, developing vaccinology or utilising raw materials that the country has in abundance to build leading enterprises.

This book is about some of those renegades; the problem solvers who have identified systems and processes that they have refined domestically before the challenging exercise of going global.

So much of our daily lives is focused on the noise of the day's political news and the failure of politicians to do their jobs that we stop paying attention to what is really important.

We tend to ignore the genius of the problem solvers and focus most intently on the stuff that frightens us.

That is, of course, human nature. We instinctively seek out information about danger, as it tells us what to avoid – it is an inbuilt survival instinct. And, because the 24-hour news cycle requires events and outrage to attract eyeballs, those best at hijacking it to get attention for their causes increasingly create drama for the cameras.

News is an enormous availability machine. Stories do not make it to the top of the agenda because they are important – they get there because they are available. In the world of television news, the more spectacular the footage, the bigger the outrage, the more likely it is to get extended airtime.

There is a very good reason to host a noisy protest outside parliament in the hour ahead of a State of the Nation Address, as there will generally be nothing happening beyond a few talking heads pontificating about something that has already been talked to death for days in the run-up to the event.

Give the editors an excuse to switch to a protest, some tear gas and a couple of stun grenades, throw in some shouty politicians, and it does not really matter what it is about, it is more compelling than the dirge that was there.

And we fall for it every time.

South Africa has a remarkable independent media, without which we would not have seen the Gupta Leaks and a host of other critical exposés that changed the course of history for the better.

Without the diligence of a handful of remarkable reporters, we would not have had the Zondo Commission of Inquiry into Allegations of State Capture or a host of other inquiries and trials that will come.

On a day-to-day basis, however, the hungry news machine is fed with a mix of distraction and obfuscation desperate to draw attention away from the real issues with which the country must contend.

This is not helped by social media agendas and the industrial-scale manipulation of truth that is willingly spread by users of platforms such as Instagram, Facebook and Twitter every day. Outrage spreads faster than fact.

There is little room for context and explanation. While newsrooms do cover events speedily and well, they are so busy doing that, that they are unable to zoom out and construct a more holistic view of the world.

In the midst of all of that noise, there are thousands of people hustling daily for survival, desperately working to put food on the table and finding ingenious ways of doing so. There is also a remarkable cohort of builders and creators who simply get on with the job of building great enterprises of the future.

They have one remarkable shared skill. As Israeli academic and author of *Sapiens*, Yuval Noah Harari puts it: 'Today, having power means knowing what to ignore.'

At no point in human history has so much worthless information been created by so many for mass consumption. The one attribute that the most successful entrepreneurs I have had the privilege of meeting over nearly two-and-a-half decades share is the ability not to ignore bad news and danger but to scythe through the irrelevant and the distractions. It is a rare but powerful skill and enables the focus that is needed to resolve real problems.

Information is power, and focusing on what matters and not what is loudest is what sets winners apart from the rest.

Long-serving National Treasury official Ismail Momoniat told the Zondo Commission in an affidavit that the economic gains achieved from 1994 to 2008 were reversed during the years of the Jacob Zuma presidency, resulting in critical economic indicators regressing to levels worse than those inherited at the dawn of democracy.

Faith in the future of the country has all but evaporated. The ever-present and pervasive sense of doom and gloom, brought by divisive politics and underpinned by the country's very real societal fractures, deepened in July 2021 when a series of protests spilled over into eight days of unfettered looting and violence. The protests were ostensibly about the jailing of Zuma for contempt of court over his refusal to give evidence at the Zondo Commission. The unrest cost more than R50 billion in damages and did incalculable harm to the national psyche.

What was worse than the violence itself was the failure of the authorities to respond in the early stages of the looting and in its aftermath, as well as the apparent unwillingness to round up some very obvious instigators. Less than six months later, parliament in Cape Town was gutted in a devastating fire, the precise cause of which at the time of writing is still to be determined. Early investigations pinned blame on a man who prosecutors claimed had accessed parliament and evaded security systems, possibly for days, before starting the fire.

Whatever sparked the fire is a moot point; what is more concerning is just how inept the state had become in protecting not only a national key point but also the very symbol and engine room of democracy itself. Like the uprising in KwaZulu-Natal and Gauteng in July 2021, parliament was a tinder-box that simply needed a spark to start a conflagration.

South Africa needs a shared vision of the future around which to coalesce. It needs to be less about promising the equivalent of the mythical city of Wakanda, made famous in the Marvel movie *Black Panther*, and more about creating an environment in which the smartest members of society can provide opportunities for others through their entrepreneurial ventures.

We need a plan. Urgently. As one of ice hockey's greatest-ever players, Wayne Gretzky, put it when he was asked to explain his success: 'I skate where the puck is going to be, not where it has been.'

Believe it or not, South Africa's National Development Plan (NDP) still exists. It has been relegated to a convenient afterthought at the end of turgid political speeches and its logo was on your vaccination certificate. Beyond that, there is little evidence that the thinking contained in the plan is being applied in any meaningful manner.

Rwanda's Vision 2050 sets a new pathway that it anticipates will guide the country to the living standards of upper-middle income by 2035 and high-income by 2050. Vision 2050 has the overarching objectives of promoting economic growth and prosperity and a high quality of life for Rwandans under the banner 'The Rwanda We Want'. There is much for which one can criticise Rwanda and its president, Paul Kagame, but a lack of ambition for his country is not one of them.

According to the Organisation for Economic Co-operation and Development, a growing number of countries are adopting strategic long-term plans. Austria, for example, integrates time frames so that ministries are forced to collaborate. In Germany, there is broad political consensus in parliament and across main political parties on the importance of strategic development goals and sustainable development. The first management rule of Germany's Sustainable Development Strategy includes the concept of intergenerational fairness, which ensures that those in power do not simply take care of their own interests but have to make decisions that benefit future generations. Greece has a permanent structure in place to ensure that planning happens regardless of who is in power. Among many other countries, in 2018, the Irish government adopted an overarching policy initiative with a medium- to long-term vision of sustainable development called Project Ireland 2040. In 2016, the government in Japan established the Sustainable Development Goals Promotion Headquarters to ensure long-term political support.

When the Ukraine prime minister, former stand-up comedian and actor, Volodymyr Zelensky, came to office, he used its inauguration to appeal to officials to think about the future each time they made a decision. The best way, he argued, was to forego official portraits of leaders such as himself and instead to adorn their offices with images of their children and grandchildren. By doing that, he said, they would make better policy choices. At the time of writing, Zelensky was leading his country's brave defence of an unprovoked Russian invasion, causing untold damage to the country, costing tens of thousands of lives and sparking a refugee crisis into Western Europe.

South Africa was on the right track when the NDP was drawn up by some of South Africa's most brilliant minds. Ironically, it was commissioned during the early part of the Zuma era and came up with a perfectly coherent view of what South Africa should look like by 2030. Its patron, Trevor Manuel, traversed the country, selling the vision for the future and receiving widespread buy-in. When he left politics, the plan lost its champion and its profile.

The existing NDP document, with its goals, hopes and aspirations, could be brought up to date with new, realistic time frames and an implementation strategy to give it a real-world relevance. Futurist Clem Sunter long ago called for an economic Codesa. While the name carries political baggage because of the many current failings in South Africa, the principle of a united view on the future is essential.

There is no shortage of capable South Africans who would willingly step into the role of an enforcer; although marketers might come up with a less abrasive title – something like Chief Growth Officer or Commissioner, with a direct line to the Presidency.

It needs to happen fast so that South Africans can buy into hope rather than despair and the growing trend of short-term contestation for a dwindling pool of resources.

Despite the pervasive sense of doom, it would be wrong to suggest that South Africa has made no progress since the Zuma years, but the findings of the Zondo Commission established what we already knew to be true and confirmed that the consequences of state capture and the hollowing out of state institutions have been devastating.

Its reverberations will be felt for years to come, particularly in failed municipalities where cadre deployment has had its most visible negative impact.

There was a week in the middle of 2021, just before President Cyril Ramaphosa was due to travel to Cornwall to meet members of the G7, when things appeared to be changing for the better. First, the country signed an extradition treaty with the United Arab Emirates, opening the way to force the return of members of the Gupta family, who were at the heart of state capture. Since then, however, there has been no further public development on this issue.

Second, Ramaphosa overruled energy minister Gwede Mantashe and empowered large businesses to generate up to 100 megawatts of their own energy needs. Eskom, the state power-er utility, has an average life of plant of over 40 years, and not even its newest power stations are operating at full capacity.

For the state to accept that it cannot fix this alone is significant.

Peter Attard Montalto, an economist at Intellidex, noted that Ramaphosa's combative approach might be a sign that Operation Vulindlela was helping to bypass truculent ministers who are re-sistant to evidence-based policy-making. Operation Vulindlela is a government-wide project centred in the Presidency and the National Treasury to fast-track structural reforms and remove obstacles and delays.

'Operation Vulindlela has been reinforced as an institutional framework that can override political blockages – this is the first and a dramatic example of this,' wrote Montalto. 'This was the president very directly overruling a minister that was close to him. This is a major signal and has rarely happened under this administration.'

The process of allowing the building of new infrastructure is tied up in departmental red tape that is frustrating even Eskom, which has plans of its own to create renewable-energy projects but needs to know that there is the administrative capacity to get the job done.

That same week in 2021, public enterprises minister Pravin

Gordhan gave away 51% of the equity in SAA to a local consortium with airline expertise. This was premised on the understanding that the government would retain the substantial liabilities of the carrier, but the fiscus would never again need to fund the national airline. It was a big step and, like the Telkom deal before it, created the potential for a model for future partnerships between government and business. Seven months after the transaction was announced, things have gone very quiet once again.

Ramaphosa visited the port of Cape Town in June 2021, with a promise of another restructuring amid revelations that South Africa's harbours are among the most dysfunctional and uncompetitive in the world. CEO Portia Derby has committed to a radical overhaul of Transnet, which runs the ports and the country's ailing rail network. While small steps have been taken to improve the delivery of a better service to importers and exporters, the ports remain a real economic constraint.

South Africa's pre-eminence on the continent is by no means guaranteed. The breakdown of governance and the deliberate dismantling of some key organs of state during the Zuma years have left South Africa at a severe disadvantage as the developed economies rebuild from the pandemic-related slowdowns that hit all countries.

Fixing the problems, though, is not a particularly complex equation, but it does require a radical departure from the thinking and destructive actions that got us into this mess in the first place.

In my first book, *The Upside of Down*, I posited that despite its problems South Africa manages to muddle through and, in many cases, entrepreneurs succeed despite the environment. If anything, it builds in a resilience that few other markets engender. Entrepreneurs tend to find a way through the chaos and uncertainty, which is brought about by a mix of outdated ideological debates within the governing party and the ineptitude of the state in creating extraordinary, world-beating enterprises. Profitable companies pay tax. Profitable companies seek further growth opportunities and hire people to make those possible. If you make it too difficult for them to do it in one jurisdiction, the owners of the intellectual property and the capital shift to places that welcome them with open arms.

South Africa's market is not for everyone. In fact, if there was any upside to the high levels of dysfunction present in the country, it is that it limits competition for individual companies as rivals go in search of more productive environments. Uncertainty around property rights, masses of regulation and the multitude of legislative requirements placed on businesses mean it is often easier to operate elsewhere.

This book is full of stories of courage and fortitude against the odds. They are stories of success in a country taken to the brink of self-destruction more often than its citizens care to remember. They are stories about extraordinary industries, companies and individuals whose raw materials, products and ideas have made a difference to the world.

They are stories of talented people building globally competitive businesses out of South Africa. Thanks to the rapid growth in the knowledge economy, their ideas and their implementation have never been less constrained by borders.

We are fortunate that the pandemic hit in the digital age – in the time of the smartphone rather than analogue. In addition, for all its marvellous attributes, the Nokia 3310 would not have been of much help if you were trying to build your business from home.

Work and global collaboration shifted from the physical to the digital world. It is a revolution whose time has come, and South African innovations and the people who created them are spread across the globe.

This book is part of that extraordinary story and that of the courageous founders looking to change the world by taking their smart ideas global and the significant advantages of having those businesses emanate from here.

There is no doubt that I have missed some epic tales. For those I have omitted, I apologise, and I will strive to include them in any future editions of the book.

Send details to info@brucewhitfield.com.

# CHAPTER 1

............

# The Economy

*The right hand doesn't know what*
*the left is throttling.* — Helena Wasserman

I was asked to address a group of beauty industry franchisees whose businesses were struggling. Government restrictions aimed at curbing the spread of Covid-19 had all but broken them. The intimacy of their treatments in confined spaces meant that many regular clients had become apprehensive about visiting at all. Located in shopping malls, their businesses had seen passing traffic plummet and they were struggling to make ends meet.

'What a wonderful opportunity you have,' I began. 'You bring joy, comfort and solace to your customers every single day. They live in the same society as you. They experience the same load shedding, the madness of the traffic, the potholes, the fear of crime and the real concern about a collapse in public services. Exactly in the same way you do. They come to you to be nurtured, to feel better about themselves. Of course, you would like more customers booking higher-value treatments and buying expensive creams and potions from your shelves. Right now, the economy is holding people back – that will take a while to return. If you can focus on the fact that you bring relief in a gloomy environment and understand the powerful positive impact you have on your customers, you will find a way to serve them even better and have them spend more of their disposable income with you.'

It was a message they needed to hear. The two years of pandemic-related economic meltdown had withered their confidence and they needed every ounce of encouragement to keep going.

They are not alone. Most service industries are operating at a fraction of their pre-pandemic capacity. In December 2021, tourism had recovered to two-thirds of the level it was at in December 2019. The industry was grateful for domestic travellers, but the big-ticket, five-star lodges were not achieving the prices they were used to because the dollar/renminbi/euro buyers of their products could not travel, and many were discounting just to keep turnover going.

It is going to take more than words of encouragement to reignite the economy in any meaningful way. At its current trajectory, it will take until at least 2024 for the economy to return to the size it was in 2019. By that time, the South African population, which grows by an average of 1.5% a year, will be 8% bigger. That is 8% more people in an economy that was already on the skids before the pandemic struck. Economic growth needs to outstrip population growth if economies are to succeed. When there is a significant growth deficit, as there has been in South Africa over an extended period, growth needs to be substantially higher to close the chasm between a gossamer-thin elite, upon whom the state depends to keep paying taxes, and the growing numbers of people excluded from the formal economy.

The South African economy resembles a giant Ponzi scheme. As long as there is more money coming in the front door than is leaving out the back, then it is okay. The trouble comes when inflows slow and outflows pick up. The best-known Ponzi scheme was run by American financier Bernie Madoff. Over two decades, he paid out market-beating returns to his A-list clientele, who depended on his successful track record to keep inflows going. It was the shock of the global financial crisis in 2008 that tipped the balance, and he ran out of money. He was unable to pay out the beneficiaries and it all collapsed in a heap. In the case of South Africa, we need to get far more people working, so as to lessen the outflow in terms of state support and to enable people to grow their incomes to contribute to the national tax take and ensure the inflow is maintained.

Richer countries make more stuff than poorer countries. It is a broad generalisation, but it has become clear over the past century or so that poorer countries tend to export their raw materials to richer, industrialised nations and import manufactured products at considerably higher prices into their home markets. Switzerland has no cocoa, but it is renowned for the quality and vast quantities of the chocolate it produces. China might not make advanced memory chips, but it does export some of the world's most affordable technologies that incorporate the intricate circuitry, which is made elsewhere in Asia.

Today, China is the world's factory and contributes about 29% of global manufacturing output, compared to the US's 17%. The

US used to be the world's biggest manufacturer, but, from the 1970s, it outsourced that function to China to get cheaper products. It worked well on both sides of the Pacific, giving consumers in the US (and the rest of the world) cheaper products and building China into the second biggest economy on the planet in three decades. It came at the cost of blue-collar jobs across industries globally, including in South Africa, where it killed off a vibrant textiles sector, for example, which was unable to compete with cheap imports.

The Covid-19 pandemic also showed up the downside of the heavy concentration of industries in limited geographies as supply chains imploded, crippling business production across the world. This could be a sign that companies will begin to diversify their manufacturing centres across multiple countries.

China earned about $4 trillion from manufacturing in 2019; this sector is also a critical driver of the American economic engine room and makes up 11.6% of US economic output. Japan produced $1 trillion from manufacturing in 2019, making it the third biggest. This was followed by Germany's largely privately owned manufacturing sector, which earned above $800 billion that year, with India growing rapidly in fifth place. By comparison, South Africa earned just $20 billion from manufacturing in the same year.

If poor countries want to get rich, noted Ricardo Hausmann, a former minister of planning in Venezuela who is now a professor of economics at Harvard University, they should stop exporting their resources in raw form and concentrate on adding value to them. Otherwise, rich countries will get the lion's share of the value through building industries that in turn create all the good jobs. With a few notable exceptions, this is precisely what South Africa does, along with many other commodity-producing nations.

We could take a leaf out of the Finland playbook. The country has more trees than it needs and therefore exports timber products, from planks to furniture and paper. Yet, those make up just 20% of its exports. The country earns twice as much from selling the technologies developed to support its forestry industry than it does out of the sector itself. Machine exports now account for more than 40% of Finland's foreign exchange earnings. Nokia, for example, was once a forestry company, which developed better and better technologies that made it efficient at processing the country's primary natural resource. Those technologies gradually found new applications, and some of the world's best-loved cellphones emerged from that stable. That is, until Apple co-founder Steve Jobs turned that world upside down.

South Africa has enjoyed some success in the beneficiation of raw materials but not on a sufficient scale to reduce its catastrophic levels of unemployment and to drive growth on a sustainable basis. The little growth that exists comes from consumption, financial services and the export of raw materials.

As Mike Schussler at Economists.co.za pointed out with increased exasperation on social media: 'When a country only produces 62% of what it did in 2011 while others produce 115% and 166% but we strike for more pay. This is the cause of poverty in SA. By the way SA produces less than half of what it did in 2005.' He cited Egypt's steel industry as an example: 'Egypt is the new king of steel in Africa. We used to produce four times as much crude steel as Egypt, now Egypt produces twice that of South Africa and if the Libyans end their civil war, South Africa may fall to number 3. Zimbabwe is no longer listed as a steel producer, they used to be number 2.'

It is no wonder many South Africans are fed up. With three-quarters of jobseekers between the ages of 15 and 24 unable to find work, the official unemployment rate rocketed to its highest level ever, close to 35% in 2021. The promise of the 1994 transition to democracy after more than 350 years of race-based discrimination has failed to materialise.

To date, South Africa has managed to keep its cash flow growing despite a dearth in tax collections in 2020. There has been a marked improvement, thanks to a boom in commodity prices that has seen mining companies pay significantly more tax than the National Treasury anticipated. But those windfalls are unlikely to be repeated and the country needs sustainable income sources if it is to thrive.

The biggest line item in the annual budget is not for education, health or policing, but in paying interest on the national debt – more than R904 million a day. Government's focus on paying out social grants and its continued debate on how to afford a basic income grant means it is only looking at the immediate need, rather than creating a long-term, sustainable growth path. For all its talk of improving economic growth and introducing jobs-rich policies, government has failed to act decisively to improve the lives of ordinary people. It focused on a short-term Band-Aid of further social grants to alleviate the worst effects of the economic fallout of Covid-19.

The country did not get to this point suddenly, by accident or without warning. The destruction of state capacity has been assured through the devastating ANC policy of cadre deployment into institutions and positions that require high levels of skill, professionalism and integrity. There has been an attempt since 2018 to claw back control, with several high-level appointments in key state entities, but the damage is deep and the evidence shows the patronage networks that mushroomed in the Zuma era are still alive and well. It remains bewildering that an inner circle of ostensibly bright and capable people could be co-opted into weakening state institutions. Yet, that is precisely what happened. There is enough evidence that the former president and several senior members of his government and bureaucracy willingly assisted in the process for personal gain.

Whether they did not understand the long-term consequences of their actions, or simply did not care, is unclear. Either way, they caused serious damage to South Africa's long-term prospects. It is almost as if they convinced themselves that there was a limited time frame during which they could mount a raid on the country's coffers, and that if they did not seize the opportunity, someone else would.

What will be critical now will be how the country chooses to deal with those who created the mess that we are in. The reality is that the problems the country faces are fixable, but it is going to take a considerable amount of goodwill and plenty of lateral thinking to do so.

When Cyril Ramaphosa assumed the presidency of the country in February 2018, he promised a new dawn. It all sounded too good to be true. And it was. Ramaphoria, as it became known, was short-lived and the country went back to its destructive habits, while the president busied himself trying to secure support within his party's divided National Executive Committee.

He did manage to stamp control on key institutions by appointing effective pragmatists to senior positions, including in the National Treasury, the South African Revenue Service and the Reserve Bank. But, by the time Covid-19 struck, he had failed to make similar progress in the security services, and his appointments to the National Prosecuting Authority are yet to yield any real benefit.

The annual State of the Nation Address (SONA) used to be a Versailles-style festival of grandiose faux optimism, full of gestures, big dreams and unlikely goals. This was only outweighed in its detachment from reality by the ostentatious show of personal wealth of MPs on a red carpet that put the Oscars to shame.

After two years of growth-crushing Covid-related lockdowns and restrictions, job losses and the continued failure of the state to grasp the nettle of a turnaround, the president admitted what has been patently obvious from the beginning. Without private-sector assistance, government will get nowhere in its efforts to grow the economy.

But his appeals run the risk of following other initiatives and ending up on the trash pile of history. Without action to support his wish for greater collaboration, it will not happen. A frustrated former Post Office CEO, Mark Barnes, disclosed at the time of the budget that he had made a proposal to government four months previously to take over the Post Office – an entity that he was on the cusp of resuscitating when he resigned over strategic differences with government, its only shareholder. Now the Post Office is dependent once again on the fiscus.

Barnes has funders, wants to incorporate unions and staff into an ownership structure and have the entity paying dividends rather than taking bailouts. The Takatso Consortium takeover of SAA was a significant breakthrough in terms of the state's desire to rid itself of long-running liabilities.

The finance minister's budget speech two weeks after SONA made the point that government was ready to tackle the mounting concerns of global investors related to mismanaged state-owned companies. Again, the proof of the pudding will be in the eating, but the willingness to close and consolidate government companies that are either unnecessary or compromised is precisely the correct signal to send, not only globally, but domestically too.

By upping the amount of money investors can put outside the country as part of their long-term savings for retirement, the finance minister sent a crucial signal – that rather than the feared tightening of exchange controls to restrict capital flows, the South African government was willing to allow the country to compete for capital. If lenders know they can get their money as and when they need it, they are more likely to make it available to a jurisdiction that respects that the money needs a return and should be allowed to flow to the best opportunities presented to it. It was a big and important signal of state intent.

A capable state is critical to the success of any economy. The South African government's insistence on putting itself at the centre of what it calls a developmental state has been nothing short of disastrous. It has neither the capacity nor the capability to pull off the China-style miracle it is so desperate to emulate. It can play a crucial role in a recovery, however, by doing a few things right.

The starting point is to get South Africans to willingly invest in their own country. Beyond the platitudes of collaboration across public and private sectors, there has been a significant breakdown of trust between public and private sectors over decades – best evidenced by the offshoring of wealth and business opportunities.

Despite numerous state interventions to narrow the wealth gap in South Africa, inequality increased rather than decreased during the pandemic. A lack of financial support for the poorest and most vulnerable in society meant they were most negatively affected by lay-offs and the least likely to be re-employed, while those with property and investible assets have seen the value of those rise through the pandemic, leaving them on average wealthier than before. The *World Inequality Report 2022* is published by the World Inequality Lab, a group of analysts that includes economist Thomas Piketty, who highlighted the impact of multi-generational wealth causing disparities in wealth distribution in his book, *Capital in the Twenty-First Century*.

The report shows in 2021, 'After three decades of trade and financial globalisation, global inequalities remain extremely pronounced ... about as great today as they were at the peak of Western imperialism in the early 20th century.'

Lucas Chancel from the Paris School of Economics describes how in 2020, during the first waves of the Covid-19 pandemic, global billionaires' wealth grew by $3.7 trillion, equivalent to the total annual spending on public health by all governments in the world before the Covid outbreak. During that time, 100 million more people around the world, including 1.5 million who lost their jobs in South Africa, were thrown into varying degrees of hardship and privation as a result.

According to the *World Inequality Report 2022*: 'The top 10% in South Africa earn more than 65% of total national income and the bottom 50% just 5.3%, which means that the upper bracket owns close to 86% of total wealth while the poorer 50% is negative and has been that way since 1990.'

The problem is not that we have rich people; the problem is that we have too many who are poor and have no way of improving their personal circumstances. Social grants are a useful tool for bridging a gap in the economy, but they are not a permanent solution to the inequality crisis. The country needs to encourage the development of enterprises that require labour to grow. Only that can create sustainable jobs.

We need to boost our export sector by making more things rather than relying on the sale of raw materials. While South Africa's key exports by value come from primary sectors, such as raw materials, before the pandemic, the World Bank described 'finance, real estate, and business services' as the strongest non-primary sector. In a recent report, the Bank said: 'Finance is South Africa's strongest sector. It has a long history of intermediating capital in global markets, has benefited from reforms in the 1990s, and has adopted global financial standards.' In fact, South African banking has long boxed above its weight. It was thanks to its superlative management and regulatory regime that in the global financial crisis of 2008, the sector was largely unaffected by the fallout from the financial engineering that very nearly broke the global economy. But that stuff is hard to replicate outside the country.

South Africa's Competition Commission is often criticised for its failure to appreciate the need for growth and is prone to restrict the dominance of large players in the economy without a plan to support credible new entrants. In its first-ever *Concentration Tracker Report*, which sought to measure the concentration and participation levels in the South African economy, it revealed that nearly 70% of 144 sectors in the economy remain highly concentrated by large firms, with 40.3% of these sectors reportedly dominated by a single firm. The structure of South Africa's economy for all its talk about opening access to new players has in fact seen it impose constraints on promising newcomers due to the high cost and inefficiency of building new enterprises and a high failure rate of new entrants into sectors across the economy. However, that concentration can be used to our advantage because it is those firms that have the capacity and the balance sheets to help support smaller industries.

One manufacturing success story the South African government is looking to build on is in the motor trade. The country has become an African hub for building various models of vehicles for global distribution for international firms such as BMW, Mercedes-Benz, Volkswagen, Nissan and Ford. According to NAAMSA, the umbrella body that represents manufacturers, there are 22 companies involved in the production of cars and commercial vehicles active in the country.

Of those, there are seven major vehicle manufacturers and assemblers of cars and bakkies, while there are several assemblers of medium and heavy commercial vehicles. There are also 21 companies involved in the importation and distribution of new motor vehicles in the country and more than 500 automotive component suppliers active in the economy.

There has been something of a shift in recent years around Gauteng being the epicentre of vehicle manufacture in the country, with a greater move towards the Eastern Cape, where Volkswagen, Mercedes and, increasingly, Ford are based. While there is a series of complex incentives designed to draw manufacturers to South Africa, the industry is a significant contributor to the economy, with manufacturing contributing 2.8% of GDP and retail a further 2.1% in 2020. That was below the figure for the previous year, owing to the disruption to exports in 2019, but the big manufacturers are investing heavily in the sector because they are incentivised to do so.

The South African government wants the big manufacturers to produce a million vehicles or 1% of all vehicles sold in the world by 2026. While mining acted as the catalyst for the development of support industries during the commodity boom years, and just as Finland earns more from the exports of the equipment that serves the forestry sector than it does from timber products, the establishment of the vehicle manufacturing sector has created an industry of component suppliers, with everything from rubber mats to leather seats and other parts that go into vehicles.

South Africa is one of five places in the world where the Ford Motor Company makes its most popular pickup, the Ranger, and exports fully built vehicles to more than 100 countries. The firm increased its investment in South Africa by a further R15.8 billion in 2021, a move it said will turn its local subsidiary into a model for the rest of the group.

Every Ford Ranger is made up of some 1 600 components. Ford currently sources an average of 43% of its components from South African suppliers as part of the Automotive Industry Master Plan, which looks to firms sourcing 60% of components locally.

It is not just the finished vehicles. The firm builds 285 000 engines and a range of components for export in Gqeberha every year. Engine parts, such as crankshafts, cylinder heads and camshafts, are cast in the UK but are processed and refined and built up into completed engines in the Eastern Cape. A total of 110 000 of those end up in the vehicles being built at the group's Silverton plant in Pretoria and are delivered by rail, while the remaining 175 000 find their way to Ford's other manufacturing facilities in countries such as Turkey, China and Thailand. Currently, the firm produces 110 000 vehicles a year, with an installed capacity of 168 000 and a goal to make 200 000 a year by 2026.

The motor industry is one example of how a blend of smart policy-making and foreign direct investment with appropriate incentives can lead to industrial development, but those are complex, long-term arrangements and do not provide any quick fixes for job creation.

The country needs other ideas and has increasingly become a magnet for inward investment by global cloud service providers in massive new infrastructure projects. In September 2021, Vantage Data Centers became the latest to make a big investment in creating an African campus. The US-based company invested R15 billion on 60 000 square metres of data space across three facilities in Johannesburg. Once fully developed, the campus will be the largest in Africa and will act as the data centre hub for sub-Saharan Africa 'due to its strategic location, IT ecosystem, fibre connectivity to the rest of Africa and the availability of renewable energy', according to Antoine Boniface, president of Vantage Data Centers, EMEA.

While its efforts to turn the sod on a massive data centre project in Cape Town have met vigorous opposition from local interest groups, Amazon announced it was looking for a site in the city for a substantial campus, while Microsoft built two data centres in South Africa, one in Cape Town and one in Johannesburg, and China's Huawei started building its two centres in South Africa in 2019.

Not everyone has lost faith in the future. Now we need to harness it. As this book illustrates, we have some extraordinary people doing astonishing things in a competitive global landscape in terms of the businesses they have built in South Africa and are taking to the world.

# CHAPTER 2

# The Quiz

*Sometimes the questions are complicated,
and the answers are simple.* — Dr Seuss

Q: Which five of the following commodities does South Africa have the world's highest resources of: platinum, manganese, chrome, gold, vanadium, vermiculite, titanium, zirconium and molybdenum?

A: Platinum, manganese, chrome, gold and vanadium.

South Africa is blessed with a wealth of natural resources. Resources exist under the surface of the earth, and reserves are those that can be accessed using available technologies. South Africa has the highest resources in the world of platinum (88%), manganese (80%), chrome (72%), gold (40%) and vanadium (32%). Gold is the outlier here as we have almost tapped out our reserves of the metal and may at some point in the future be able to extract more of the resource if prices rise and technology improves. We have the second highest resources of minerals like vermiculite (40%), commonly used in soil mixes, as well as by professional gardeners and nursery workers to improve seed germination; titanium (17%), which is as strong as steel but weighs half as much and is used in everything from prosthetics to surgical tools and bike frames; and zirconium (19%), which is good for steel alloys, lamp filaments and even some deodorants.

South Africa also has good resources of so-called battery metals, which are increasingly important as the world weans itself off fossil fuels and needs to store the energy from renewable resources. Nickel is an important component of batteries, and South Africa is one of the five main African producers, alongside Côte d'Ivoire, Zimbabwe, Madagascar and Zambia. It also has copper and cobalt resources that are critical in global battery manufacture.

We are nowhere in terms of molybdenum resources, but its story is one of the most compelling (see Chapter 11).

**Q: Is Kreepy Krauly South African?**
A: No. Well, yes. Sort of. Not anymore.

It was designed, developed and made in South Africa by a mechanical engineer from the former Belgian Congo, Ferdinand Chauvier, and sparked an innovation revolution in pool care from this country. Most international innovations from South Africa, including Kreepy Krauly, are now owned by global businesses outside of the country in which they were created.

**Q: Which South African company beat Neil Armstrong to the moon?**
A: Pratley.

Pratley Putty was used in the Ranger space programme, which predated the Apollo missions as NASA ran tests ahead of the first moon walk. So Pratley did make it to the moon before the first humans set foot there. It was used by a company that wanted to become the agency for Pratley Putty in the US – a move the US company, which is significantly globalised, turned down, but its product, a world leader at the time, made it to the surface of the moon.

### Q: Who was Hans Merensky?
A: A geologist and a keen farmer.

His name lives on in the trust Hans Merensky created just before his death, midway through the twentieth century. The world's richest known platinum reef is named after him, while the name of the estate he bought in Limpopo Province, Westfalia, is the label borne by most of the world's avocados (see Chapter 4).

### Q: Which company is the world's biggest producer of avocados?
A: Westfalia Fruit.

With its origins in South Africa, the company is now headquartered in London and is the single biggest avocado supplier on the planet, with operations on 5 continents and in 16 territories supplying customers in 40 countries, 12 months of the year (see Chapter 4).

### Q: What fruit is available fresh only from South Africa in September and October each year?
A: Cherries.

The cherry window has been closed with production by ZZ2 in South Africa of cherries during those months when previously the fresh fruit was not available anywhere else. The details of this marvellous little stopgap are in Chapter 4.

Q: What do the series *Black Sails, Outlander* and *Homeland* have in common?
A: Large parts of each were filmed at the Cape Town Film Studios on a piece of land wedged between a wetland and a smelly water treatment plant between the N2 highway and the newly widened R310 to Stellenbosch (see Chapter 13).

Q: Where is the world's biggest single-site gold refinery?
A: Germiston.

The privately owned refinery has been in operation for a little over a century and the history tells us it has processed more than a quarter of the world's known gold. Since 1967, it has also produced the highest number of gold blanks, about 60 million for the Krugerrand range of investment and, more recently, silver coins. Located in Germiston, due to its proximity to one of the continent's biggest and busiest railway junctions, it was able to move products in and out of the facility with relative ease. Before it opened in 1921, gold had to be sent to London for processing, so the move saved producers a fortune in time, transport and security costs. Its proximity led to the creation of Rand Airport – the country's only international airport until 1948. Local gold production peaked in 1971, when the country produced 1 000 tonnes of gold, equal to 80% of global gold production at the time.

**Q: Which is the world's most widely owned gold coin?**

A: The Krugerrand.

The gold blank discs produced at the Rand Refinery are transported to the South African Mint in Centurion, where they are date-stamped and have the image of Paul Kruger punched on their surface. The creation of the coin was a smart mechanism to encourage ownership of bullion and provided an increasingly isolated apartheid government with a source of much-needed hard currency income. It was the world's first modern, investment-grade bullion coin. The one-ounce Krugerrand weighs 33.93 grams – 5 grams more than the gold in it as a result of its 8.33% copper content, which is included to harden the coin. Its diameter measures 32.77 mm and it is 2.84 mm thick. It was the first gold coin to offer one full troy ounce of high-purity gold (91.67% fine, or 22 karats).

Because it was first to market, the South African Krugerrand represented the lion's share of gold bullion coin trades during the early 1980s. It carried 90% of the global coin market at the time. It had first-mover advantage and, as a result, it remains the number-one choice for private gold coin ownership.

Fifty million ounces of Krugerrand coins of various sizes have been sold globally, by far the most of any bullion coin in terms of volume (see Chapter 3).

**Q: Which was the first city in the southern hemisphere to install electric streetlamps?**

A: Kimberley.

Within three or four years of a diamond rush, sparked by the discovery of the Eureka diamond near Hopetown, Kimberley was South Africa's second biggest human settlement, made up of tents, corrugated-iron buildings and later more permanent structures. Within a decade, it was rich enough to be the first city in the southern hemisphere to install electric streetlamps.

**Q: What were Frikkie Fish Sticks?**
**A: South Africa's first fish fingers.**

It was a product made by South African fishing company I&J from 1955. The original fish stick was not coated, and it was sold as a rectangular block of plain fish. Its mascot, a cartoon fish character called Frikkie, holding a top hat and carrying a Fred Astaire-style cane, was created to persuade a generation of children to eat fish. It was only later that the fish stick took on a crumb coating and was renamed the fish finger. That term was first referenced in a recipe given in a popular British magazine in 1900, and fish fingers are most often associated with the UK as the gateway drug to full-sized fish and chips.

**Q: Where was the world's first Nando's outside South Africa?**
**A: Tuart Hill, Perth.**

Fernando Duarte invited his friend Robbie Brozin to Chickenland, a humble Portuguese eatery in the heart of Rosettenville, south of Johannesburg in 1987. The legend goes that after just one bite of the peri-peri marinated chicken, they knew they had an opportunity to build a substantial franchise operation. Little did they know just how transportable that concept would become, thanks not only to the quality of the product, but also to some remarkable branding that has allowed it to box far above its weight category in new markets around the world (see Chapter 9). The UK expansion started in 1992 – that country now has the largest number of Nando's outlets in the world.

### Q: Which is South Africa's most planted wine grape varietal?
### A: Chenin blanc.

In addition to being used to produce increasingly excellent chenins, the varietal is used extensively in blends and is also a key component of the country's growing brandy industry. While pinotage may have been created in South Africa through the masterful crossing of pinot noir and cinsault vines by Abraham Perold, Stellenbosch's first professor of viticulture, in 1925, chenin is more widely cultivated. Cabernet sauvignon is the most planted red grape variety, followed by pinotage (see Chapter 6).

### Q: What is the value of automotive exports from South Africa annually?
### A: About R200 billion.

In 2010, South Africa exported $1.8 billion worth of cars to the US – more than Sweden and Italy. Automotive exports reached a peak in 2019 of R201.7 billion, but it declined nearly 13% amid the Covid-19 disruption of 2020. According to the *Automotive Export Manual*, the value of total automotive exports from South Africa declined by R26 billion, or 12.9%, from the 2019 record to R175.7 billion in 2020. Automotive exports account for nearly 14% of the value of all exports from South Africa.

**Q: The diamond polisher of which stone had a nervous breakdown after working on it?**

A: The Cullinan diamond.

At 3 106 carats, the uncut Cullinan diamond was about the size of a standard 330 ml Coke can. It was named after Sir Thomas Cullinan, owner of the Premier diamond mine near Pretoria, where it was found.

Fellow broadcaster David O'Sullivan's grandfather was one of the first people ever to hold the stone: 'My grandfather, Gerry O'Sullivan was a messenger boy at the Cullinan mine. As the story goes, one day he was running an errand when he saw a couple of men holding a muddy rock. They called him over and gave it to him. "Now you have held the world's biggest diamond," he was told.' Journalist Chris Moerdyk's great-grandfather, William McHardy, was general manager of the Premier mine in 1905 when the stone was unearthed, and he is the proud owner of one of four quartz copies of the stone made in 1908 to commemorate its discovery.

The diamond was gifted to King Edward VII in 1907 by Prime Minister of the Transvaal Colony, Louis Botha. It was sent to Holland to the king's most trusted diamond cutters, Asscher, where it was cleaved into nine separate stones. Asscher's favoured diamond polisher, Henri Koe, and two of his colleagues worked fourteen-hour days for eight months to finish the stones, using fifteenth-century technology – a scaife, or polishing wheel.

The diamond was finally divided into 105 individual stones, and the two biggest are part of the Crown Jewels stored in the Tower of London. The Great Star of Africa, at 530 carats, is the world's biggest polished diamond and forms part of the royal sceptre; the Lesser Star of Africa, at 317 carats, is in the Imperial State Crown.

On completing the job, Koe had a nervous breakdown. He was sent to South Africa to recuperate.

## Q: Which South African town intercepted a church?
## A: Adelaide.

Not long after the end of the South African War, parishioners at Adelaide in the Eastern Cape prayed for a miracle. The NG Kerk in the town had been commandeered during the war by the British garrison as a headquarters because it was the sturdiest building in town. The woodwork in the church was in a sorry state of disrepair and nothing short of divine intervention would provide them with the materials they needed. One day, as if by a miracle, those materials arrived by ox wagon. There was timber, a pulpit and matching chair. The grateful parishioners, their faith replenished, set about making the necessary improvements to their church. Years later, a letter arrived from a congregation from Adelaide, the capital of South Australia and now that country's fifth most populous city: 'It is with trepidation that we enquire whether a consignment of oak wood, which we ordered from England about two years ago for our new church, has not, perhaps, by mistake been delivered to your town in South Africa, instead of ours.' The Eastern Cape Adelaide admitted receiving the wood and, in a gesture of Christian charity, the Australian congregation did not ask for compensation. Evidence of that fortuitous mistake is on show at the NG Kerk in Adelaide, South Africa, to this day.

Q: Which 80-tonne, 1960s' South African invention protects American riverbanks against storm surges?

A: The dolos.

It could become a useful tool in the looming battle with rising oceans. The interlocking blocks of concrete are used to protect sea walls and preserve beaches from erosion. They work by dissipating, rather than blocking, the energy of waves. Their design deflects most wave action energy to the side. The dolos was designed in 1963 and first used in 1964 on the breakwater at the port of East London. Dolosse are also being used in rivers in the Pacific Northwest of the US to control erosion, prevent channel migration, and create and restore salmon habitat. East London harbour engineer Eric Merrifield took credit for the design, but his subordinate, Aubrey Kruger, claimed to have created the prototype on his lunch break at home one day when he cut three pieces of broomstick, nailed them together into an H-shape and turned one of the sections 90 degrees. But it was Merrifield who won the Shell Design Award and the Associated Science and Technology Societies of South Africa's Gold Medal.

Q: Which South African battle's name is most exported?

A: Spioenkop (Afrikaans spelling).

The main grandstand at Liverpool's home ground is called The Kop in honour of Liverpudlians who died on the slopes of Spioenkop during a particularly bloody battle in the South African War. It goes down as one of the British Army's most significant defeats during the three-year conflict. There were 243 fatalities and 1 250 wounded or captured in the ferocious fighting. Leeds United's club mascot is called Lucas the Kop Cat, and there is a village in Nottinghamshire called Spion Kop. There are also said to be numerous hills across Australia bearing the name Spion Kop in honour of that bloody battle fought on the hill in KwaZulu-Natal. In addition, it is famous for the fact that three prominent global leaders of the twentieth century all traversed that field during the fight: Winston Churchill, as a war correspondent; Mahatma Gandhi, as a stretcher-bearer; and Louis Botha, as a soldier. That single battle might therefore have played a formative role in shaping the contemporary history of the world in the years to come.

### Q: Which South African construction firm rescued miners trapped underground in Chile, and built Africa's first high-speed underground railway and Dubai's first seven-star hotel?

A: Murray & Roberts.

South African engineering skills were respected globally, and it had a healthy construction sector until the immediate aftermath of the 2010 FIFA World Cup, which coincided with the early stages of the state capture project. When 33 miners, 32 Chileans and a Bolivian, were trapped 688 metres underground for 69 days in the San José mine near Copiapó in the north of Chile, Murray & Roberts played a significant role in their painstaking rescue. It was also the lead contractor on the development of the Gautrain and, as an early participant in Dubai's building boom, Murray & Roberts won the contract to build the iconic Burj Al Arab, which it completed in 1999.

The company saw a boom decade in South Africa up to the

World Cup in 2010, but a collapse in government spending on infrastructure forced it into a significant rethink about its future. The firm closed its infrastructure and building businesses as part of a strategic disposal of assets in 2016 in order to focus on the global resources market instead, concentrating on three core sectors: underground mining; oil and gas; and power and water.

**Q: Who was the first South African to make it to space in a privately funded aircraft?**

A: Mike Melvill.

Mike is less well known than Mark Shuttleworth, who, after cashing in on his internet security business, Thawte, just before the peak of the dotcom era, travelled to the International Space Station in 2002. Shuttleworth was the second space tourist on board the Soyuz TM-34 mission with the Russian space agency. He was labelled the 'Afronaut' and the 'first African in space'.

Melvill, a test pilot, was the first commercial astronaut, and the first person to travel into space aboard a privately funded spacecraft. He was educated at Hilton College in KwaZulu-Natal, and his family emigrated to the US in 1967. On 21 June 2004, Melvill piloted SpaceShipOne on its first flight past the edge of space, becoming the first person to pilot a privately built aircraft into space and making history as the first commercial astronaut. In 2021, billionaires Jeff Bezos and Richard Branson both succeeded in achieving weightlessness as part of their efforts to encourage space tourism for the super-wealthy.

**Q: Who were the first South Africans to be named *Time* magazine Person of the Year?**

A: Nelson Mandela and F.W. de Klerk.

Pretoria-born Elon Musk not only became the richest person in the world in 2021 but also adorned the cover of *Time* as Person of the Year, becoming the third person born in South Africa to receive the honour. In 1993, Mandela and De Klerk were joined by Israeli Prime Minister Yitzhak Rabin and Palestinian President Yasser Arafat in a special Peacemakers' edition.

**Q: Which is the world's second biggest cider producer?**

A: Distell.

The makers of Savanna and Hunters are the second biggest producers of apple cider in the world after brewer Heineken, which has the world's largest side hustle in Strongbow and Bulmers. In 2021, Heineken made an offer of R40 billion to the shareholders of the local drinks company, which is also known for Amarula (see Chapter 5).

**Q: What are PGMs?**

A: Platinum group metals.

The six platinum group metals are ruthenium, rhodium, palladium, osmium, iridium and platinum. They have similar physical and chemical properties and tend to occur together in the same mineral deposits. Despite the price of platinum and the considerably higher number of industrial applications it has than gold, it is not regarded by investors in the same light as the yellow metal. Platinum metals are good for jewellery. They are resistant to wear, barely tarnish and are also useful in motor-vehicle manufacture, in auto-catalytic converters as a means of reducing the pollution effects of the internal combustion engine, and increasingly in new battery technologies being developed to store energy generated from renewable sources such as wind and solar (see Chapter 3).

**Q: What South African product had to drop the 'r' off the end of its name to avoid antagonising British patent lawyers?**

**A: Appletiser.**

Marketed for decades in the UK as 'Appletise', the company was founded in Elgin by Italian immigrant Edmond Lombardi in 1966. It was later taken over by SABMiller and, more recently, by Coca-Cola. It dropped the 'r' rather than fight expensive battles in the UK market, which had an existing product called Tiser (see Chapter 7).

**Q: Which is the world's second biggest agricultural exporter?**

**A: The Netherlands.**

Sorry, a trick question in a quiz showing off South African successes, but it is just too interesting to leave out. The Netherlands is a leader in efficient and sustainable agriculture – and the second largest exporter of agricultural goods in the world. High-tech farming methods, such as hydroponic watering systems and geothermal energy, limit its impact on the environment and maximise yield. In 2017, the Netherlands exported $111 billion worth of agricultural goods, including $10 billion of flowers and $7.4 billion of vegetables. With its rich agricultural heritage, South Africa is the world's second biggest citrus exporter, after Spain.

# CHAPTER 3

# Mining
# – The Backbone of Everything

*This gold will cause our country to become*
*soaked in blood.* — Paul Kruger

Minerals were being mined, processed and beneficiated south of the Limpopo River long before the diamond and gold rushes of the mid- to late nineteenth century. The industry is a key jobs creator and generator of foreign income, tax and royalties for the fiscus.

Veteran mining journalist David McKay, the editor of *Miningmx*, says that while the industry has provided the critical backbone upon which the economy was built and remains pivotal to its long-term future, it has a downside. 'The industry is woven into South Africa's history of subjugation and struggle and so it is tempting to believe in its absence the country would be more peaceful, cleaner and with an agrarian economy supplying peninsula cities, like they have in Australia. But the reality is that the country would have had a less centralised economy. And with the concentration of capital comes vibrancy, innovation and progress, as well as cruelty, hardship and despair. Without mining, South Africa would be another country; certainly, a less interesting one.'

The golden rhinoceros of Mapungubwe is small enough to fit into your hand. Its discovery in 1934 at a royal grave site close to the border with Zimbabwe provided evidence of a wealthy thirteenth-century kingdom that had trade links as far north as present-day Tanzania. Three of the 27 burial sites excavated in the 1930s contained gold objects, including animal figurines, such as those of rhinoceroses, a crocodile, an ox and a wild cat, as well as fragments of other unidentified animals – two of which were eventually reconstructed in 2009. There were other artefacts resembling regal regalia. It is believed that the economy of the region was based on cattle herding, agriculture, hunting and gathering, as well as long-distance international trade. There were also pieces of Chinese porcelain among the treasures, connecting Asia–East Africa trade to the kingdom and dispelling colonial myths about the lack of African development, culture, settlement and trade.

For better or for worse, South Africa is incredibly rich in natural resources, with large reserves of some of the most valuable minerals on the planet. The first industrial-scale mining began in the 1850s with the establishment of a copper mine, followed by diamonds and then the world's biggest gold discovery on the Witwatersrand. It contributes about $13.5 billion to South Africa's GDP. Platinum group metals (PGMs) are the second most produced mineral category in South Africa after coal, which saw production begin at about the same time as gold and was used to power the mines and their supporting industries. It might be a filthy business, but coal generated a quarter of all mining revenue in 2020. The country has proven coal reserves of about 9.9 billion metric tonnes.

Mining remains the cornerstone of the South African economy. In the early 1960s, it contributed about 35% of GDP in a highly concentrated mining and agricultural economy. Today, it makes up just 8.2% of the economy, but it remains pivotal as an employer and export revenue earner. It provides 450 000 jobs, and it makes up about 60% of the country's exports, the biggest of which remains coal. South Africa mines more than 300 million metric tonnes of the stuff annually; that is the equivalent of the weight of more than two million blue whales or 50 million decent-sized elephants.

A total of 61% of the coal mined in South Africa is burned locally to generate electricity. The balance is shipped offshore, mostly to Pakistan, although China is opening up to local producers as a result of trade tensions between it and its regular supplier, Australia.

The second biggest mineral by volume is iron ore, followed by chromium and manganese ore. By comparison, platinum exports amount to just 138 metric tonnes and gold is 97 metric tonnes. That is fewer than 30 decent-sized elephants, but, thanks to elevated prices, worth a lot more than the equivalent amount of coal.

Despite renewed efforts to reduce the globe's dependence on coal, which is the world's biggest single pollutant, it remains the largest single source of power generation globally. Coal-fired power stations are still being built on a large scale in developing regions, such as Southeast Asia, although the Secretary-General of the United Nations, António Guterres, appealed to the world's richest nations via the virtual Davos gathering in January 2022 to ban the building of new coal-fired power stations, as a means to force a change of thinking on future energy security.

South Africa is well positioned there, too, thanks to its enormous reserves of PGMs, some of which are used in new energy storage technologies and in a relatively fast-growing sector, hydrogen. Globally, the demand for hydrogen as a source of cleaner energy is growing as Western governments face increasing pressure to decarbonise, in an effort to limit the longer-term effects of climate change.

South Africa, says PwC, is in an extraordinary position to revolutionise its own economy and could become an exporter of cost-effective green hydrogen to the rest of the globe. Fewer than a dozen countries produce it, and South Africa has good platinum reserves to do so. The infrastructure required to export hydrogen is similar to existing natural gas networks and is already being piloted in Australia and Japan. South Africa could leverage its existing and new infrastructure to do the same and could become a major player in the production and export of hydrogen-based fuels, chemicals and products.

The South African government sees the potential in the sector and has identified it as a 'big-frontier' investment opportunity for the country. It has appointed Sasol to be the anchor developer of the planned Boegoebaai Green Hydrogen Special Economic Zone, near Port Nolloth, close to the Namibian border. Sasol also has plans to develop green hydrogen production facilities in Gauteng.

But it is not just hydrogen.

A small start-up with a plant in the middle of the old Free State goldfields could turn into this decade's richest source of natural gas. Renergen, listed on the JSE, has significant levels of methane, which is converted into liquified natural gas and helium.

Gold miners used to burn off the gas as a waste product, and its usefulness is a more recent discovery. These reserves, some of the richest in the world, were discovered quite by accident. It is likely that when government granted Renergen the licence to exploit it, it did not quite realise the full extent of the opportunity the company was seizing upon.

Stefano Marani and Nick Mitchell bought the gas rights on an 87 000-hectare piece of land near Welkom in the Free State in 2012 for just $1. Their original plan was to set up a small power generation unit for a nearby mine. On further examination, they discovered not only a significant resource of methane but also attached to that a rich concentration of valuable helium.

Renergen is gearing up to be a significant global producer and counts several of the world's oil and gas majors as clients as it gets production underway. The reserves are helium rich; there is a concentration of 2% to 4% helium in the gasses Renergen taps out of mostly disused gold mines. Compare that to operations in the US, the world's biggest producer, where concentrations are as low as 0.3%, and those in Qatar, the world's second biggest producer, where they are even lower.

In 2019, the global helium market was worth $10.6 billion. Marani thinks he can supply 10% of that, thanks to current reserve estimates of nearly 10 billion cubic metres of the stuff – enough for 1.5 trillion party balloons. The best part is that the gas emerges from beneath a massive dolerite cap via a natural fissure and does not need to be extracted using fracking, as is the case in many parts of the world. Experts expect a helium rush from private companies, as reserves in the US are running out.

Although it is thought to be the second most abundant element in the universe, it is extremely rare on Earth. It is typically produced as a by-product of natural gas processing, itself a result of decomposing uranium reserves. That helium exists in the Free State is a result of billions of years of asteroid strikes, specifically that of the meteor that hit earth near present-day Vredefort, causing the geology of the Witwatersrand and the Free State to be pushed to the surface. This first enabled it to be mined for gold and now tapped for gas, which in the heyday of metal sales was simply burned off as a waste product.

The most labour-intensive commodity sector is platinum. If the South African mining industry employed 100 workers, 39 would work in the PGM sector, 21 in the coal sector and 20 in the gold sector. The iron-ore sector has far smaller requirements and would hire just 5 of every 100 employees, with the remaining 15 working in smaller industries, including lime works and stone quarrying.

In 2019, Stats SA reported that PGMs had, for the first time in a decade, overtaken coal as the most significant contributor to total mining sales as a result of sharp rises in the prices of palladium and rhodium.

PGMs' primary industrial use has been in autocatalytic converters in the motor industry to reduce harmful emissions from internal combustion engines. As the global vehicle industry looks to alternative sources of energy to drive their motors, the metals are also finding application in battery technologies, ensuring ongoing demand.

Platinum-based fuel cells are proving to be more cost-effective, cleaner and more reliable than alternatives, such as diesel generators. The platinum-based fuel cells are making a real positive impact on rural households across South Africa. Electricity in homes and schools improves the quality of education, and the ability to pump water for irrigation facilitates farming, creating potential for fuel-cell, mini-grid electrification.

PGMs have found application in many other unexpected ways, including in the treatment of cancer. The first platinum-based chemotherapy drug discovered by researchers was Cisplatin, which, 40 years later, continues to have applications in certain types of cancer treatment. The airbags in your car are coated with platinum-cured silicones to protect them from the explosive activation systems and enable them to remain folded and ready for deployment, without deteriorating, in case of an accident. Airbags also contain an initiator sensor that uses a fine platinum wire, coated with explosive material to facilitate release. There are platinum-cured silicone mixtures used in a range of everyday products, from shampoo to lipstick and in plasters for wound healing. Platinum catalysts are used to make petrochemical feedstocks, the basic raw materials for the manufacture of plastics, synthetic rubber and polyester fibres used to produce clothes and blankets. They are even in technologies that help keep food fresher for longer in a high-tech, palladium-containing sheet placed in the bottom of packaging. This sheet absorbs ethylene, the gas emitted by produce in the ripening process, and extends the shelf life of fresh food.

By comparison, gold has little use in the real world beyond the belief among investors that its value will provide protection against the ravages of inflation.

Nearly a millennium on from Mapungubwe, the Krugerrand is the world's most widely held gold coin. More than 60 million Krugerrands have been minted since 1967 and give ordinary people around the world a way to own physical gold.

Things started slowly for the Krugerrand. From 1967 to 1969, just 40 000 coins were produced. That increased sharply to 200 000 by 1970. In 1974, more than a million coins had been sold – a number that rose sharply to six million by 1978. In the early 1980s, Krugerrands made up 90% of the international coin market. At that time, South Africa was by far the world's biggest producer of gold and mined 70% of the world's metal.

The timing of its launch was impeccable. When US President Richard Nixon took America off the gold standard, introducing the fact that the value of a currency was no longer linked to the price of gold, the ability of investors to hold bullion grew in popularity.

American investors bought tens of millions of Krugerrands until about 1985, when the US banned the importing of new coins as part of economic sanctions against South Africa. The American Eagle gold and silver bullion coins followed in 1986, mimicking the model created by the Krugerrand. Canada minted the first Maple Leaf coin in 1979, and China minted the one-ounce Panda in 1982. By 2018, more than 50 million ounces of gold Krugerrands had been produced, while the American Eagle has seen 20 million ounces created since its original minting.

The brand equity of the Krugerrand remains strong. With the increase in uncertainty around the global financial system and worries about hyperinflation, which has sparked a revolution in cryptocurrency speculation, there has also been a boom in demand for gold. Prices have rocketed in recent years, causing the Mint to issue a new range of one-ounce silver Krugerrand bullion coins at the beginning of 2018, as well as, in 2017, a 50th anniversary platinum version as a proof collectible.

Archaeology suggests gold was first used by cultures in what is now modern-day Eastern Europe around 4000 BC to make decorative objects. Today, the metal is mined on every continent, except Antarctica, and is dominated by a small group of majors. The ten biggest gold mining companies in the world account for 22% of global production and mined $48 billion of the stuff, extracting nearly 27.5 million ounces among them in 2020, according to data from Mining Intelligence.

There are still three South African gold mining companies in the global top ten. Although AngloGold Ashanti no longer has mines in the country, it remains headquartered here for now. Gold Fields only operates the South Deep mine in South Africa since spinning off the rest of its mines into what is now increasingly a platinum producer, Sibanye-Stillwater. Sibanye has warned it will probably close the last of its South African operations by the end of this decade. Thanks to its investment in American-based PGM producer Stillwater in 2017, the group created a globally competitive, lower-cost, lower-risk producer of the metals. There was a brief period in early 2022 when the value of the company was higher than that of its former parent. To be fair though, it was primarily due to the dealmaking subsequent to the unbundling, rather than the value of the original gold mines.

The top three gold miners, Newmont (US), Barrick (Canada) and Polyus (Russia) account for nearly half of the world's production annually. Newmont operates mines in Nevada, Colorado, Ontario, Quebec, Mexico, the Dominican Republic, Australia, Ghana, Argentina, Peru and Suriname and alone makes up 21% of the gold produced by the top ten firms. China is now the world's biggest single producer and accounts for 11% of global production, despite the fact that there are no Chinese firms among the world's top mining companies. There is mounting evidence of Chinese investment into African and South American gold mining projects as its own resources come under pressure. Russia is a growing producer of the metal and is expected to produce more than China by 2029.

It is yet to be seen what the long-term consequences of Russia's imperialist ambitions will be on that country's economy and on that of the region in which it has direct influence, and how it will play out globally, especially when it comes to food and fuel price inflation.

According to the World Gold Council, 6 500 years after it was first discovered, more than 90% of the gold mined annually is destined for jewellery and investment in the form of bars and coins. It has little practical application beyond some limited technological uses and in dentistry because it has no reaction on the human body.

There is yet to be a movie about a heist involving gangsters purloining a load of iron ore or driving a coal truck off the road and filling the boot of the getaway car with the spoils. But there are plenty of blockbusters about those who go to great lengths to crack a safe filled with sparkling gemstones – diamonds especially. For all the glitz, glamour and Hollywood appeal of diamonds, their sales make up a tiny proportion of the global export of South African minerals but garner a disproportionate amount of attention – and that is no accident. It is all linked to the skills of a gifted 1940s copywriter.

Up until the 1860s, diamonds were rare. That was until fifteen-year-old Erasmus Jacobs found an unusual pebble on the banks of the Orange River near Hopetown in the present-day Northern Cape. More stones were found as fortune seekers descended on the scrubland around the Colesburg Kopje, 127 kilometres north of the first diamond discovery that led to the creation of Kimberley – the scene of the world's biggest diamond rush and the single largest crisis for the industry up to that point. Suddenly, diamonds were not as rare as had once been thought. There was no mass market requirement for the stones, which were the preserve of royalty and the super-rich. What made them sought after in the following century was truly a stroke of genius.

The legend goes that farm kids played with the pretty-looking stone for some time until, one day, Erasmus's mother gave it to her neighbour, Schalk van Niekerk, who suspected it might have value. Van Niekerk entrusted the diamond to a travelling salesman by the name of Jack O'Reilly, who, after failing to get any interest in it in the nearby towns of Hopetown or Colesberg, had it sent by post in a plain brown paper envelope to William Atherstone, an amateur mineralogist in Grahamstown.

It was eventually cut into what would become known as the Eureka diamond and was bought by the governor of the Cape Colony, Sir Philip Wodehouse. It remained in England for nearly 100 years, changing hands at Christies as part of a bangle in 1946 and, finally in 1967, when De Beers bought it for the people of South Africa. The first diamond discovered in South Africa remains on display at the Kimberley Mine Museum.

The first serious discoveries occurred on a farm called Vooruitzicht, belonging to two brothers called De Beer, and it became the richest source of high-quality gem diamonds in the world. Up until then, their value had depended on scarcity. From 1871 to 1914, when it closed operations, the mine at Kimberley would yield 13 600 000 carats, equivalent to 2 722 kilograms of diamonds.

Ancient religious texts, including the Bible, the Quran, the Hindu Puranas and even Buddhist writings, contain references to rare and valuable gems. The earliest written references to valuable gemstones go back to ancient Egypt. We know, however, that even our earliest ancestors also liked pretty baubles. They were unable to access and process any of the 200 gemstones we know of today, but there is archaeological evidence in caves across Europe that early man used amber as an adornment. There is also evidence to suggest it was traded in northern Europe during the third and fourth millennia BC.

The ancient Greeks learned to work metal and used semi-precious stones to make jewellery, and it gained traction under the Romans. Pliny the Elder described the properties and uses of crystals and minerals that were known and used in the ancient world, including how diamonds were employed to scratch other gemstones to test their relative hardness.

The establishment of trade routes saw the distribution of stones such as rubies, sapphires and emeralds from Asia into Europe. But, during the Middle Ages, adornments lost their lustre under the influence of the Catholic Church, which preached against worldly pleasures, while itself building up considerable reserves of valuable bejewelled gold and silver ornaments.

Around the fourteenth century, royalty, intent on exhibiting their power by showing off wealth and status, became more ostentatious as stones were increasingly being mined and traded across empires. By the seventeenth century, master craftsmen had worked out how to cut facets into precious stones to show off their real beauty, but such stones remained the rare preserve of religious and political elites.

The discovery at Kimberley changed everything. The scale of that and subsequent discoveries meant that what had been exceedingly rare was now at risk of becoming worthless. If you have ever tried to sell a piece of diamond jewellery, you will quickly discover that it depreciates considerably faster than a new car driven out of the showroom. It meant, wrote Edward Jay Epstein in a 1982 article entitled 'Have you ever tried to sell a diamond?' in *The Atlantic*: 'Diamonds had little intrinsic value – and their price depended almost entirely on their scarcity.'

That scarcity needed to be engineered, and who better than De Beers, which since its early days in Kimberley had succeeded in tying up most of the world's supply of the stones? The way it did so was to manage supply and create demand through some devastatingly clever marketing, the legacy of which lives on to this day.

It was not until the middle of the twentieth century that it became customary for women to wear a diamond as a symbol of their engagement to be married. De Beers controlled about 85% of the world's diamond sales and needed to create a market for polished stones. What better way than to make a connection in the minds of newly engaged couples that their prospective union was dependent on their announcing their betrothal with a sparkling diamond ring. The bigger, the better. Size mattered and was directly proportional to the value of the union. American men needed to feel a compulsion to purchase a diamond engagement ring.

Before the Second World War, in the bleak aftermath of the Great Depression, fewer than 10% of engagement rings had a diamond in them. By 1990, 80% of engagement rings around the world contained diamonds. This was largely thanks to a young copywriter called Frances Gerety, who, late one night more than 50 years earlier, wrote down: 'A Diamond is Forever.' She worked for a New York-based ad agency called N.W. Ayer, which was hired to polish the image of diamonds. Gerety is said to have thought the line was 'okay', and initially it was not met with over-whelming enthusiasm. But it captured the sentiment De Beers was seeking to disseminate: a diamond, like your relationship, is eternal. It also discouraged people from reselling diamonds. The last thing De Beers wanted was a secondary market in the stones it sold at a hefty premium.

Pop www.adiamondisforever.com into your browser later and see where it takes you. Spoiler alert: the De Beers website; the concept remains at the centre of its marketing to this day.

Long before social media created influencer culture, N.W. Ayer was doing it with precision. Diamonds made it into movie scripts and onto the big screen. As Hollywood grew in influence, so did the ability to utilise its films as a distribution mechanism for the idea of the American dream. Movie stars were adorned with diamonds, and the ad agency offered stories and society photographs to selected magazines and newspapers that would reinforce the link between the gems and romance. They success-fully moulded public perceptions, and De Beers laughed all the way to the bank. It created demand through convincing young couples that a betrothal was meaningless unless it was accom-panied by a sparkling piece of compressed three-billion-year-old carbon, created 160 kilometres below the earth's surface.

The ad agency put a price on love. One of its campaigns in the 1970s went: 'How else could two months' salary last forever? A diamond is forever. De Beers.' Men were being told what to spend and women were given a target as if that is what was required to have a meaningful relationship.

Genius.

From 1939 to 1979, De Beers' wholesale diamond sales in the US increased from $23 million to $2.1 billion. Over those four decades, the company's ad budget soared from $200 000 to $10 million a year. Every one of De Beers' advertisements featured an educational tip called 'How to Buy a Diamond'. The instructions said: 'Ask about color, clarity and cutting – for these determine a diamond's quality, contribute to its beauty and value. Choose a fine stone, and you'll always be proud of it, no matter what its size.'

The agency saw tremendous success from its early campaigns. In just four years, from 1938 to 1941, it reported a 55% increase in US diamond sales.

De Beers' cartel strategy ended up costing the company a $250-million fine in 2005 to settle class action suits brought against it in the US for price fixing – but it was a small price to pay for control of an entire industry and its global supply chains for the better part of the twentieth century.

By the time it made the settlement, the writing was on the wall for De Beers' global dominance amid new discoveries of diamonds in Canada, Russia and Australia. The settlement meant it was able to return to the US market. Settling made sense. In the early 1980s, De Beers controlled roughly 85% of both production and global sales of rough diamonds, but the US made up more than half of the world's diamond market, and De Beers wanted a piece of the action.

The idea of controlling the market had started with its founder, Cecil John Rhodes, who formed the first cartel with the top ten merchants in London's historic diamond district. His successors perfected their control of the global diamond supply chain and maintained their dominance in a way that was unprecedented across any industry. It created the London-based marketing arm, the Central Selling Organization (CSO), which bought the production of the thirteen mines owned or co-owned by De Beers in South Africa, Botswana, Namibia and Tanzania. It bolstered the 44% of the world's diamond output it controlled directly by purchasing another 25% of global production from Russia and Canada, which were shipped to the CSO.

There, the company's 500 sorters would combine all of the stones and separate them into 14 000 categories and then into lots called boxes, and every five weeks it would distribute these among an exclusive clique of 125 'sightholder' partners from across the world, who, without argument or dissent, would take their allocations home to their respective cutting centres, where they would be processed and polished into the cut diamonds we are all familiar with. Only then would they make it to market.

De Beers' dominance was diluted with the fall of communism when Russia brought Siberian diamonds to market and with the substantial discoveries in Australia and Canada.

So, instead, it moved to brand its diamonds in the same way as Nike was doing by adding its swoosh to running shoes, and firms around the world started investing heavily in brands. De Beers looked to do the same by inscribing what it called its 'Forever' mark on its very best diamonds. It was not just a diamond; it was a De Beers diamond, and the mark was a sign of the quality of a stone that came from ethical sources, rather than from the killing fields of the illicit diamond trade made famous in the movie *Blood Diamond*.

GENIUS

So, rather than controlling every diamond on the market, it sought instead to make the diamonds it did produce more valuable.

When De Beers entered Japan in the 1960s, diamonds were marketed as a token of 'modern Western values'. In 1967, when the campaign started, fewer than 5% of Japanese women had a diamond as a symbol of betrothal. That number grew to 60% by 1981.

Growing demand from China and stable markets elsewhere means that the global appetite for the stones remains positive. In a good year, South Africa will export about 2 tonnes – or 10 million carats – of diamonds. It is a big number. The Big Hole at Kimberley yielded a total of 13 600 carats over its entire 43-year lifetime.

Today, the global diamond mining industry is dominated by three companies: Alrosa from Russia, Rio Tinto in Australia and, of course, De Beers.

Mined diamonds are mostly processed in and sold via the major global diamond centres in Antwerp, Dubai, New York, Hong Kong, Mumbai and Tel Aviv. In contrast to precious metals, there is no universal market price per carat of diamonds. Despite that, global diamond prices have increased more than tenfold since 1960 to the prices today.

South Africa's diamond production is worth anything from R13 billion to R17 billion a year. During 2019, 91% of the country's rough diamonds were exported, half to the United Arab Emirates, 30% to cutters in Botswana and 16% to the European Union, with the balance spread across India, Israel, Switzerland, China, Thailand and the US.

62

The country's largest source of rough diamonds is the De Beers-owned Venetia mine in a nature reserve near Alldays in Limpopo. It has another 25 years ahead of it, thanks to a decision to switch from an open-pit operation to underground mining.

While South Africa is richly endowed with mineral resources, its current failure to maintain critical infrastructure restricts its ability to compete effectively and puts a cap on the volume of minerals that can be exported. While the country's Sishen–Saldanha line developed a reputation over two decades for superlative performance in getting iron ore from the middle of the country to the port of Saldanha, even that rare success story has started to fray at the edges. Equipment breakdowns, cancelled trains and delays in shipping have choked exports of iron ore from Saldanha in the west and coal from Richards Bay in the east.

Exxaro reported its 2021 results could have been 30% higher were it not for the criminal disruptions on the line to Richards Bay. While measures were being taken to combat theft and the damage to rail infrastructure, the response was slow and resulted in lost revenues for the company, lower returns to shareholders and fewer taxes for government. The new listing Thungela Resources also commented in its 2022 results about the opportunity cost of inadequate rail infrastructure affecting its sales volumes and the frustration at not being able to take advantage of a boom in global demand for coal. In response, Transnet CEO Portia Derby appealed for patience as she sought to dial back on the damage wrought by a decade of mismanagement of the entity, which saw its rail network eviscerated and ports become some of the least efficient in the world.

Anglo American-controlled Kumba Iron Ore, the country's biggest miner of the globally sought-after commodity that is central to steel production, reported in 2021 that it was struggling to get its product to market. It blamed poor-performing ports and rail bottlenecks for causing its stockpiles to rise as exports had been choked through inefficiency of the system run by Transnet. As stock levels at mines rose, it forced Kumba to slow down production.

Sasol and Thungela Resources both reported they were struggling to move coal to ports. It proved to be a significant lost opportunity as China ran short of coal and suffered significant rolling blackouts through a large part of its industrial heartland. As prices rose, South Africa found itself unable to fully exploit the opportunity.

Exports of just coal and iron ore earned the country $15 billion in export revenues in 2020.

Part of the problem is a highly concentrated and inefficient bureaucracy. In May 2019, the Department of Mineral Resources merged with the Department of Energy, creating an economy-critical super-ministry. Covid-19 understandably caused disruptions to mining, but the sector recovered quickly to find that the systems it had used before the crisis to facilitate the movement of its products had deteriorated and needed urgent attention.

A report by PwC found: 'The mining sector in South Africa has been negatively impacted by underinvestment in rail infrastructure and decreased efficiencies related to the transportation of key bulk commodities (coal, iron ore and manganese). Transnet, as the SOC [state-owned company] responsible for maintaining the rail and port network, has been operationally challenged by locomotive unavailability, coal line shutdown interruptions, power outages and derailments, combined with vandalism and sabotage of rail equipment and pervasive cable theft.'

The report added that the difficulties were crippling exports at a time when commodity prices were booming. Mining companies saw the biggest improvement during the Covid-19 pandemic, thanks to higher commodity prices, and dividends from the sector rose from R43 billion to R76 billion from 2020 to 2021, despite the failures at Transnet. It could have capitalised on the price boom far more had the proper infrastructure been in place.

According to Stats SA, more than 300 million metric tonnes of coal are exported annually, making it the country's biggest commodity export in terms of volume. Seventy-five per cent of mineral exports are made up of coal, followed by iron ore, then chromium and manganese ore. Other higher-value commodities make up a tiny proportion of exports but generate far more in terms of foreign exchange. The country exports just 138 metric tonnes of platinum and less than 100 tonnes of gold, but the value of those exports generated significantly higher tax revenues for the fiscus than had been anticipated at the start of the crisis. The reality is, as with so much in South Africa, it could have been much better.

The mining market is dominated by export sales. More than 61% of sales were from exports in 2019. Each commodity differs. While 96% of manganese was exported, nearly two-thirds of coal was consumed locally and mostly by the hungry carbon dependency of Eskom.

PGMs have become some of South Africa's most valuable exports. They are used in the automotive sector, in coins and bars, and in fuel cells and batteries, as well as in a range of other industries.

Because South Africa is the world's biggest producer of PGMs, the Covid-related disruptions in 2020, which led to a 15% drop in production, pushed up prices at a time of increased demand: rhodium rocketed by 187% and palladium by 43% in dollar terms and accounted for nearly three-quarters of the value of PGM sales. A decade before, platinum had been the key commodity and had made up 68% of sales.

The PGM sector is the largest contributor to mining in terms of sales and overtook coal as the number-one export commodity from South Africa for the first time in 2020. PGM sales amounted to R190 billion – that is worth more than iron ore and gold sales combined. Sanctions imposed on Russia in response to its invasion of Ukraine saw the export of minerals, including valuable PGMs, disrupted, pushing up prices to the benefit of South African producers.

South Africa is the third largest iron ore exporter and the sixth largest producer of the commodity in the world, mostly from Kumba Iron Ore's largest mine at Sishen in the Northern Cape. Kumba has continued to invest heavily in the project, and the mine is expected to last until 2039. About 96% of the country's iron ore exports travel along the 860-kilometre dedicated railway line to the deepwater port at Saldanha.

Despite this environment, in January 2022, the JSE rose above the 75 000 mark to record levels, buoyed, in part, by some of the baby steps of reform taken since Cyril Ramaphosa came to power and by the fact that there had been a boom in commodity prices as a result of pent-up demand. This was brought about by the pandemic and the global breakdown in supply chains, and it led to shortages of key minerals everywhere.

More than two-thirds of the earnings of the JSE's 40 biggest companies come from outside South Africa. Anglo American has South African interests, but it digs far more holes beyond South Africa's borders than within it; Naspers remains heavily dependent on the profitability of China's Tencent, thanks to its acquisition of a stake in that company long before it became successful; and firms such as Aspen Pharmacare operate in more than 50 territories.

Like so many of the commodities South Africa produces, few are beneficiated at home. Rather, raw materials are exported to big, industrialised economies where they are efficiently processed into finished goods for import.

The lesson for Africa will come from Aliko Dangote, the continent's richest man, who, in 2022, began to refine Nigerian oil into fuel after generations of drillers simply exported the stuff elsewhere, forcing one of the world's biggest oil producers to import diesel and petrol. The facility, which cost an estimated $19 billion to build, has an installed capacity of 650 000 barrels per day, and its output is sufficient not only to meet the country's own fuel demands but also to turn it into an exporter of refined crude. In that lies a lesson for other African economies.

# CHAPTER 4

# Agriculture – Growing with the Best in the World

*Farming looks mighty easy when your plow is a pencil and you're a thousand miles from the corn field.* — Dwight Eisenhower

There is a six-week window from mid-September to the end of October when the only fresh cherries available anywhere in the world are produced in South Africa. The 'cherry window' is small, and the 200-tonne harvest starts at the Muriti farm near Rustenburg, followed five days later at a farm called Kareebosch near Polokwane, and soon after on a farm in Gauteng and another at Belfast in Mpumalanga.

Size matters. The bigger, the plumper, the juicier, the better, and the goal is to harvest when the fruit exceeds 24 mm in diameter. Most of the crop is then ready for air transport to the UK, India and the Middle East.

The last cherries of the season used to be from Lake Okanagan in Canada. This crop finishes in mid-September, and traditionally the 'global new crop' only started in November, originating from Chile.

Now Limpopo-based ZZ2, better known for its tomatoes, is crashing the party, producing varieties under licence from Californian firm Zaiger Genetics, which allows it to plug the global supply gap as it harvests from September to mid-November, becoming the start of the global new crop season, or should that be the end of the last one?

It does not really matter.

ZZ2, one of the country's biggest fruit and vegetable producers, saw a gap and stepped into it, knowing that despite the growing global trend towards seasonal, local crops, there is a big enough market that still expects their favourite food all year long.

Agriculture is critical from a food security perspective. Since South Africa is a net exporter of a range of agricultural commodities, agriculture is a valuable foreign exchange earner, though it is a far less significant force in the economy today than it was in the 1960s.

In 1961, agriculture contributed 11% of GDP. Back then, South Africa's economy was heavily dependent on labour-intensive mining and farming. That has changed considerably in the intervening years. Now agriculture makes up just 2.4% of the economy, but it does generate about 10% of the country's export revenues – around $10 billion a year – a number that is forecast to grow as global demand for its produce expands.

South Africa has by far the most modern, productive and diverse agricultural economy in Africa, but its ownership is highly concentrated, based first on the apartheid legacy of forbidding black people from owning land and, second, due to the enormous consolidation in agriculture driven by the high cost of increased mechanisation and the need to be globally competitive. That has also seen a dramatic decrease in the number of active farmers on the land. In 1994, the Transvaal Agricultural Union estimated there were 120 000 commercial farmers active in South Africa. Today, there are about 32 000. Fewer than 7 000 generate 80% of agricultural output.

South African agriculture has come on in leaps and bounds since my grandfather was in his prime. A *Who's Who in Agriculture* publication from the 1960s describes his operation like this: 'Farming on Mathejespan [*sic*] is most intensive, but great care and attention has always been paid to the preservation of the veld, and the productivity of the arable land.' He was clearly big on sustainability and knew future generations might want to benefit from his legacy. He was one of the first people to import a tractor between the wars, and he brought in animals from the UK to improve the genetic pool of his beef herd. He was edgy for his time but would hardly recognise the complexity of the increasingly globalised markets and the large companies today that own vast tracts of land and produce an inspiring array of high-margin crops for export.

A growing number of the country's agricultural practices and the people who have created them are among the best in the world, but South African agriculturalists could learn a thing or two from the Dutch about productivity and intensive farming as pressure builds on feeding a fast-growing global population.

The Netherlands is the world's second biggest exporter of

agricultural goods after the US, which has 237 times the space and 20 times the population of Holland. But it is the scarcity of space that is driving one of the world's smaller countries to lead much-needed changes in how farming is done for the future.

Holland is crowded. Its land and labour are expensive. So, it has had to figure out how to work within its constraints. It has developed a remarkable industry, which, in 2017, exported $111 billion of agricultural goods, from flowers to vegetables. That is eleven times more than South Africa managed.

Not bad for a small country.

A quarter of the Netherlands lies below sea level, as a result of seven centuries of land reclamation from the North Sea. With a population of 17.6 million people, the Netherlands is the sixteenth most densely populated country in the world and the second most densely populated country in the European Union. That does not suggest there is much space for farming.

One example of its extraordinary innovation is the story of Duijvestijn Tomaten, which produces 100 million tomatoes a year from an area not much bigger than fourteen football pitches. Since 2011, the firm has been using geothermal energy to heat its greenhouses. Water is delivered using hydroponics and the plants are grown in small bags of rockwool substrate, made from spinning together molten basaltic rock into fine fibres, which contain nutrients and allows the plants to soak up water even when moisture levels are low. The farm also pipes waste carbon dioxide into the greenhouses from a nearby Shell Oil refinery – that helps the crops to grow and reduces climate-changing emissions being released into the atmosphere.

Its exports are aided by its superlative infrastructure and the fact that it has an enormous geographical advantage because of its position in northern Europe. It has some of the world's best-performing ports and a well-connected rail system, which means it is able to get its produce to foreign markets, mostly within the EU, without much trouble.

This is a long way from one of the world's biggest investment scams: the 1600s' Tulipmania, when punts in rare bulbs reached fever pitch and ruined thousands of speculators. Today, the country runs a perfectly legitimate $10 billion-a-year trade in cut flowers and is the world's biggest exporter of tulips, bulbs and a wide range of seeds.

South African agriculture is nowhere near that level of evolution. Its smartest operators, however, are progressively adopting a global mindset and its biggest exports include citrus, wine, table grapes, maize and apples, but it also exports wool, increasingly to China, along with nuts, sugar and mohair.

Most farming in South Africa is large-scale, dry-land agriculture, reliant on the vagaries of a more unpredictable climate and the ever-present uncertainty of land tenure. In 2021, the governing ANC abandoned plans to change the constitution to facilitate much-needed reform after it failed to secure a required two-thirds majority in parliament to do so. It has said it will resort to using existing legislation to facilitate a change of ownership more than a century after the 1913 Natives Land Act, which deprived black South Africans of land ownership in their own country.

Rather than restrict investment and progress in agriculture, the ANC appears to have galvanised the industry into being proactive about bringing more black farmers into the sector. But it is not easy for new entrants, as the industry requires vast amounts of capital for players to be competitive. It is also no longer the jobs panacea it once was. It contributes just 5% of formal employment, which, considering it is just a little more than 2% of the economy, is helpful, but it is low compared to other parts of Africa. The employment rate in agriculture is declining due to greater automation and mechanisation, which is aimed at keeping the sector globally competitive.

And despite its vast open spaces, the fact that it is drier than many of the world's biggest food producers means only a fraction of the country's land is suitable for commercial crop production – around 15%.

Even with these barriers, it is a leading producer in a range of agricultural commodities. According to the UN's Food and Agriculture Organization, South Africa is one of the world's largest producers of chicory roots (4th), grapefruit (4th), cereals (5th), green maize and maize (7th), castor oil seed (9th), pears (9th), sisal (10th) and fibre crops (10th).

The sticky label on the piece of fruit you absent-mindedly pick off before washing and devouring the fruit represents a mixture of courage, optimism and enormous risk appetite, which encapsulates the rich and textured story of South African agriculture.

South Africa is the second biggest citrus exporter worldwide after Spain and is a leading global player in the avocado and macadamia nut markets.

The country has come a long way since the sanctions-busting Outspan oranges that eventually became a rallying point for the global anti-apartheid movement in the 1970s. The first orange and lemon trees arrived at the Cape from St Helena in 1654. They were planted in the gardens of the Dutch East India Company and used as a key ally in the fight against scurvy – a disease caused by a lack of vitamin C that afflicted sailors making the long journey from Europe to Asian markets. Citrus exports to Britain began in the immediate aftermath of the South African War in the early 1900s amid predictions, even back then, that the country could become a major global producer if it were to use irrigation. The number of cases exported exceeded one million for the first time by 1925. By the 1930s, all South African citrus was exported under the Outspan brand, owned initially by Percy Fitzpatrick, most famous as the author of *Jock of the Bushveld*. His descendants, the Niven family, still farm citrus in the Eastern Cape to this day.

Citrus comes from three main areas in South Africa: the Western Cape around Citrusdal, the Northern Cape along the banks of the Orange River and the Sundays River Valley in the Eastern Cape. South Africa is a major producer. You would swear it was the Italians in the world's number-one position considering how much PR the country does about lemons and the things it makes from them. Celebrations are held throughout Italy to mark the lemon harvest in April and May each year; no postcard of the picturesque Amalfi Coast is complete without bright yellow lemons in the foreground; and you have not lived until you have sipped an icy Limoncello. We clearly could do more to beneficiate our agricultural products, but for now we need to be satisfied that 2.25 million tonnes, or two-thirds of the annual crop, of lemons, limes, oranges, grapefruit and soft citrus get to international markets.

Citrus exports have grown by more than 40% in the past decade to about R20 billion annually and this trajectory is set to continue. The Citrus Growers' Association expects an increase from the current 150 million 15-kilogram cartons per year to 200 million by 2025, and 255 million by 2030.

One of the single biggest citrus exporters is the Sundays River Citrus Company (SRCC), owned by its 105 growers in the Eastern Cape. It dates back to 1924 but has really begun scaling up operations in the past decade or so, bringing much-needed jobs and income to the country's poorest province. It exports fresh fruit to Europe and the UK but is excluded from the US due to a chemical it uses to prevent black spot on its fruit. The US is, however, a big importer of South African lemon juice as well as lemon oil, made from the rinds of squeezed fruit and used in the formulations of fizzy drinks such as Coca-Cola and Pepsi.

Argentina and Mexico supply more than half the citrus juice imports into the US and South Africa just under 10% – which makes it an important market for Venco, a firm owned by five of the Sundays River Valley's biggest producers. It processes between 80 000 and 100 000 tonnes of oranges and lemons into a range of products, including citrus concentrates that are either frozen or preserved and exported in drums or big soft bags similar to those used in the wine trade, cold-pressed oils from the peels, and a range of bulk concentrates and citrus pulp.

South African fresh citrus enters the US duty-free under the African Growth Opportunity Act and accounts for 4% of total US citrus imports, making it the fifth biggest supplier to that country. South Africa's fruit exporters to the northern hemisphere have the significant benefit that they are counter-seasonal producers to those in wealthier northern climes.

Today, the labels of SRCC, Westfalia, ZZ2 and Kromco are as likely to end up on the tables of Dallas, Dubai or Delhi as they are in Durban, Dullstroom or Delmas.

Apples make up 46% of the country's deciduous fruit exports, according to Hortgro Pome, formerly the South African Apple and Pear Producers' Association. The South African apple industry has grown markedly over the past 50 years.

When you head out of Cape Town on the N2 highway, battle your way through the traffic jam in Somerset West and climb the majestic Sir Lowry's Pass into the Overberg region, the core of the country's expanding apple trade, you will pass the enormous Kromco processing facility on your left-hand side. It was founded as a cooperative in 1971 and had 60 members, with average apple farm sizes of 30 hectares. Today, it is a private company with eleven shareholders and the average farm size is 160 hectares. In South African farming, in sharp contrast to the Dutch example, scale is everything.

The 25 200 hectares of orchards produce more than 458 000 tonnes of apples for export, worth more than R10 billion a year.

That is double the volume and value of pears that make up about a quarter of deciduous exports. There is increasing global demand for higher-priced but lower-volume stone fruits, such as peaches, plums, apricots, nectarines and, of course, cherries.

Deciduous fruit is a commodity business. Consumers buy on varietal rather than place of origin. The fruit is traded in bulk, and provenance, to the majority of consumers in most parts of the world, does not really matter. One Golden Delicious apple does not vary markedly from another, no matter where it is grown, unlike wine, which trades on its terroir and country of origin. Because deciduous fruit is a commodity, you have to be cost-competitive. The South African industry has succeeded in striking that balance to compete with the best in the world by producing the right quality fruit at competitive price points.

Commercial agriculture is not ever going to be the mega-employer it once was, simply because machines are far more effective, accurate and efficient at doing jobs such as grading, sorting and packing. That technology comes with a hefty price tag. Kromco, for example, has two automated pre-sorting lines that required an initial investment of R400 million. Considering the massive volumes of fruit that need to be processed, speed is of the essence to ensure that the product is in optimal condition when it reaches consumers' hands. Any delays or breaks in the cold chain can be devastating for a crop and the reputation of a producer.

'Our packhouse can handle numerous varieties, qualities and pack configurations with the necessary flexibility to service our customers' needs without compromising on quality, speed and cost,' says Paul Clüver Jnr, whose family is a long-term shareholder in the enterprise, which distributes to 45 countries.

South Africa's opportunity to grow exports to China is significant, and local apple growers have had access to that market since 2015. While volumes are small compared to the demand from the US, the industry sees it as a strong growth market.

The pandemic-driven global logistics crisis has had a major impact on all exporters. It is made worse by the fact that South Africa's ports are rated as among the most inefficient in the world. The Durban harbour was ranked by a World Bank report in the bottom three of the world's 351 competent container-handling facilities, while Ngqura in the Eastern Cape, and Cape Town were also given low rankings.

The industry has opened up markedly since the advent of democracy in South Africa. The UK has always been an important market for South African fruit producers. In the 1990s, the major supermarket groups had most of the country's export-quality product sewn up between them, with Tesco, Sainsbury's, Waitrose and ASDA controlling almost 90% of the purchasing power. Producers all planted and delivered pretty much the same assortment of fruit and, after the emerging markets crash of the late 1990s, consolidation became the order of the day. That has led, says Clüver, to South Africa becoming increasingly commercial and a world-class operator.

ZZ2 is not only useful in terms of being the only cherry producer in the world for six weeks in September and October every year, but it is also successful in that it produces nearly half of the country's annual tomato crop. Westfalia has diversified across multiple geographies and is the world's single biggest avocado supplier, with operations on 5 continents and in 16 territories supplying customers in 40 countries for 12 months of the year.

Two decades ago, Westfalia had 1 200 hectares of avocados in the hills around Tzaneen supplying mostly European supermarkets. Now it has about 2 000 hectares of avocado orchards in southern Africa alone, from which it delivers 5 million cartons of Hass, Fuerte and Ryan avocados every year.

It is privately owned, controlled by the founding Hans Merensky Trust, and includes the state-owned Industrial Development Corporation among its key shareholders. Because it is privately owned, it does not publicly disclose financial information, nor will it discuss its global land leases. However, London-based CEO Alk Brand says it reports in dollars and its revenues are 'substantial'.

Westfalia has come a long way since it was founded by geologist Hans Merensky, who also had a penchant for farming. Merensky's influence is still felt to this day in mining. The first platinum nuggets of significance were found in South Africa in 1924, and it was Merensky who discovered two deposits, each about 100-kilometres long, in what is now known as the Bushveld Igneous Complex. This discovery started with test work in the area around Mashishing (formerly known as Lydenburg). With funding from friends, he searched out payable platinum deposits from a base on the farm Maandagshoek, where he secured 23 claims. These mines have produced about 75% of the world's output.

His work saw the Merensky Reef named after him, and he

later identified the eastern limb of the Bushveld Complex. He established the Merensky Trust in 1949, three years before his death, and it continues to oversee extensive forestry and agricultural holdings worldwide. He bought the original Westfalia estate in 1929 and set about rehabilitating the poorly managed land, which had been overgrazed and where exotic vegetation had crowded out indigenous plant species.

Today, the world's biggest avocado producer carries the name of the original estate.

The avocado ripening cycle begins annually in Israel from 1 October, with Spain and Chile coming on stream at the same time. Westfalia has sales offices as well as ripening and packing facilities in the UK, France and the Netherlands. It now operates avocado estates in southern Africa, Mexico, Chile, Portugal, Colombia and Peru, as well as in California. It has the world's biggest avocado-growing footprint, allowing it to service customers in the UK, Europe, North America, Latin America and southern Africa all-year round. It is looking at new growing opportunities in Latin America and Asia.

With the exception of its business in Chile, nearly 100% of its farming and growing operations are dedicated to avocado production. That makes it quite dependent on the millennial trend of high-priced avocado toast remaining a healthy meal of choice in perpetuity. It does trade other agricultural commodities from third-party suppliers, including mangoes, blueberries, pomegranates, apples, grapes, stone fruit, citrus, cherries and passion fruit, which it is also able to supply globally. It has developed beneficiation capacity for excess product, which means it has a range of avocado oils, purées and guacamole, while also making dried fruit to extend the life of its fresh produce.

'Like any other fruit, avocado trees produce only for a number of weeks per year, so to enable our customers to be supplied all year we have established our own farms and source from independent growers in many parts of the world,' says Brand. 'We make sure our avocados are available for local consumption and for export and our technical and agronomy teams have identified the areas where we can grow avocados sustainably.'

It is a dominant supplier in each of the sixteen territories in which it operates, which means that it has direct lines of communication to the biggest retailers and food service suppliers within those regions.

'We have a sophisticated distribution network, and our packing takes place in world-class and high-tech packhouses, where value is added through our own ripening rooms creating ready-to-eat avocados in line with local taste preferences,' adds Brand.

Key to Westfalia's success has been the decision to fund the world's largest private avocado research programme, which has enabled it to develop industry-leading rootstocks to grow new varieties sustainably under vastly different conditions in many parts of the world.


Like Westfalia, the ZZ2 Group is privately owned. However, it remains headquartered in Limpopo.

The Van Zyl family started their farming operations in the region more than 100 years ago. They trace their ancestral roots as far back as Willem van Zyl, who worked as a fresh produce supplier for the Dutch East India Company until he was sacked for insubordination in 1702. He bought land in Franschhoek, where he farmed fresh produce, wine and livestock. His descendants left the Cape in the migration northwards during the 1830s, settling eventually in the region east of Polokwane in 1880. His descendants today focus primarily on tomatoes and avocados but also run mango, onion, date, cherry, apple, pear, stone fruit, almond and blueberry businesses in the Western Cape, Eastern Cape, Gauteng, North West Province, Mpumalanga and Namibia.

The name ZZ2 originated in the aftermath of the South African War when it became a requirement that all livestock should be clearly branded. The Van Zyl family was allocated the ZZ2 moniker, which they later used, dipped in red paint, to stamp their identity on pockets of potatoes, and the name stuck. ZZ2 was registered as a private company in 1966. Tomatoes are exported to Réunion, Dubai, the Seychelles and Oman, while around 3 000 tonnes of avocados go to Europe. The rest of the produce is sold through the fresh markets in Johannesburg and Cape Town. It plants 60 000 hectares of crops annually and employs around 8 000 people in South Africa, most of whom are based at its headquarters.

It has a substantial herd of mostly Pinzgauer cattle. They are not only used for beef production but are also a critical part of the crop life cycle. The firm works on a seven-year rotation, so land used for tomatoes is left fallow for cattle to roam across and fertilise naturally as they return nutrients to the soil between crop cycles. With concerns about global warming and the water shortages likely to ensue, the firm also sets aside vast conservation areas to guard natural water resources for an unpredictable future.

ZZ2 is the biggest tomato producer in the southern hemisphere, delivering about 160 000 tonnes to market annually. Nearly half of all tomatoes consumed in South Africa carry the ZZ2 brand, due to its wide geographical spread and its ability to produce all-year round. It is also invested in a juicing factory where it processes sweet Romanita tomatoes into juice and is seeking export markets. It only exports fresh tomatoes to parts of the Middle East and Africa when there is a hiccup in global supply chains, because the short lead time of rapidly ripening tomatoes complicates logistics and the cost of export make them uncompetitive in most markets.

The company manages to produce avocados all-year round and is expanding its 1 000-hectare footprint for production, while its own nursery operation can produce up to 300 000 trees a year, enabling it to export to the UK, Europe and Asia.

The big global drive is on so-called superfoods, which are in demand worldwide. In addition to avocados and cherries, ZZ2 also has apple and pear orchards, along with blueberries, Medjool dates and a vast array of nuts, although not on anything like the scale or at the reach of Westfalia.

China absorbs most of South Africa's macadamia nut crop. The global industry is quite small, making up just 1% of all tree nuts produced annually. This means the dominant players are leading the growth trajectory. A total of 97% of what is produced in

South Africa is exported. Macadamias South Africa, known by industry insiders as SAMAC, started in the 1970s when growers began to collaborate to tackle common industry-related problems. It has played a vital role in globalising the South African industry and building it into a significant player that vies with Australia, from where the nuts originate, as the largest international producer. The industry has grown from 1 211 tonnes of nuts to nearly 60 000 tonnes in 2019. As macadamias have increased in popularity, the value of the product has risen from R32 million to nearly R5 billion. The industry is expecting more than a tenfold increase by 2027, by which time it anticipates annual macadamia production of 721 000 tonnes.

Macadamia nuts need a hot, subtropical climate with little humidity to survive. The majority of the trees in South Africa are planted in Levubu and Tzaneen in the Limpopo Province, in Hazyview, Nelspruit and Barberton in Mpumalanga, and in coastal KwaZulu-Natal. Most of the rootstocks are created in Australia and Hawaii.

The trees flower from August to September and harvesting runs from March to July. Unlike with other tree crops, it is difficult to tell which macadamia nuts are ready for harvesting, so farmers wait for them to drop before they are gathered off the ground in a labour-intensive process. Increasingly, tree-shaking machinery is being used that allows the nuts to drop immediately into nets, which speeds up processing.

All these enterprises require patience to bring orchards to production. Deciduous trees reach their full potential about five years after planting, while it takes that long for macadamias to start producing nuts and up to fifteen years before they deliver on their maximum production capacity. Macadamia trees need a lot of management to ensure good nut quality, as they are susceptible to many pests and diseases. Properly managed trees can yield about 12 kilograms of nuts each a year. Orchards need to be vast to be commercially viable. Almonds are equally difficult to grow and originate from Asia and the Middle East. They require the same sort of frost-free tropical climate as the macadamias do to thrive.

Farming is increasingly capital-intensive and requires a policy environment that encourages farmers to take a long-term view. The land debate is a long way from settled in South Africa. Government has made some progress at restitution for those with historical claims on property after being dispossessed in terms of the 1913 Natives Land Act and being forcibly removed by the apartheid government. The issue has become a political time bomb. Yet, ZZ2 and others have chosen to work within an imperfect system and are earning the right to continue working the land in the areas where they are active. Due to the labour-intensive nature of what they do, they are significant employers and taxpayers in a country short on jobs and revenue.

'We are actively participating in constructive and enabling reconstruction and development programmes involving landowners who have acquired land in accordance with the land reform programmes and "Permissions to Occupy" from traditional leaders,' says Tommie van Zyl, CEO of ZZ2. 'We are working on a large project with the Makgoba community in Tzaneen, which includes large-scale, commercial farming projects, entrepreneurial, medium-sized farming projects for individuals or families, and micro or communal projects.' There is also a strong collaboration with the University of Limpopo to train agronomists, soil scientists and horticulturalists, who will ultimately benefit the region as they qualify and begin to work as professionals in the food industry.

But climate change brings considerable risk. The group maintains weather stations on all its farms, and its century-old records reveal dynamic and oscillating weather patterns that are impossible to predict with any certainty. ZZ2 manages what it can with new cultivars, improved production techniques, moving to different locations, concentration of growing periods, utilising protective structures for shading or rain cover, properly designed packhouses, cooling technology, efficient logistics and even refrigerated transport.

'We need our government to make marketing and import protocol agreements with countries, especially in the East where we can compete with our products. This will have a massive impact on job creation,' comments Van Zyl, who is frustrated at the constraints imposed by an inflexible bureaucracy that could do considerably more to facilitate the movement of products across borders.

Getting products to market is also a challenge. The choice between air freight and shipping is determined by costs and the scarcity value of the different products. Cherries and blueberries are high-value, much-sought-after products that warrant air freight, whereas deciduous and citrus fruits are more commoditised and are shipped by sea freight to markets.

Firms like the UK-based, privately owned BerryWorld contract supply in South Africa through a locally owned subsidiary, and independent farmers utilise 2 000 hectares of land to grow licenced varieties, such as Flavourburst, for the company. BerryWorld South Africa supplies the UK, Ireland, Europe, South Africa, Asia, the Far East and the Middle East.

This requires a complex series of carefully managed relationships, starting with individual growers, some of whom share in the ownership of the varietal licences. Fruit farming is a long-term game. The right land needs to be sourced, prepared and planted and then careful management needs to bring the trees to optimal production in about eight years. That is, if the increasingly erratic elements behave.

South Africa produced about 20 000 tonnes of blueberries in the 2022 season, of which more than 90% was for export. It is a rapidly growing industry that generates about R2 billion in sales annually.

'The countries South Africa is able to export to are limited,' says BerryWorld sales manager Stefan Viljoen, 'as we are either heavily tariffed or do not have the correct phytosanitary protocols in place – that is, technical controls for pests and pesticides.' The industry maintains it has the proper protocols but government sign-off is slow. As a result, blueberries from South Africa are only sold in the UK and EU, with limited volumes in Southeast Asia and some in the Middle East. Other markets, such as China, Japan and South Korea, are still closed to blueberry imports. Production in South Africa is a tenth of what happens in Peru at the same time and a lot less than that of Chile, which comes to market as the local season ends. That keeps a lid on pricing, despite a high standard and quality delivered from South Africa.

BerryWorld South Africa sources fruit directly from 35 dedicated growers that range geographically from Zimbabwe to Limpopo and Mpumalanga and down to the southern and Western Cape.

'There is little risk of blueberries going the way of ostrich feathers,' says Viljoen. When the *Titanic* sank in 1912, the most valuable cargo on board was a shipment of feathers, which was insured for $2.3 million in today's money because, in 1912, only diamonds were worth more by weight than the feathers. The global hat craze needed feathers, and it made farmers in Oudtshoorn, the ostrich capital of the world, filthy rich. The industry boomed in the early part of the twentieth century, thanks to northern hemisphere fashion demands requiring millions of plumes. But it disappeared almost as quickly as it started, partly as motoring replaced horse-drawn transport and hats were simply not practical in open-air vehicles driving at speed. In addition, a combination of austerity and women needing more sensible headgear in their commute to factories as they took over jobs from fighting men, made them impractical. What we have left is the majestic sandstone 'ostrich palace' homes of Oudtshoorn, reminding us of how fleeting some international trends can be.

Blueberries, argues Viljoen, are not that kind of trend; they are part of a global movement toward healthier eating.

ZZ2 started its cherry orchards in 2015, and it produces about a dozen varieties each of apples and pears around the Ceres and

Langkloof regions of the Western Cape between November and May each year. It has planted 63 hectares of almond trees and it runs joint ventures with established growers. Its rapidly growing date business along the banks of the Orange River in Namibia sees it produce moist and meaty Medjool dates. The abundant water supply, combined with the intense desert heat, creates ideal conditions for production.

The firm continues to invest heavily in infrastructure. During the pandemic, it built one of the world's biggest single avo-handling facilities, not only to process its own produce but also as part of a strategic partnership with Mission Produce and contract exporters Core Fruit, which sends 236 varieties of fruit and nuts through 105 harbours to 65 countries from South Africa.

Agriculture is a sector in which confidence is key and security of tenure is imperative if a new generation of farmers are to keep investing in long-term production. So far, so good, from an industry point of view, but, under pressure, governments, like that of Robert Mugabe's in Zimbabwe, can resort to extraordinary measures, such as that country's destructive land reform programme, in order to hold onto power. That fear is never far from the minds of South African farmers. By the very nature of their existence, being dependent on the elements and pricing for their products, which is beyond their control, farmers tend to be some of the most extraordinary optimists anywhere. Thank goodness.

CHAPTER 5

· · · · · · · · · · · · ·

# The Big, Bold Booze Bonanza

*In wine there is wisdom, in beer there is freedom,*
*in water there is bacteria.* — Benjamin Franklin

SABMiller is without doubt South Africa's most successful corporate export, but it did not export beer. Instead, it transferred systems and well-trained executives to head up new acquisitions around the globe, as it embarked on its early 1990s emerging markets brewery acquisition spree. It was, for a time, the second biggest brewer in the world. When Anheuser-Busch InBev bought it in 2016, the *Financial Times* billed the more than $100-billion takeover as the third largest acquisition in history and the biggest in the UK at the time.

The company had taken full advantage of the once-in-a-lifetime opportunity presented by the almost simultaneous collapse of apartheid in South Africa and communism in the USSR. This opened up African and Eastern European markets to the world's strongest players, of which SAB, by virtue of its monopoly in South Africa, was one.

Unlike the distressed brewers it bought, especially in Eastern

Europe, it had not allowed itself to become complacent about its dominant position in its domestic market. Over the years, it managed to fend off competition from the likes of Louis Luyt's Kronenbräu 1308 and Anton Rupert's wine and spirits business, Distell.

It was SAB's pedantic focus on processes and branding that made it one of the most efficient brewers in the world, and it transplanted that ethos to every new market it entered.

Rob Forsyth, a portfolio manager at Ninety One, studied global brewers and beer markets for more than two decades. 'At its core it was an operationally obsessed company with tight operating metrics, while a firm like Naspers [which tried a similar model of exporting its talented South African leadership to manage acquisitions in China] at its core is an investment-focused company, with capital allocation a priority in a more regulated media industry,' Forsyth explains.

The brewing company, described to me once as the 'best non-certificated MBA' in existence thanks to its high standards, superlative training and absolute focus on the minutiae of brewing, was able to drive fast turnarounds in markets with strong, well-loved brands.

Despite the immense complexity of entering new jurisdictions, the company did a few simple things in each market that immediately set the flywheels of its businesses moving. It refreshed brand identities and introduced new bottles to replace over-used, chipped and damaged ones that should have been recycled and replaced long ago. It also improved distribution, ensuring that its products were always available when and where customers wanted them. And, critically, as it learned in South Africa, it marketed the hell out of its brands, building customer loyalty.

Across Africa, the company made beer more affordable. Mark Bowman, then MD for Africa for SABMiller, said at a presentation in 2012: 'Beer is very expensive in Africa. We talk about $1 a serve, which equates to three to five hours of work for most Africans.' So, it set about halving the price of a beer so that workers could afford one in less than two hours of work.

At its peak, the company produced nearly 30 trillion litres of drinks a year – 240 million hectolitres of beer and nearly 50 million hectolitres of soft drinks. Six of its brands were among the world's top-50 consumed beers in the world.

What SABMiller did most successfully was understand the power and heritage of domestic brands and the association of people with their favourite drink, whether it was Tyskie in Poland, Ursus in Romania or Dreher in Hungary.

Unlike rivals, such as Heineken, Carlsberg or Budweiser, it did not seek to have a global flagship brand because it believed that beer was fundamentally a local business. At its peak, SABMiller produced more than 200 brands, including some of the world's most-loved premium beers.

The company mopped up businesses, mostly in emerging markets, but also added premium brands to its portfolio, such as Holland's Grolsch and Italy's Peroni. Many South African companies have bitten off more than they can chew in the US and the jury is still out on whether SAB's decision to acquire Miller was the correct strategic move or whether it could have concentrated its efforts better elsewhere. Still, it created the profile SABMiller wanted. It served beer on every continent and that made it immensely attractive to AB InBev, which would significantly overpay for the assets, many of which, due to the complexity of competition laws, they would be forced to sell to rivals as they battled to derive value from the deal.

Like so many other South African businesses, SAB owed its origins to mining when it was founded in 1895 to slake the thirst of fortune seekers from across the globe. Within two years, it became the first industrial company to list its shares on the fledgling stock exchange. In 1999, it shifted its primary listing to London, providing it with the base from which to raise capital for its global expansion.

SABMiller had always been ambitious, first in dominating the domestic market with an unparalleled focus and applying that to its global growth strategy, which started with an initial flurry of small deals in the early 1990s. It bought Miller in 2002, and in 2005 it bought Colombia's Bavaria, giving it a firm foothold in Latin America. In 2007, it bought Grolsch, and, in 2008, it combined the Miller Brewing Company with the US business of Molson Coors. Its last big deal was the 2011 purchase of the Foster's Group. When the controlling Heineken family rejected its offer to buy that business, the writing was on the wall and the global number one, AB InBev, bought its biggest rival, SABMiller.

By the time SABMiller was taken over, it was distributing beer in more than 60 countries across six continents. It also produced the world's highest volume beer, Snow, ironically drunk at room temperature in China, overtaking Budweiser as the world's most consumed beer. Its company-owned brewing operations in Africa spanned 31 countries, while it operated joint ventures in Vietnam and Australia and was the second biggest brewer in India.

It had an aggressive strategy to drive volume and productivity in major markets, while optimising and expanding established positions in developing markets, all the while looking for new opportunities to enhance its reputation as a global brewer amid voracious global consolidation. Where possible, it sought to have first-mover advantage and, when it hit the ground in a country, it moved fast to consolidate that advantage, all the while looking to cut costs in every part of every operation it took over.

In addition to providing it with the access to capital markets it needed, the London listing gave SABMiller global credibility and the moniker 'British brewer', while the Miller deal provided it with status and scale in North America and a dollar-based income stream to offset the more volatile markets in which it was seeing strong growth.

In 2020, Heineken, which had long been testing African markets from its first brewery in sub-Saharan Africa at Sedibeng outside Johannesburg, cancelled plans for a second facility near Durban because the country was gripped by alcohol bans as one of the government measures to limit the spread of Covid-19. It felt like the company had lost faith in the country, but it soon made a bid for Distell, best known as the distillers of local brandies and the world-renowned Amarula cream liqueur. A little-known fact is that Distell is the world's second biggest cider maker after Heineken. Yes, Heineken is one of the world's biggest brewers, but it also happens to be the single biggest cider maker in the world, producing nearly 6 million hectolitres of the stuff in eighteen countries annually. The Distell deal dramatically widened the gap between Heineken and its nearest rival even further.

Distell was attractive to Heineken for a number of reasons. Distell had plenty of local and regional brands of cider, wine and brandy, but, mostly, it had an established African distribution platform. At the time of writing, more than a quarter of its revenues were generated outside of South Africa – 17% from other African markets and nearly 10% from other countries, mostly in Latin America and Europe. That global exposure proved a godsend during South Africa's repeated alcohol bans during the Covid-19 pandemic.

Following the deal, Heineken has a 10% share of South Africa's beer market and 43% of the higher-margin premium segment, and, thanks to the Distell portfolio, it now controls around a quarter of the local drinks market.

Distell does not disclose specifics about revenues and volumes but counts Amarula among its top-ten revenue earners and one of the biggest fifteen sellers in terms of volume. In a company that has a significant number of high-volume wine labels in its stable, as well as the big-selling Hunters and Savanna cider brands, that is significant.

After the political transition in 1994, wine was Distell's key export focus, and its value-for-money wine brands, including the staple Tassenberg, Drostdy-Hof, Nederburg and J.C. Le Roux labels, along with Viceroy brandy and Amarula, earn its biggest revenues from the rest of Africa, whereas its Latin American and

European markets have seen a surge in spirits exports since its 2013 acquisition of Scotland's Burn Stewart.

Burn Stewart owns Deanston Distillery in Perthshire, Bunnahabhain, on the Isle of Islay and Tobermory on Mull. It also produces the Islay-influenced Black Bottle and Scottish Leader. That deal not only added Scotch whisky to Distell's offering but also improved the group's ability to access international markets via the existing distribution arrangements the whisky business already had, and its spirits business has seen margins double.

Distell has been rationalising its portfolio. In addition to selling the neglected Plaisir de Merle to Rose Jordaan, who cut her teeth in wine-making at the family farm Bartinney just up the road, it has been ruthless with brands that no longer fit the portfolio. Despite winning the vodka trophy at the International Wine and Spirits Competition in 2007, Mainstay, distilled from molasses, was discontinued in 2020. A staple, or mainstay, ahem, of every middle-class liquor cabinet of the 1970s and 1980s, it no longer fitted the group's premium spirits portfolio. The vodka category has low barriers to entry and it was not worth the time and energy required to sustain a brand for it to continue. It was part of a new focus on doing fewer things better.

Distell reaches many customers via third-party distribution arrangements outside South Africa, but it has also built its retail offerings and, although late to the digital revolution, is increasingly seeing sales via e-commerce. Like many businesses that dominate their category anywhere, it had allowed itself to become complacent and was not innovating its product ranges nearly often enough – an area CEO Richard Rushton says is receiving particular attention.

Whereas smaller, more focused rivals are able to experiment and change strategic direction quickly, the nature of the traditionally conservative, large corporate means it becomes considerably harder to do. Consumer tastes have been developing quicker than Distell was able to transform its operations, and the group has had to undergo a significant shift in culture to take more risk in developing and getting new offerings to market.

'We are now more willing to use our intuition and experience to back up the strategic choices that we make. At the same time, we have upped our execution game from soil to bottle and we focus relentlessly on raising the bar and keeping our customers happy,' Rushton said.

Going beyond borders requires a sea change in thinking. Many failures across sectors and businesses that have sought to globalise have not taken local conditions into account in the markets they target. Part of Distell's success has been a result of empowering local teams to make big calls because it is impossible to dictate decision-making in Belfast, Brussels or Berlin from the southern tip of Africa.

Local knowledge is critical. The global expansion of local restaurant concepts has learned this the hard way. Finding the right partner in a foreign jurisdiction that understands your brands and ethos is important for success, and identifying the right people to drive the domestic business and support staff there is pivotal. It is about thinking local, while applying relevant lessons learned elsewhere (see Chapter 9).

Distell has subjected itself to a great deal of introspection in recent years – cutting what did not work and focusing deliberately on its strengths.

The global liquor trade is evolving fast, and consumer trends are changing quickly. Covid-19 and the restrictions on social interactions have led to a blurring of consumer behaviours and habits. Vaccine inequity also means that markets are volatile. Added to that, regulators in different parts of the world are increasingly sticky about the rules governing alcohol consumption.

'We are confident in our ability to win on the African continent versus international markets, where the large multinationals dominate. This is because the demographic dividend across Africa plays to our portfolio strengths,' Rushton said.

The pandemic also exacerbated the fault lines in societies, and none more so than in emerging markets and in South Africa. Different parts of the world recovered faster than others and that impacted on a range of risks in its primary markets, affecting everything from currencies to incomes impacted.

Unlike AB InBev, which substantially overpaid for SABMiller, Heineken was not going to do the same and offered R40 billion for the business, much to the chagrin of minority shareholders.

Best known for being a brewer, Heineken controls two of the world's most popular cider labels, Strongbow and Bulmers, which it relaunched with a promise to use only British apples in an increasing global trend towards regionalisation in the cider trade. It owns a big New Zealand producer and will now add

Savanna and Hunters to its portfolio mix.

It is that regionalisation that Laura Clacey and her British-born husband Karol Ostaszewski are playing into. They started Sxollie Cider in the Elgin Valley in 2014, with a plan to beneficiate local fruit for a global consumer. It was a time of experimentation by a number of players in the belief that the boom in craft beer and craft gin would surely follow in the cider market. The local craft cider experiment seemed to fizzle out even before Covid-19, but the pair had far bigger ambitions than just South Africa, which consumes only 2% of its total production. The experience from South Africa was invaluable and provided them with an 'in' with one of their biggest UK customers today, Nando's.

'Beer, gin and wine had enjoyed their craft moments, but cider was very much a sleeping giant, still awaiting that great re-awakening. It was a growing consumer trend, and the drive towards provenance drew us to making a cider from a single estate, using apple varieties that we know and love, such as Granny Smith and Golden Delicious,' says Ostaszewski.

With the growing global trend of sustainability and food provenance, the pair hit on a cider made only from naturally sweet eating apples, with no added sugar, concentrates, flavourings or colourants. Interestingly, by not adding sugar, they were able to steal a march on UK producers striving to get their products as carbon-neutral as possible. Because the UK imports all its sugar, this adds to the carbon footprint of the finished product – omitting sugar solves that problem, even for an import.

'We wanted to change people's perceptions about one of the world's oldest beverages, which had lost its way. Downward price pressure led to producers cutting corners in production, diluting the integrity of an amazing drink that should deliver a taste profile that reflects the apples. We also wanted to make the global community aware of the incredible raw materials in South Africa. Much has been made of commodities such as gold, platinum or chrome, but we wanted to focus on the delicious apples that take advantage of abundant sunshine and fertile soil. We could then add value to the apples and showcase Sxollie, with apples as its sole ingredient,' Ostaszewski says.

A total of 98% of what Sxollie produces in South Africa is exported – without fizz, in 26 000-litre flexi-tanks – to the UK, which has a strong cider-drinking culture. It is bottled in Liverpool, where the stock lands some three weeks after leaving Cape Town harbour. Thanks to a deal with top-end grocer Waitrose, it has a national reach, and Sxollie is now also sold in every one of the 450 Nando's outlets in the UK and Ireland.

Relative to the big producers, Sxollie is tiny. It aims to produce and export 5 million litres of cider – about two Olympic swimming pools full – to the UK market a year. That country has a market worth a staggering £3.2 billion a year. The first step is to crack the code in the UK and create a strong foundation for a broader global push.

Like any start-up, it is mostly about the hustle and working on a shoestring budget to create a viable business. The biggest hurdle is getting consumers to try something they do not know from a place that is not famous for producing cider and has an intimidating-looking name. The cider category in the UK had been in a slump, and, even at events such as Taste of London, there was a reluctance to give a product no one had heard of a try. Just as the publishers of the Stieg Larsson trilogy, which began with *The Girl with the Dragon Tattoo*, seeded public transport and benches with apparently discarded copies, knowing that once people read them, word of mouth would do the rest, the Sxollie focus was simply to ensure as many people as possible tried the product.

The reality is that setting up and running a business in South Africa is far tougher than in the UK, but the pair persisted, based on the fact that the quality of the apples was so good that it justified the pain of operating in the country.

From the bureaucracy of getting a licence, to the low access to start-up capital or loans, to the complicated banking rules and regulations, it is easy to see why South Africa performs so poorly in the Ease of Doing Business index. They were also faced with huge consumer challenges, as the South African market had become accustomed to mass-market, cheaper options, making it difficult for them to get acceptance of their higher-priced premium product. They were apprehensive about expanding into the UK and were uncertain as to whether their product would find a market.

'Nobody is doing single varietal South African cider in the UK. We are using eating apples, not cider apples, so it is a completely different product,' Ostaszewski says.

So, while the product was created and perfected in South Africa and will continue to be produced here, the UK market makes it a logical place to use as a headquarters because of its demographics and high levels of disposable income, as well as being a significant investor base.

Sxollie is already exported to Norway, Denmark, Ireland and Singapore, and Australia is on the radar for expansion.

The last place you would expect to find a sorghum-based, pilsner-style beer called Tolokazi would be in the UK, but necessity, as they say, is the mother of all invention. It was not Apiwe Nxusani-Mawela's plan to sell her beer in that market. When her microbrewery shut down in the midst of South Africa's draconian liquor bans during Covid-19, she was approached by the chief marketing officer of Edinburgh-based subscription service Beer52, which introduces its 100 000 customers to brews from around the world. They put her in touch with a brewer in Croatia, which made 200 000 cans of Tolokazi, and the product made its way into the hands of British beer drinkers. Subscribers rated the beer, which is described on its website as a 'classic pilsner style brewed with sorghum malt. Crisp, with sweet, bready malt characteristics and medium supporting bitterness. Floral and earthy aromas from local hop varietals.' A score of 3.8/5 was given, the same as was given to another South African craft brew, Devil's Peak Pale Ale.

Now that South Africa's biggest drinks makers are both owned by global multinationals, the new frontier has to be in the wine trade, currently made up of hundreds of independent producers. South Africa's 360-year-old wine industry, famed for pleasing the palates of Napoleon during his exile on St Helena following his defeat at Waterloo, as well as the eighteenth-century author, Jane Austen, could be on the cusp of something really big.

# CHAPTER 6

· · · · · · · · · · · ·

# South African Wine
# Comes of Age

*How do you make a small fortune in the wine business,
start with a big one.* — GT Ferreira

South Africa's wine industry needs its *Sideways* movie.

The film is less about wine and more about male friendship, mid-life crisis, human frailty, infidelity and love – but most people remember the wine and the scenery. If the Californian wine industry and Napa Valley tourist authority did not fund the movie, they should have. Its benefit to both was enormous. A 2009 study by Sonoma State University found that the film had a big, direct impact on the US wine industry. Not only was it a boost for the industry, but it also increased sales and the production of pinot noir by 170%.

Wine does that. It creates a powerful association with the place it comes from. France has been producing wine since at least the sixth century BC and makes about 8 billion bottles of the stuff each year. To fans of the ancient art, it is the epicentre of global wine and it uses this to its great advantage. The French have also long since worked out that the 23-day 2 000-mile Tour de France, for most of us, is less about the technicalities of cycling and the gruelling feats of endurance over weeks of torturous peddling, and more about the exquisite scenery and the aerial shots of the châteaux of the Loire Valley and the seemingly endless vineyards along the route.

The Tour is billed as the world's biggest annual sporting event, but its real value is in tourism, with up to 11 million people lining the roadside and millions of TV spectators worldwide wishing they were there.

South Africa is seeking to do similar things with events like the Cape Town Cycle Tour, the eight-day Cape Epic and the Comrades Marathon – but none quite captures the magnificence of a place in the same way that the longer format of the Tour de France does.

What we do have is wine. Researcher Julien Couder at the Grenoble Alpes University writes: 'Wine choice is strongly driven by the perception of its terroir of origin. Terroir has the ability to carry symbolic meaning, expertise, authenticity, etc., which will infer on the wine's perception. Nevertheless, to market a product with its terroir of origin, practitioners have to stay close to the image a customer has of this place. Otherwise, it could lead to cognitive dissonance and strongly distort the way their product is perceived.'

That is why South Africa needs a great story about wine – a sense of romance, mystery and intrigue.

Individual estates tell their own stories well. Anglo American-owned Vergelegen makes much of its Willem Adriaan van der

Stel origins, steeped in Dutch colonial history and slavery and as one of the first examples of corrupt money being used for self-aggrandisement in South Africa (I tell the story in *The Upside of Down*). Groot Constantia trades off the fact that it was the first registered winery in the country, and its products have garnered fans through the ages.

According to Wines of South Africa (WOSA), the country has nearly 2 800 farmers cultivating more than 92 000 hectares of vines. The industry provides livelihoods for nearly 270 000 people. It is tiny by global standards. Italy, France and Spain are the world's three biggest producers and together provide about half the world's wine. South Africa is the eighth biggest, yet it provides just 4% of global supply. It is interesting that South Africa is only fifteenth in the world in terms of vineyard plantings, so it is a very efficient maker of the stuff compared to higher-volume producers.

Despite its size relative to the rest of the world, it is critical particularly to the economy of the Western Cape and is a catalyst for tourism, export revenues and international investment. Despite that, the industry complains it does not get the support or recognition it should from central government.

In 1994, the *Cape Times* quoted the then Western Cape minister of agriculture, Lampie Fick, as saying wine farms would mostly disappear from Stellenbosch, needing to be converted to vegetable and fruit farms to serve the needs of growing urban populations. 'With increased demand for agricultural land to house more than double the current metropolitan population, it should be a foregone conclusion that the vegetable pantry for

Cape Town will move from the Cape Flats,' Fick said at the time. He was wrong.

But politicians have long not liked the influence of the wine industry and the elitism of the sector. It is not a significant direct contributor to GDP. Its worth is about R55 billion a year, which is just 1.1% of annual GDP. It may have something to with the fact that nearly 30 years into democracy the industry is still largely controlled by a handful of wealthy white landowners and has not seen the racial transformation of ownership that government would like. It also comes from a dark period in South African history, built off the back of slavery, the 'dop system' (the part-payment of wages in cheap wine creating a dependence on liquor) and fuelled by low-paying jobs.

It may be a small cog in the complex machinery of South Africa, but it is a critical one.

One of the industry's compelling exports beyond the bottled liquid is the fact that it is a source of valuable foreign direct investment. The internationally renowned wine expert, Michael Fridjhon, wrote about the extent of foreign ownership of the South African industry in *Business Day* in 2021, arguing strongly that the wine estates in which foreign buyers have invested are better off than when they were bought. 'In the mid-1980s, as the late Hans Schreiber was buying up high-profile viticultural real estate in Stellenbosch, a serious concern was expressed – in newspaper columns and not just at jukskei competitions – about the sale of heritage sites to foreigners. Remember that this was in a time of enforced isolation. PW [Botha] ruled with an iron fist in a chain-mail glove. Presumably those who were editorialising believed that he would simply wave his tungsten-plated arm and the foreign investors would be sent on their way with their deutschmarks in their pockets and their tails between their legs,' he wrote. 'Their sentiments were hardly original, or even uniquely South African. When the British Pearson Group acquired Bordeaux First Growth Chateau Latour in 1963, the French establishment tried to persuade the president to block the sale. De Gaulle is said to have responded, "They can't very well take the soil with them."'

Fridjhon went on to list the large number of estates in foreign hands, pointing out that in each case the properties were better off for being under wealthy ownership and citing Delaire Graff as a prime example. When Laurence Graff bought Delaire, the farm was run-down, and the few vineyards that were left were infected with a virus that limited its prospects significantly. Around the same time, Glenelly in nearby Ida's Valley was bought by the French wine family of Pinzgauer. It had no vineyards and was comprised of rotten infrastructure and what was billed as wetland resembling more of a swamp. Both, points out Fridjhon, are now world-class properties with wines to match.

'Without foreign owners, we would be in the vinous dark ages,' says Fridjhon.

What the investment has done is raise the bar for the rest of the industry and led to a proliferation over three decades of a significant number of new labels and farms, as well as the impressive expansion of the wine-growing region into places like the Swartland, Elgin and the Hemel en Aarde Valley. Nearly half the Constantia wine route is owned by international buyers, as are a host of properties further inland, such as Morgenster, Vergenoegd, Avontuur, Ken Forrester, Taaibosch, Pink Valley, Ernie Els, Stellenzicht, Alto, Dornier, Hazendal, Saxenburg, Spier, Asara, Stark-Condé, L'Avenir, Laibach (until January 2022), Warwick, Uitkyk, Le Bonheur, Neethlingshof, Quoin Rock, Marianne and Oldenburg. And that is just Stellenbosch; many more in Paarl and Franschhoek have foreign capital.

The reason wine needs capital with deep pockets is that it can take a significant amount of time for properties to reach their full potential.

But, South Africans have also been shopping as estates have come on the market. In January 2022, premium single estate red wine producer Kanonkop bought neighbouring Laibach. Kanonkop, with its 100 hectares of vines, could not keep up with demand and the farm next door provides precisely the same growing conditions, with a further 40 hectares of vines, which meant the estate could expand and grow its volumes without compromising on its high-end Paul Sauer flagship blend, cabernet and pinotage varietals. Like most estates, Kanonkop produces a second, more affordable range; its Kadette offering from younger vines than those used in the top-end estate production rides on the coattails of the premium offering and is available in more than 40 countries.

Named Kanonkop after the hill from which a cannon was fired in the seventeenth and eighteenth centuries to announce the arrival of sailing ships into Table Bay, it is a fourth-generation family-owned wine estate, which is now in the hands of brothers Paul and Johann Krige. The cannon shot was a signal to farmers to load up their wagons for the 50-kilometre journey to the harbour in Cape Town to sell their produce. The first commercial wines were bottled on the property in 1973, and the Laibach acquisition is the first expansion since then. Kanonkop's global appeal is that despite its youth relative to centuries of history entwined in the châteaux of Burgundy and Bordeaux, its winemaking style is more traditional than that of many of the lighter, new-world wines. Few South African wines age well. Kanonkop is an exception.

In 2020, Rose Jordaan bought the beautiful but unloved Plaisir de Merle property on the picturesque border between the Paarl and Stellenbosch wine areas from Distell. The company was tidying up its assets in preparation for a bid from global brewer Heineken and was intent on getting out of farming. Factories producing cider and Amarula yield a far better return than the wine business, which comes with significant management issues and has far too many things that can go wrong, making earnings volatile and unpredictable. The property is well situated in the heart of the winelands; up the road in one direction is tech billionaire Koos Bekker's Babylonstoren, and on the other side is the extraordinary Boschendal estate, once owned by imperialist Cecil John Rhodes.

Rose Jordaan used her architectural training to build the Bartinney wine business, and set about learning about the importance of biodiversity in the vineyards. She pulled up centuries-old bluegum trees and other alien vegetation. The water table rose, resulting in an eruption of natural springs throughout the property. She restored the indigenous fynbos and proteas on the farm, which led to a return of animal and insect species to the property.

'This won't be done in my lifetime,' she says. Rose is starting an enormous project to get the best wine the land will produce and also to bring back as much of the property as is viable to a more natural state. 'It's about a long-term commitment to South Africa,' she says. About a third of the 980-hectare property was under vines when she bought it. Distell produced wines under the farm label, but its primary purpose was to supply grapes to the company's other brands, such as its Durbanville Hills range. The centuries-old buildings on the estate were run-down and used as storage.

Like Bartinney, Plaisir de Merle was also covered in alien vegetation. Now rebranded Plaisir, it is unusual in the winelands in that it has rich red clay Hutton soils that are good for moisture retention compared with the sandy soils and flinty shales of many other properties in the area. It also has another critical asset – an abundance of water.

'Years of neglect meant a lot of the vineyard had leafroll virus, the rivers and mountain were congested with alien invasive trees, and the estate was tired and not getting enough feet through the doors to make it viable,' she muses.

The sale price was not disclosed, but the property had been on the market for some time. The domestic economic crisis brought about by a series of lockdowns and alcohol sales bans had put many properties on the market, and Rose pounced when the price reduced to a level at which she believes she can make it work.

Wine industry players will tell you that producing great wines requires exceptional focus. Corporate ownership of the estate meant it lacked a vision and purpose. Most of the buildings were boarded up and in a state of serious disrepair. Those have been restored, keeping as many original characteristics as possible as decades of grime have been peeled away to reveal original features, such as timbers, murals and wall designs.

Critical to sustainability, though, will be to restore the land. Rather than slash, burn and remove the aliens, which have denuded soil quality and sucked up ground water for generations, the trees and vegetation have been chipped and the carbon-rich mulch returned to the soil to help it regenerate after years of commercial farming with herbicides and pesticides.

The level of grape plantings will be reduced as some vineyards are restored to the indigenous fynbos to create organic buffer zones between the commercial grape crops and to create ecological corridors for plant diversity and animal movement.

'A healthier living environment means healthier vines and better wine,' Rose says.

Much of the work that has to be done does not yield a short-term benefit. Thirty years ago, the wine route was a sleepy place where small groups of people would go from farm to farm, tasting and occasionally picking up a bottle of what they might have tried. Increasingly, wine farms are about attracting crowds of people for a broad range of experiences, and everything from farm stays to globally competitive dining experiences are on offer. Some of the country's most highly rated restaurants have become destinations in themselves, and this is a critical part of South Africa's tourism economy. Rebuilding these wine farms is about making the properties better to visit and, one day, when the world's visitors once again descend on South Africa and the winelands, Rose wants to be ready.

For South Africa, wine is an international calling card. WOSA estimates about 19 million glasses of South African wine are drunk globally every day. About half the country's annual wine production is exported. All wines for export must be granted a licence, and samples of each batch of wine destined for foreign countries must be sent to the Wine & Spirit Board at Nietvoorbij in Stellenbosch, where they undergo detailed tasting tests and chemical analysis in the laboratories before licences are granted. An official seal is given to each bottle by the Wine & Spirit Board, which verifies that the claims made on the label regarding origin, vintage and grape variety are true. The 2010 vintage bore a world first in the form of a new seal that traces the wine from vine to bottle, certifying a wine's integrity as well as sustainability.

Rose Jordaan is going for the full 'instagrammable' experience and has created walking and cycling trails, as well as good food catering for a range of tastes and price points. Her aim is to turn the farm into a destination, raising footfall and the possibility of greater wine sales. While the traditional 'wine route' still exists, a younger generation of visitors are looking for intimate experiences they can share with their friends across the world. 'Covid has woken people up to the fact that life may be shorter than expected; be here now!' she says, and that is precisely what she is trying to achieve on the property.

'South Africa has the most exciting prospects with regards to wine excellence. For the first time in many decades, the world is noticing that our premium wine offering is not only comparable to the best in the world but is significantly better consistently. The move away from volume to premium value as an export driver has been very difficult, but the tide has turned,' Rose explains.

Nearly three-quarters of the country's wine exports are done in bulk containers and are bottled, branded and distributed at their destination. This bulk wine is of inferior quality to branded bottles of estate wine you would recognise. The bulk wine generates less than R2 billion a year in export revenues, so the opportunity lies in the lower volume but considerably higher value premium product, which earned R7.2 billion in 2020. There are signs that the strategy to promote better wines is paying off. Producers are getting more recommendations than ever before from some of the world's biggest wine pundits.

The UK is South Africa's single largest international wine market, absorbing about half our exports, and 2021 proved to be a bumper year for our product in that country. According to Majestic Wine, the UK's largest specialised wine retailer, sales of South African bottles rocketed in December 2021, plugging a gap left by tougher-than-normal growing conditions in New Zealand. It said like-for-like sales were up 41% on the year before, and South African wine had been the biggest mover of the previous six months. It anticipated the renaissance would be a long-term trend.

It certainly does not hurt that some of the world's pre-eminent wine writers publish their opinions in the British media. Eight of the 40 white wines UK-based wine critic Jancis Robinson recommended to *Financial Times* readers for Christmas 2021 were South African, and most were from Elgin and the Swartland.

Despite three of its member countries producing half the world's wine, the EU absorbs about 30% of South Africa's wine exports. There has been exponential growth in the market in China in recent years due to trade tensions with Australia, which has traditionally had the Asian market sewn up. The US is also showing good growth, especially in the premium segment, owing to the duty-free benefits of the African Growth and Opportunity Act.

That is only half the story. Wine is also a key driver of tourism. The better South African wines do globally, the higher the likelihood of a positive spin-off for wine tourism. Tourism itself is an export in that it earns substantial amounts of foreign exchange. At the start of the Covid-19 pandemic, one of the very first budgets to be cut was that of South African Tourism, the government-owned body tasked with promoting the country as an international destination of choice, but its potential as a driver of growth and jobs is significant.

Tourism also has a positive impact on the domestic wine industry itself. According to Vinpro, nearly 15% of the wine industry's total turnover is a result of tourism, which includes visits to cellars and dining and accommodation in the winelands, while smaller, emerging players are more heavily dependent on visitors than larger, more established properties are.

When liquor sales in South Africa were negatively impacted by a series of bans on the sale of alcohol domestically, the crisis precipitated a serious rethink of exports, and the sale of premium wines increased markedly as producers needed to find new markets. The overall value of South African wine exports in 2020 increased by 7.7% to just over R9 billion, with sales of chenin blanc and pinotage rising in double digits.

For local producers focused on export markets, the opportunity is enormous. Boutique producers such as Vilafonté, launched in 2005 as a small-scale, 42-hectare joint venture between US wine fundis and local farmer Mike Ratcliffe, are seeing an exponential increase in interest in the wines they produce. Being recognised as Outstanding Producer of the Year by the International Wine & Spirit Competition has also been a boost. It is one of the few competitions entered into by the world's best labels, making the recognition all the more outstanding.

The secret of Vilafonté's success is focus. It only produces three high-quality wines at different price points, labelled Seriously Old Dirt, Series C and Series M, from cabernet, merlot, cabernet franc and malbec vines. But wine does not sell itself, and Ratcliffe has focused much of his energy on creating a market for his product. Limiting volumes has created demand, which means that every vintage is quickly sold out after each year's carefully choreographed launch.

The industry appears to be reaching a tipping point, where the country's top ten to fifteen producers are starting to be recognised as being among the best in the world.

Ratcliffe is seeing his wines in Emirates Business Class and alongside other premium producers, as well as in some of the world's top-end retailers. The focus over the next decade, he believes, will be on regional specialisation and a drive towards serving a global premium market. Areas such as the Hemel en Aarde Valley are likely to home in on pinot noir and chardonnay, Stellenbosch on cabernet, and the Swartland region on chenin blanc and cinsault, while the Constantia Valley is producing exceptional sauvignon blanc.

'There is a new-found confidence in South African producers, which is good to see, now we need to convert that confidence into pricing, which will come,' Ratcliffe says. Many of the world's great wines are produced in significant volumes of 60 000 to 100 000 cases. When a local producer in South Africa makes an exceptional wine, their four barrels are consumed locally before it even gets spoken about globally. To get global acceptance, the South African industry needs regional specialisation and considerably higher volumes so that the great wines can be simultaneously experienced at tables in Tokyo and New York, and not simply become a footnote on a wine writer's fantasy Christmas list.

Pricing is everything. While it may hurt your sensibilities to spend R700 on a bottle of Kanonkop's iconic Paul Sauer or more than R1 200 on The Jem from Waterford, the quality of those wines is exceptional by any measure. In the US, you might pay R20 000 for a bottle of wine from Harlan Estate in Napa Valley or R70 000 for a bottle of Screaming Eagle cabernet from another well-known Napa Valley estate. The Argentines, who also have a perception problem on bulk exports of wine, have managed to get premium pricing on premium wines, and a bottle of Catena Zapata Estiba Reservada will set you back more than R7 000. The French will let you have a Château Margaux for more than R15 000, the Australians a bottle of Penfolds Grange for R11 000, and the Italians a bottle of Sassicaia for R4 000. There is a global market for exceptional wines at exceptional prices and South Africa's top producers are finally finding their way into those elite circles.

Eben Sadie's Columella has achieved over R2 000 per bottle in the US, but that is rare, although there are signs that a decade of hard work by producers in collaboration with WOSA is seeing better pricing applied to top-end local wines.

You do not need to be labouring in the vineyards to be part of the wine industry.

Nicolò Pudel dreamed up the idea of a specialised wine delivery business in 2014. At the time, he was running Pier2Pier, helping premium South African wineries develop their own digital platforms and e-commerce applications. That is where the idea to sell only top-end wine online came from. No one else was doing it. So he launched Port2Port, with three fundamental goals: a cutting-edge online shopping experience; world-class customer service; and vintage-specific, highly detailed wine-related content.

The global wine trade has barely changed since the early 1600s. It is an age-old industry, constrained by capital and know-how, struggling to optimise its supply chain model and stay abreast of digital developments, and that has happened at the expense of producers. The mission was to make it easier for producers to connect with their customers online. Wineries, for all of their glamour, are generally low-margin businesses, not only because of escalating input costs but also due to the high cost of distribution. Many South African wine producers have struggled to connect with international clients, who might have once visited the properties and have a warm disposition to the brand but no easy way of keeping tabs on what their favourite estates are up to.

'We had set ourselves the objective to bridge the gap between wine lover and producer and give the people behind the labels a voice, thus enabling them to tell their story first-hand. Soon Port2Port was not only a store; it also became a shoppable wine publication. A wine destination for the wine lover, built by wine lovers,' says Pudel.

It is a marriage of an ancient art form and modern technology. It turns out tech and tradition are a good combination. Many retailers sell wine online. Port2Port's biggest differentiator is that its content has cultivated a loyal and engaged customer base. It makes its money off commission and says it keeps it the lowest in the industry; because we no longer have time to waste figuring out how applications work, the effort has gone into making it highly intuitive.

'We want to change the way people buy and sell wine online and are aiming to make the same impact Uber had in the transport industry, Airbnb in hospitality and YOOX in fashion.'

Port2Port opened in the UK in April 2020, but the company has not been able to visit the UK yet due to Covid-19. Despite this, it saw the proof of the value of its systems as it was able to list 700 different wines in two weeks – 400 of them South African – without anyone present in the UK. Today, the UK still represents only 10% of overall revenue, but the goal is to tap into a receptive market and have a 50% revenue split between local and international markets by 2025.

The site carries nearly 3 000 wines from more than a dozen countries, and part of its strategy is to offer the largest selection of wines available, with virtually infinite supply.

'The wine industry is just at the beginning of a radical transformation phase. Distribution models are being disrupted and technology is the number-one driver. What started happening in other industries, such as travel, accommodation and transport a few years ago, only just started happening in wine,' says Pudel.

Unlike big retail stores that have to carry costly stock of each of the products they sell, Port2Port is a marketplace: it allows buyers and sellers to connect on its platform but fulfilment is done by the label. The website manages the real-time shipments from over 200 vendors, making it, as far as I can tell, the only fine wine marketplace in the world.

The biggest shock for many South African enterprises is the level of competition they face in foreign markets. They may think they operate in a competitive environment, but Pudel, and others featured in this book, all admit to being taken by surprise by the level of contestation for customers in their new markets.

'In South Africa, doing a great job at what you do is usually enough to stand out, whether it is on selection or customer support. Do it well and you will most likely succeed. Overseas, the game is completely different. Businesses strive to excel in everything they do and lots of them are really good at it. In the UK, wine retail goes back centuries; they basically invented the wine trade as we know it. As such, the marketplace is crowded with new and old businesses competing for the same piece of pie, and it is tough competition,' Pudel says. 'The key lesson we learned is to find an identity as quickly as possible and stand by it. Port2Port today is the UK's largest South African fine wine store.'

South Africa's wine industry is nearly as old as the colonial project itself.

The first vineyard was planted in 1655, and the first wines flowed from its grapes four years later. It led to further plantings at Boschheuvel, today known as Bishopscourt, and the aptly named Wynberg. Jan van Riebeeck strongly encouraged farmers to plant vineyards, although they were initially reluctant to do so. The Dutch did not have the rich viticulture heritage of the Spanish, French and Italians, but it was the enthusiasm of later governors like Simon van der Stel that saw the industry take hold. It would not be until the arrival of a small but dedicated band of French Huguenots, escaping religious persecution some decades later, that the industry really flourished. That legacy lives on, and producers for the first time are starting to achieve prices commensurate with the quality of what they are delivering to global markets.

# CHAPTER 7

# Juice Juice Baby

*It's a great advantage not to drink among hard-drinking people.*
— F. Scott Fitzgerald

If Italian immigrant Edmond Lombardi had gone with his first instincts when he arrived in South Africa, he would no doubt have become a successful Karoo sheep farmer and wool producer. Fortunately for us, he went apple farming near Elgin in the Western Cape instead, but not before going on a big detour first.

When asked in later life why he had chosen apples over sheep, he responded: 'Animals die.'

Lombardi and his British-born wife were en route by ship to Australia. During a stopover in Cape Town, they hired a car and explored the region. Family legend says it was she who fell in love with the rolling hills of the Elgin Valley, which reminded her of the Cotswolds. So they stayed, abandoned the idea of sheepherding and went apple farming instead.

Born in France of French and Italian parents, Lombardi began his working life in Nice at a haberdashery company that traded fabrics between Nice and Monte Carlo. He later worked as a waiter in Paris and in the UK where he learned to speak English, and there he spotted an opportunity to enter the marble trade. Always the opportunist, he supplied the stone to satisfy Edwardian England's desire for marble and gained experience quarrying for the stone – a skill that would prove useful later. But the rise of Mussolini and fascist control of the Italian economy conspired against him. He packed it in and embarked on the journey that saw him settle in South Africa.

Lombardi knew nothing about farming but was undaunted. Following his brief flirtation with sheep, he bought Applethwaite Farm in Elgin; taking the first steps on his way to creating his empire.

'His farm was not yet profitable, so he put his quarrying experience to use, buying a clay quarry and making bricks with a partner, George Ratcliffe, who also invested in the farm. Belville-based Brick & Clay went public, my father and George Ratcliffe parted company, George keeping the brickworks and my father the farm. By then the farm was running profitably. I was in school and my mother had named it Applethwaite after a village in England,' remembers his son, Dave Lombardi.

He would add to his land holdings over the years and steadily increased the number of dams at his disposal to guarantee water supply. He had many critics, who saw him as overinvesting in the enterprise. Right from the start, Lombardi's approach to farming was different. He did not carry the multigenerational baggage that can afflict those in agriculture, and, probably because he did not know what he was doing, he harnessed expertise from Stellenbosch University to maximise the viability of the land to produce the crops he needed. His commitment to technology and using only highly rated engineers and professionals to develop his water systems drew criticism of the amount of money he was pouring into the venture. But Lombardi continued undeterred.

While there was a solid market for first-grade and second-grade fruit, the third-grade produce that went into the informal trade was impacting on margins. It made up about a quarter of the crop but generated just 5% of the income. Lombardi went to the US and sent a young Dave to Europe to look for ideas. Both returned with plenty. Apple juice was not at the top of the list. They briefly considered making apple sauce: 'Although the products I came back with were good, my father's marketing gut feel said otherwise. So, this time Lombardi made a trip to Europe, and in Switzerland he had his other Eureka moment. He discovered a clear, sparkling apple juice that looked just like Champagne. It is a long costly story, but once more he engaged the best people: Professor Luthi, head of the World Fruit Juice Organization, was hired as visiting technical director; he engaged Dr Nino Costa, who had worked at Nederburg as the local technical director; and he engaged the services of Stellenbosch University Food Tech laboratories and staff. That is how Appletiser, the Champagne of fruit juices, was developed,' Dave explains.

The first factory, built by German engineers and Swiss juice technologists, could process the 3 000 tonnes per year of Applethwaite's own under-grade fruit. No sooner had he started, however, when a new factory was necessary within two years to absorb about 60 000 tonnes of fruit brought in from the region.

Appletiser was launched in 1967, and the non-alcoholic sparkling apple juice gained plenty of attention. The *Sunday Times* wrote: 'Elgin apple drink is a success: Cape Garden Factory with Italian flavour', with publications describing it as the 'Champagne of fruit juices'.

On a good day nowadays, the Appletiser factory at Elgin can produce half a million litres of the drink. The process, in as much as the company will disclose, begins with the crushing of selected apples, using a combination of pressure to extract the juice and heat to evaporate the water in the apples in order to leave behind what in the days of old man Lombardi was called 'the muti'. It is also described as 'the aroma', but Coca-Cola calls it less romantically the 'beverage base'. His genius was getting those early scientists, who lived in a specially designated house on his property for months on end, to develop a concentrate that was consistent, regardless of the apple crop, and could be stored for use throughout the year.

Unlike KFC's secret herbs and spices or the Coca-Cola formula kept in a safe in Atlanta, Georgia, in the US, Appletiser is derived from a natural product. Nowadays, with the volumes being bigger than ever before, the consistency of the taste, odour and appearance of Appletiser and the other variants, Grapetiser and Peartiser, are ensured by the final blending of the beverage base by Conco, which is the concentrate supply point, owned by the Coca-Cola Company.

The concentrate, once produced, is stored in a massive warehouse refrigeration facility, where temperatures are at −20 degrees Celsius. Bottling and canning occurs on site in Elgin, where the concentrate is combined with a mix of deflavoured apple juice and water. The water is sourced from dams Lombardi built on the property. Impurities are removed by the farm's own built-for-purpose water treatment plant on site. Even the oxygen in the water is extracted to ensure that it does not lead to discolouration of the juice – you will know that the moment you break the skin of an apple, it starts to go brown as it reacts to the oxygen in the air.

The Coca-Cola Company bought a 50% stake in Appletiser in 1979. Two years later, Appletiser added a red and white Grapetiser to its portfolio, using another plentiful fruit from the Western Cape. Appletiser was first launched in the UK as 'Appletise' because the owners of a rival product called Tizer objected to its full name being used in that market. Later, they came to a settlement, enabling the company to standardise its branding.

Another big ownership change occurred in 2016. AB InBev bought SABMiller, which in turn owned Coca-Cola Beverages South Africa. One of the regulatory requirements of the deal was that the drinks bottler should get an empowerment shareholder, so a 17.5% stake in Appletiser was sold to investment holding company African Pioneer Group, while a 4% stake went to a manager of the operation, Sipho Madlala. That deal has enabled Coca-Cola to take ownership and double its global reach. The product is sold in 30 countries, including the UK where it is sold through large supermarket chains, Belgium, Spain, Japan, Hong Kong, Australia and New Zealand.

And it is all thanks to an Italian immigrant whose wife liked the rolling topography of the Elgin Valley and decided to stay.

While it may no longer describe itself as 'the Champagne of

fruit juices', thanks to EU rules on geographic descriptors being banned for use outside specific areas, its heritage and consistent quality has allowed Appletiser to be strategically positioned as a premium product. And despite its high natural sugar content in the fruit it uses, it can stand by its 'no sugar added' moniker as part of its marketing in a world seeking healthier consumer choices.

The biggest lesson Appletiser has learned as it has globalised is that it was not competing in the juices market but rather in an altogether more lucrative zero-alcohol adult drinks segment. The problem its modern-day marketers are seeking to solve is not that of a thirst quencher – which water does better – or a quick energy boost, which brands such as Red Bull and Monster energy drinks have cornered, but as a drink that elegantly marks an occasion better than a mainstream fizzy drink or something alcoholic and that allows you to avoid the intrusive 'so why are you not drinking?' question.

Appletiser has the advantage of having the global marketing and distribution might of its owner, the Coca-Cola company, behind it, yet it has targeted a specific high-value market niche where there is a definite gap for its product, and it is a gap other entrepreneurs have also spotted.

The global zero-alcohol adult drinks market is growing in leaps and bounds, leading to international campaigns such as 'Sober October' and 'Dry January' for those looking to give their bodies a break from alcohol.

According to food and beverage data analysis group Tastewise, in 2021, web searches for non-alcoholic beverages were up 47% from the same period the year before. Tastewise also reported that restaurant and bar mentions of non-alcoholic beverages were up 52%.

Market research company Fior Markets estimated that the global non-alcoholic beverages market would grow from $923 million in 2020 to more than $1.7 trillion by 2028, escalating at a compound annual growth rate of 8.19%. There are more non-alcoholic drink beverage options than ever before. Besides beer and wine, consumers are buying up dry spirits, botanicals and premixed mocktails.

So, how did a guy with a degree in property development from the University of Cape Town get into the high-end, non-alcoholic drinks business? The origins of South African-created alcohol-free gin and tonic, The Duchess, are tied to the global financial crisis and the fact that Johannes le Roux's qualifications were not in demand because of a collapse in global confidence in property, banking and high finance. The global financial crisis led to one of the biggest crashes in property prices in history. The qualifications that should have set him up for life were not worth the piece of paper they were written on.

But as I pointed out in *The Upside of Down*, a disaster really is what you make of it.

Le Roux needed a job – or a big idea. He chose the job as the first employee in a start-up advertising agency that grew to ten people in two years. While it was a useful introduction to the world of business in a highly creative environment, he wanted to go out on his own. Mark Twain once quipped, 'write what you know'; in the same way, many people starting their first enterprise are advised to do what they know. Le Roux knew the drink of choice for many South Africans was brandy and Coke, so his start-up focused on delivering a consistent supply of that tipple in draught format.

'While bartending as a student, I had an idea to launch a brandy and Coke on tap. I called it Brannas Draught, and it would be my first venture into the beverage business. There were no guidebooks to launching your own beverage brand, and I learned from failing and winning,' Le Roux says.

If the purpose of a business is to grow it and sell it, his first venture was a big success. After twelve months, Brannas Draught caught the eye of KWV, which bought a significant stake in the business.

Using the money he had earned, the lessons gleaned and the momentum he had built up in his first business, Le Roux started looking for the next beverage idea and went to Amsterdam to do market research on trends in the drinks space.

The craft gin revolution was gathering speed and fancy gin and tonics were all the rage. But something far more significant was happening: the shift towards alcohol-free options for adults seeking to reduce their booze intake but not detract from social occasions.

Since The Duchess launched in 2016, the category has exploded, and the brand now sells a range of alcohol-free adult drinks across seven countries and is expanding. Global drinks giants might not be the world's great innovators, focusing rather on volume and distribution of existing products, but they can spot a good idea. In 2019, AB InBev, the world's largest brewer, made its first investment and followed it up with a second, alongside Rand Merchant Bank, in 2021.

'No good idea will ever go unfunded,' says entrepreneur Nic Haralambous, who encourages young people to start their own businesses. 'If you can't raise money, your idea just isn't good enough.'

Le Roux was exactly on point and on trend, and his minimalist branding grabbed the imagination of drinkers in multiple markets. Since its launch, The Duchess has sold 8 million bottles and, in 2020, expanded its range to include alcohol-free wine spritzers that have the mouthfeel and flavour profile of wine, infused with flavours such as elderflower, just without the kick and tapping a more health-conscious adult market.

Part of the rapid growth of The Duchess has been due to the dearth of alternatives. By interpreting market signals well, Le Roux hit a sweet spot and supplied a consumer desire, giving him an early-mover advantage. That advantage is only maintained, however, for as long as consumers stay loyal, because new entrants enter the market. His challenge now is to stay relevant and continue to innovate in what is becoming an increasingly contested category.

More than half The Duchess sales are from exports. It produces exclusively in South Africa and sends the finished product to its expanding network of international customers. By 2025, Le Roux wants 90% of his sales to be outside South Africa.

Like most new products, The Duchess found its early customers at farmers' markets across Cape Town and gradually built retail demand, first locally, then nationally and more recently in international markets. No one on his team in the early stages had any experience in producing, launching or branding a beverage for global distribution. That is the advantage of starting modestly and building as experience grows. Critically, the focus remained on the customer: 'We think of the consumer and their life experiences first and then mould our products to those occasions,' he says. 'Nothing of value is created alone or in the short term.'

Many South African businesses have crashed and burned in their overseas expansion efforts. Australia has chewed up and spat out the ambitions of many who should have known better than to assume that market was in any way like South Africa or that their products or services would easily transcend borders.

'Even in our globalised world, each country has its unique culture and approach. In order to succeed in other territories, you need to present your product in a way that they understand the value,' adds Le Roux. 'In most cases, this means working with local partners that are aligned with your vision but have the local knowledge you don't have.'

Breaking into new markets requires visibility and needs some calculated risk-taking. Part of the early success of The Duchess in international markets, especially in the UK and Europe, occurred in 2018 when Le Roux was asked to address the Global Soft Drinks Conference in London on the topic of speaking to the 'Beyond Alcohol Generation'. It was a high-risk strategy because he was ahead of the market, but now the idea has gained more mainstream appeal. Putting himself out there to tackle a potentially contentious topic at the early stage of the development of a new trend required guts – but it paved the way into new markets that are hard to penetrate, especially in fast-evolving consumer markets from far away.

Monster energy drink has taken the world by storm and has a South African connection. It has 39% of global market share of the energy drinks market versus Red Bull's 43%. Chairman and Monster co-founder Rodney Sacks grew up in Johannesburg and studied law at Wits University. He became the youngest person at the time to be made a partner of Werksmans, one of the country's largest corporate law firms. He stayed for twenty years, becoming a senior partner, before emigrating to California in August 1989. In less than a year, a consortium led by him and fellow South African Hilton Schlosberg bought a drinks business called Hansen Natural Corporation. Its performance over more than a decade was fairly pedestrian as they developed Monster by supporting high-adrenaline sports. They eventually sold a stake to Coca-Cola and the company changed its name to Monster Beverage Corporation in 2012. In 2015, Sacks swapped its natural drinks, which included Peace Tea and various juices, for Coca-Cola energy brands such as Full Throttle and Relentless, and Coke in turn opened its global distribution arm to Monster.

Sacks has been in the top 400 of the Forbes list of dollar billionaires. By March 2021, Monster was the top-performing company on the S&P 500 Index over the last 30 years, delivering a total return of 295 805% to shareholders, outperforming the likes of Apple, Microsoft, Netflix and Amazon. And in January 2022, the company announced plans to enter the alcoholic drinks market, offering $330 million for craft beer and hard seltzer producer CANarchy Craft Brewery Collective. It was a cash deal and extends the global trend of soft-drink companies branching out into alcoholic drinks as the lines between categories shift. Coca-Cola tied up with brewer Constellation Brands to launch Fresca-branded, ready-to-drink cocktails, while PepsiCo partnered with Boston Beer to launch a Mountain Dew-branded alcoholic beverage.

Sacks's path to success and wealth is rare, but it is not only in the ready-to-drink premium alcohol-free category that small ideas are flourishing globally. Sometimes you can create a niche for a product you sell in categories you never considered viable.

One of South Africa's great indigenous exports is rooibos tea. If ever there was a South African crop ripe for beneficiation, it would be the dried and fermented reddish-brown leaves of *Aspalathus linearis*, a plant found exclusively in the Western Cape region of South Africa, where it has been consumed for centuries. It might not be everybody's cup of tea, but it is sold as a satisfying, healthier, caffeine-free alternative to coffee and  black and green teas, and is finding some traction as iced tea, red espressos, lattes and cappuccinos.

Up the N7 highway, on the road towards Namibia from Cape Town, you will come across an unassuming-looking roadside rest stop that not only provides weary travellers with sustenance on their long journey north or a final stop as they head south before getting to their destination, but it also offers an astonishing rooibos tasting experience.

Mientjie Mouton grew up on a rooibos farm in the Citrusdal area. In the aftermath of apartheid, as many of the commercial constraints of the old marketing boards were broken down and agriculture deregulated, she saw an opportunity to market her product directly to international players. About half of South Africa's annual 20 000-tonne rooibos harvest is exported. Mouton's company, Carmién Tea, does more than 10% of that and exports 98% of its annual production, most of it in bulk and much of it to Europe, especially the Netherlands and Germany, as well as the UK, where it is referred to as 'bush' tea. There is also a growing market in Asia, where Japanese consumers are developing a taste for the product.

There is a small, but rapidly growing market for specialist packaged teas that are sold by Carmién in South Africa via the mega pharmacy groups. They carry exotic flavours, such as 'floral berry' and 'masala', a blend of spices infused into the tea bags at a processing plant, which, since 2006, has been 50% owned by farmworkers.

They are not alone in leveraging the much-vaunted benefits of rooibos.

Grant Rushmere's beverage career began in selling specialty African coffee. He was fed up with seeing newly harvested African beans being bagged for export to countries outside of the continent, where they would be roasted and sent back in bags for African consumers at a considerably higher price. He started

Afro Coffee to use the beans, create a brand and thus deliver value back into Africa. Rushmere sold Afro Coffee to Red Bull, which is headquartered in Salzburg in Austria, and today there is a store and online presence in that city.

He turned his attention to rooibos because its naturally sweet, tannin-free taste profile made it a good base for flavoured iced tea. He called it BOS, reflecting the heritage of the product but also creating a colloquial play on words. Going 'bos' is to go mad, but in a nice, crazy, fun-loving way.

Enter Richard Bowsher, who had recently begun farming rooibos in the Cederberg after selling his tech business, Streaming Media, in San Francisco. He was looking for brands to invest in and, like Appletiser's Lombardi decades before, he wanted to add value to the raw material grown on his 6 000-hectare farm, Klipopmekaar. The name of the farm describes the red sandstone topography of the region, where it appears as if some long-dead civilisation of giants spent its days piling stones on top of each other.

Like many other producers in the region, Bowsher was farming, producing, processing and exporting hundreds of tonnes of rooibos directly to specialty and premium tea brands worldwide. Few people were actually doing anything to beneficiate the crop locally, beyond stuffing the dried leaves into teabags.

His business started out doing pretty much what every producer in the region was seeking to do: deliver top-quality product to the world's biggest processors of tea. Brands such as Ronnefeldt of Germany and TWG Tea of Singapore make creative use of rooibos in a range of high-value blended teas. Bowsher built a rooibos production and export business that sought to differentiate through quality, sustainability, transparency and direct global supply to premium tea brands.

BOS produces a range of iced teas sold in an assortment of formats, from cans to bottles, as well as branded packages of loose leaf and bagged rooibos. Currently, 40% of its sales are global, with a short-term ambition to raise that to 60%.

'To create a successful brand you need to have greater meaning and be more than the sum of your parts. Rooibos and our South African heritage allowed us to represent Africa, and the spirit of Africa, and contribute to consumers around the world. When people think of Africa, they think of safaris, maybe African art or curios. It's up to us as Africans to share what we are really about and FMCG [fast-moving consumer goods] products allow you to do this just as you find with French wines, Japanese sushi or Champagne – it's up to us to take brands that are immersive of our culture and share them with the world,' says Will Battersby, now CEO of BOS Brands.

Rooibos has been awarded geographical indication status by the EU, which means, like Champagne, rooibos can only be called that if it is produced in South Africa.

Global operations are managed from Cape Town, where staff deal with third-party distributors in each market and know how to get unusual brands into retail supply chains. All production for sale domestically, as well as for export to Asia and the US, is completed in South Africa, while some of its iced teas are manufactured in Europe for that region.

'BOS was a conscious response to an opportunity to create a brand in the iced tea space that was just as cool, just as emotive as

Red Bull. The idea is to make being healthy fun,' says Battersby. 'The biggest lesson was to realise that you have to start all over in each market. In some markets, things did not go as well because we started thinking our brand resonated with consumers before putting in the hard yards of brand-building – you have to do the start-up work in each market. This takes time and investment and there are few shortcuts.'

It is also tempting to enter highly competitive iced tea markets that already have a proven track record for consuming your product. But, says Rushmere, they have found it easier to enter less competitive markets where the brand can stand out as a premium alternative to mainstream products.

'Our greatest intrinsic strength or advantage is rooibos. From a product perspective, perhaps belatedly, we are now driving the tea aspects of our brand by expanding our tea range into flavours and launching BOSpresso, extracting opportunity in the hot beverage space,' he concludes.


Think 'hot chocolate' and the brands produced by the global giants of Cadbury and Nestlé will probably come to mind. You would expect that it is hard to drive a wedge into a market that is dominated by large companies and create a brand new business doing what they do. It is usually the other way around. The small guy has the idea and that is quickly appropriated by the corporate.

It turns out it is possible to find a niche in a market dominated by global heavyweights – you just need a great product, a desire to disrupt, superlative branding and time.

The co-founder of NOMU, Paul Raphaely, tells it like this: 'On a dark and stormy night in Cape Town, I was minding my own business in a bar in Long Street when it suddenly dawned on me that 21 years after starting the company, Tracy Foulkes and I had 2 kids, 3 dogs, 8 fish and a medium-sized food concern, employing 70 people and exporting 200 products to 20 countries, in 7 categories.'

Raphaely is the marketer, and Foulkes is the product creator and innovator.

'It all happened very fast, as things did in those days, when a good idea, presented beautifully, and placed easily in direct line of sight of droves of foreign visitors, soon became an export brand, long before making real headway in the local market.'

It started out as a business selling dressings and a range of herb and spice rubs through Cape Town retail stores. The products carried clear, contemporary branding and were distinctly identified as local. Foreign visitors to South Africa were instrumental in creating demand in their home countries as the products they bought on holiday ran out and they wanted to replenish supplies. Within four months of its launch, and even before making it to the shelves of local retailer Pick n Pay, products were being packaged for delivery to the UK, Sweden, Denmark and Holland.

The rapid international uptake was a welcome complication as they set out to develop a range of quality, innovative and good-looking products in a drab market that required a shake-up.

The company today produces more than 200 products and its

single biggest line by far is hot chocolate. The launch of NOMU Skinny Hot Chocolate came about because Raphaely wanted to reduce his own sugar intake but not give up his chocolate addiction. And in the same way as The Duchess has leveraged the trend towards alcohol-free adult drinks, NOMU was able to carve a niche in a market that was going off sugar, either because of a rise in global diabetes cases or simply from a weight and general health perspective.

'Perhaps it was just a function of newness and obvious visual distinctiveness on the shelf, but Skinny raced forward to become our number-one seller and has become a must-have specialised product in the dietetic- and diabetic-friendly space, while also still satisfying a broader, more general consumer appetite for quality and flavour in hot chocolate,' says Raphaely. Across its brand, hot chocolate makes up 35% of total sales and 20% of its exports.

It also pays to stay humble: 'We try not to lose sight of the fact that we do just make hot chocolate. It's not some lofty, moral pursuit, but the letters and communication we receive from customers from around the world are so amazing and heartfelt, that sometimes it does feel like we are achieving something else. We might be bringing a little light and a little fun, with products that have an authentic and more personal story behind them,' he says.

Before the global financial crisis, 80% of NOMU sales were international. That dipped to below half and has been in recovery mode since then.

Third-party agents and distributors have done a great job of getting products to market, but online demand is growing too, with Amazon in the US and the UK leading the way as consumer shopping patterns change.

The trick, however, is developing and maintaining strong, direct relationships with customers as much as possible as online channels depersonalise so many of the contacts that created the markets in the first place.

The global growth opportunity for specialist products is immense, and some are gaining traction faster than others. A proliferation of venture capital firms looking for smart ideas to take global suggests that the genius of these small firms is likely to resonate in international markets. The strength of the brands is not that they are specifically South African, but that the products themselves are world class and in an increasingly competitive FMCG environment. Independent producers such as these are finding markets in a world dominated by a handful of global giants.

# CHAPTER 8

· · · · · · · · · · · ·

# Fishing Where the Fish Are

*Sell a man a fish, he eats for a day, teach him to fish and you ruin a wonderful business opportunity.* — Karl Marx

Just 1% of South Africa's annual 670-tonne commercial West Coast lobster catch makes it onto domestic dinner plates. Approximately 90% is exported live to markets in China and Japan. The balance is exported in whole frozen form or as frozen lobster tails to China, Japan and the US. And it is not just rock lobster. The country exports far more of the fish caught and bred in its waters than is consumed domestically, and there is growing demand internationally for fish. Firms such as Sea Harvest and I&J have been supplying fish to global markets for 50 years.

More than 60% of Sea Harvest's annual revenue comes from exports of just one type of fish: wild Atlantic Ocean hake caught off the West Coast. Two-thirds of the catch is exported to the EU, with the main markets being Spain, Italy and Portugal, where it is a prominent staple on Mediterranean menus. Whereas South Africans consume an average of 10 kilograms of fish per person each year, the average person in Portugal eats six times as much.

A quarter of Sea Harvest's catch is exported into the Australian fish and chips market, while the balance is sent to the US and the UK. Those markets are willing to pay a premium for healthy wild fish certified as coming from sustainable sources.

The Sea Harvest group's Viking Fishing's mussels and oysters are sold locally, while the abalone harvest goes exclusively to Hong Kong, where the Chinese community, including visitors from mainland China, pay top dollar for wild Cape abalone. Chinese consumers devour 180 000 tonnes of the stuff annually, most of it local and low grade.

There are fourteen abalone farms in South Africa, three-quarters of them in the Western Cape. The industry earns about R700 million a year and supplies just 3% of farmed product, suggesting it represents a considerable growth opportunity. I&J is a pioneer in South African abalone farming and has a 600-tonne capacity per year from its Walker Bay plant in Hermanus.

Scientists at the University of Cape Town are experimenting with a wide range of technologies to diversify production of seafood such as sea urchin, popular in sushi restaurants in Japan, and even seaweed for export.

South Africa has four big commercial fishing firms, which require government licences to operate their fleets in domestic waters. All are growing their exports to global markets that are increasingly hungry for fish and a range of other seafood, including abalone, rock lobster, mussels and oysters.

Premier Fishing counts its customers in Asia, Europe and

the US, which has a particular fondness for West Coast rock lobster. Sea Harvest's two abalone farms have capacity to produce 500 tonnes a year, most of which will be sold in Hong Kong and China. It is usually sold fresh, but a pandemic-related breakdown in global supply chains and international container shortages saw the firm shift a growing proportion of its production to canned product, while also exploring options to dry and freeze product. A combination of Covid-19 and pro-democracy protests in Hong Kong disrupted exports for AVI-owned I&J, while the country's biggest fishing company, Oceana, which already had substantial canning facilities before the pandemic disruptions, was able to hedge against some of the breakdowns in supply chains.

What is critical about all of the country's big fishing businesses is that they are an important life-support industry to the small, often remote communities in which most of them are located. According to the Food and Agriculture Organization (FAO), large fisheries in South Africa produced more than 600 000 tonnes of fish, of which only a tiny proportion was taken out of inland waters. Nearly half of the catch was made up of anchovy, a quarter of hake and a smaller proportion of pilchards.

The local fishing industry employs about 28 000 people in the primary sector, with more than 80 000 jobs directly linked to the success of the sector. Despite a strongly stated government focus on aquaculture, its contribution to the economy, while growing fast, is small, at less than 7 000 tonnes.

In 2016, about 2 500 tonnes of seaweed was harvested, mostly to be made into feed for abalone, but there is growing demand for the crop globally, which one European start-up is turning into a possible plastics alternative for the future.

The industry is not without its challenges, particularly when it comes to conservation and the long-term viability of fish stocks as a resource for commercial exploitation. Globally, pressure is mounting on the oceans as unethical fishing practices wreak havoc on natural environments and on fish numbers in international waters. The FAO estimates that approximately 85% of the world's fish stocks are either overexploited or exploited to their maximum. The World Wildlife Fund's *Fisheries: Facts and Trends South Africa* report suggests that the position here is similar, with nearly 50% of its marine resources fully exploited. A further 15% of marine resources are overexploited, including important commercial species such as West Coast rock lobster and Indian Ocean yellowfin tuna populations.

The picture is healthier for the large-scale commercial fishing enterprises as the report says offshore marine resources are in a relatively stable state, but the status of many of South Africa's linefish species is poor, with almost 70% of the commercial species considered collapsed and at less than 10% of their pre-fishing populations.

Some 97% of the world's small-scale fishermen, many of whom come from impoverished communities that rely wholly on the sea for their livelihoods, are vulnerable to predation themselves. Historically, middle-men have acted as a go-between in the industry between those who catch the fish and the markets they reach. It made many communities vulnerable to exploitation by unscrupulous operators. That has led to the development in South Africa of a global innovation in Abalobi, a non-profit, public-benefit organisation begun in the country by Belgian Serge Raemaekers, Abongile Ngqongwa and Nicolaas Waldeck. Abalobi uses technology to help small-scale fishermen create sustainable businesses through identifying the source of the fish they catch, helping them to reach markets and providing software to assist them in running their small businesses.

Since its genesis in 2015, Abalobi has expanded its influence beyond South Africa's borders, working with like-minded organisations in the UK, Ireland, the US, Portugal, the Seychelles and the World Wildlife Fund. Raemaekers co-founded Abalobi as part of a University of Cape Town research project in 2017 to connect fishermen to markets and vice versa – enabling them to trade directly with one another. It solves a generations-old problem: 400 chefs and 8 000 private customers. Mutually beneficial, fishing communities get paid a fair price and customers get a sense of well-being – in the name of sustainability.

Fisheries play a critical role in providing direct and indirect livelihoods for over 140 000 people in South Africa, and fish protein is critical to the survival of many food-insecure traditional fishing communities.

While commercial fisheries contribute only about 0.5% to South Africa's GDP, the areas in which they operate make them a critical force in ensuring livelihoods in many remote coastal areas can be maintained.

The biggest export for the country's commercial fishing companies is wild-caught hake.

'The provenance is the selling proposition for both the Cape hake and Cape abalone,' says Felix Ratheb, CEO of Sea Harvest. 'It is wild-caught, the last hunted protein. It is naturally organic, with no antibiotics. The hake from South Africa is sustainable and has been certified by the gold standard in sustainability, known globally as the Marine Stewardship Council [MSC].'

Logjams at South Africa's inefficient ports, exacerbated by the supply chain disruptions brought about by Covid-19 lockdowns and restrictions in different parts of the world, have made getting product to market more complicated, especially when fishing and fruit seasons overlap. But exporters from all industries have found ways to muddle their way through an inefficient bureaucracy and inadequate infrastructure. However, the breakdown in supply chains has added to the cost of exports, especially airfreight, where there was a dramatic decrease in the number of available cargo spots on aircraft and air freight charges tripled from $3 per kilogram to $9.

Just 15% of Sea Harvest's annual hake catch is sold through retail, while a significant 25% goes into the food service and growing domestic fish and chips sector. And yes, the better cuts are exported.

The advantage for large-scale domestic fisheries is that wild-caught fish demand exceeds supply, and this will continue as populations grow and consumers call for healthier diets. It would be trite to suggest that the annual regulated catch sells itself – but demand is strong and South Africa is seen as a world leader in sustainable fishing. The growing risk along vast, hard-to-police coastlines like South Africa's is that unlicensed foreign vessels can easily trawl domestic waters with little concern of being caught and being held to account. As international fish stocks dwindle, that likelihood will increase.

South African fisheries compete globally against rivals in New Zealand, Iceland, Norway, Argentina, the US and China. Alaskan pollock, for example, is the largest whitefish resource and makes up about half the world's catch, with most of that going to Germany for processing into fish fingers, while cod and haddock are the joint second largest resources and serve northern Europe and the UK.

Exports in South Africa have been helped through beneficial trade agreements with major markets. The European Partnership Agreement and the African Growth and Opportunity Act (with the US) mean products enter those markets duty-free.

Increasingly, however, fishing companies have been diversifying into new markets and product lines in recent years. In early 2022, Sea Harvest announced a A$70-million acquisition of a Western Australia-based prawn specialist, MG Kailis, which it will house in a newly registered, wholly owned subsidiary of Sea Harvest Australia called Sea Harvest Marine. Oceana owns the US-based Daybrook Fisheries and is a big producer of fishmeal for the international animal feed trade and oil products for the healthcare sector.

Fish lends itself to beneficiation and is both labour- and capital-intensive. At 2021 prices, a deep-sea trawler cost in the region of R250 million, and you need a fleet in order to get economies

of scale. It costs about R2 billion to set up a factory to process
fish into products, from frozen cuts to fishcakes and other boxed
goods, as well as using what is left for fishmeal. South Africa's
bigger producers have made that fixed investment in the country
over decades and export to ALDI in Germany, Waitrose in the
UK and Coles in Australia.

Humans eat nearly 145 million tonnes of fish a year. Of that,
40% goes to China, where people consume an average of 26 kilograms a year, which is 50% higher than the global average,
according to the FAO. The next biggest consumers are the EU,
Japan, Indonesia and the US.

According to the FAO 2020 edition of *The State of World
Fisheries and Aquaculture*, the consumption of fish is significantly outpacing population growth. Since 1961, demand for fish has
grown an average of 3.1% a year against a population growth
rate of 1.1%. Today, more than half the fish on global markets
is farmed. Aquaculture, or fish farming, produces about 52% of
the world's fish. In addition to increased production, there have
been technical developments in terms of processing and logistics,
reduced raw material waste and better utilisation, but the biggest factor is that living standards are improving as humanity is
urbanising at the fastest rate in history.

Fish farming has reduced pressure on global stocks of wild fish,
but there are limited suitable water resources for sustainable fish
farming. Water quality is of increasing concern and stocks are vulnerable to outbreaks of aquatic animal diseases.

While wild fish stocks in many parts of the world have been eviscerated by unsustainable fishing practices for decades, there is clear

evidence that fish stocks can recover, as they have off Namibia, if managed properly. Tough regulation on catch sizes may hurt short-term profits, but it ensures the longevity of the resource.

The 2020 FAO report, for example, highlights how tuna catches reached their highest level of around 7.9 million tonnes in 2018, and the fact that two-thirds of these stocks are now fished at biologically sustainable levels – a 10% improvement in two years.

South Africa's small commercial fishing industry is part of a complex and growing global system that primarily serves the high-consumption northern hemisphere, which is becoming increasingly dependent on the resources of the global South. In that lies a significant long-term opportunity for countries like South Africa, which has the potential to engage in considerably more fish farming along its 2 800-kilometre coastline between Namibia in the west and Mozambique in the east. For now, though, its competitive advantage is in exports of wild-caught fish and seafood.

It is a sector with enormous unrealised potential beyond the wild fishing industry. Corporate players are tentatively expanding aquaculture, but the scope is considerably larger than we have at present. In a world of agricultural subsidies, it would make sense for higher levels of government backing for businesses that can deliver ocean caught and farmed produce internationally. Many coastal communities survive thanks to fishing but could become thriving hubs with appropriate backing.

# CHAPTER 9

# Food, Glorious Food

*If anything is good for pounding humility into you permanently, it's the restaurant business.* — Anthony Bourdain

South Africa's biggest restaurant export began with a regular lunch date between two work buddies. There was one joint they preferred above all others. Chickenland, in the unpretentious deep south, slightly worn and weary Rosettenville suburb of Johannesburg, served food like nothing they had ever tasted. It was an unfussy Mozambican-style takeaway that served delicious peri-peri chicken. It was located about as far away from the glitz and glamour of the high-flying social set as you could get.

Apartheid was dying, but its chief custodians were not quite ready to hand over power. The country was financially, morally, socially and ethically bankrupt. There was also a significant risk of civil war. A business strategist with an MBA from a prestigious global university might have recommended starting such an undertaking elsewhere or going into the flak-jacket business instead. Few would have considered it the ideal location from which to launch a global restaurant chain.

However, that is precisely what happened.

It has been 35 years since Middelburg-born Robbie Brozin, and Fernando Duarte, of Portuguese heritage from Mozambique, decided to buy Chickenland. They named it Nando's after Fernando's son and started the long and uncertain growth path that today sees the firm own and run some 1 300 restaurants in more than 30 countries.

Brozin had a regular middle-class white South African up-bringing in the small Mpumalanga town. The family moved to Johannesburg when he was twelve. He went to school, completed his obligatory period of conscription and studied commerce at Wits University. He was, it is safe to say, an unexceptional student. He came from an extended family of accountants but struggled to get his head around numbers and failed accounting several times before eventually being awarded his degree. He tried auditing for a while at PwC, but, by his own admission, he was not destined to keep tabs on others' businesses. Three years later, he joined the family business, Teltron, the South African agency for Sanyo electronics.

Like many entrepreneurs of the day, Brozin's dad was an im-porter and got caught on the wrong side of a collapse of the rand when the country defaulted on its debt in 1985, and he was forced to sell his business to Premier Milling.

The deal brought a change in culture that left Robbie Brozin miserable. He hated the hierarchical strictures of being owned by a large corporate. He resented wearing a tie and being told what grade of carpet, size of desk, pot plant and number of air conditioners he was entitled to as a result of his status in the business.

So he left, a week before the birth of his first son. He had no job or immediate prospects, beyond knowing that whatever he did next, he would need to work for himself.

Brozin might not have had the head for numbers that his accountant father had, but he did understand the basic premise of business being that you needed to buy something and sell it at a higher price. So, armed with the steely confidence of youth, Brozin and Duarte hatched a plan over a plate of their favourite chicken to buy the business.

Neither knew anything about the restaurant trade. Neither had delivered a plate of food to a customer in their lives. But they had distinct skill sets: Brozin was a good marketer and Duarte was an IT whizz and was strong technically. The pair envisaged at the start that Duarte would run the shop and Brozin would simply be an investor. But the bug bit and Brozin developed a taste for operations, discovering that he had a flair for service and motivating teams to deliver their best work.

The genius of Nando's was the founders' understanding that they were onto something special and took the view from the start that it should have a clear identity and a strong brand personality. Demand grew and, by the time they reached three stores, they needed capital. Brozin's dad sold shares in Teltron and, while he did not ever formally join Nando's, he was instrumental in the early days of helping to shape the business and the accounting disciplines of what it would become.

The move to the UK was strategic. The decision to stay was opportunistic. The first partners in that country did not work out and the founders considered withdrawing. It came about courtesy of one of the early Nando's kitchen staff who offered to connect Brozin with the Enthovens, the family behind insurer Hollard, which also operates across four continents.

Family patriarch Dick Enthoven was spending half his time in South Africa and the other half in the UK. He agreed to meet the owners of the restaurant, and they must have made a considerable impression. Either it was the chicken, the vibrant atmosphere or perhaps it was Brozin's tireless enthusiasm that sealed the deal quickly. Enthoven agreed to invest.

The first Nando's in the UK opened as a fast-food service in Ealing Common in 1992, but the growth really kicked off a year later under UK CEO Robby Enthoven, who changed the format to its current standard sit-down concept adopted across the globe.

Dick Enthoven's faith in the pair was handsomely rewarded and, according to global business news service Bloomberg, in 2015, Nando's accounted for half of his $1.1-billion fortune.

In the early days, there was no real business plan, and the history books on Nando's suggest there was an element of the founders flying by the seat of their pants, but Enthoven was the patient wingman. They ran out of money three times, and three times Enthoven extended them some more, until one day he called them to order.

It was the early 1990s and there was still no certainty that the negotiations between the government of the day and the newly unbanned political parties, dominated by the ANC, would yield any sort of peaceful result. The assassination of Chris Hani, leader of the South African Communist Party, in the driveway of his home at Dawn Park in Boksburg on Gauteng's East Rand, could so easily have tipped the country into a full-blown civil war that would have dashed all hopes of a negotiated settlement. There certainly would not have been the extraordinary fifteen-year period of unbroken economic growth that followed all the way up to the global financial crisis in 2008.

As it turned out, cool heads prevailed, and the timing of the creation of Nando's turned out to be fortuitous, as they had the fair winds of growth compounding in their favour during the early days of their existence.

It was the torturous emergence of a young democracy that helped shape the company's brand identity. Right from the start, it was about inclusion, tolerance and acceptance – values that helped it grow, not only in South Africa but also in the UK and later aided its American expansion. The brand was bold, cheeky and prided itself in speaking truth to power – something that would stand it in good stead as it entered new markets over time.

Nando's generates 'talkability', and this makes it a prime candidate for social media. Its Facebook page has been liked nearly 5 million times, on Twitter in the UK alone it has 1.2 million followers and more than 500 000 in South Africa, while on Instagram it has more followers in the US than in its home market and 400 000 in the UK.

The group was in its infancy when it began its international expansion. Unlike most other businesses, which first ensure they have a proven business model that has exhausted domestic growth opportunities, Nando's did things differently. The founders and their new investor had faith that their product was good enough to go global. It was not all smooth sailing. Its earliest

UK operators tended to be South African emigrants who had a strong affinity for the brand, but they themselves had very little in-country experience or knowledge about the environment in which they were operating and made lots of mistakes in the early days of expansion.

From the beginning, Nando's chose to push boundaries and that generated a significant amount of positive PR for the firm. It found an ad agency prepared to do the same, and set about creating a robust brand, which, while good for growth, meant there was pressure to do philanthropic work long before the company could properly afford it.

Brozin recalled in the 2019 documentary *Plucked*, made using two decades of Nando's adverts to tell its story and evolution through a period of enormous social and political change, that the brand has always boxed above its weight. He remembers getting a call to go on a trip with Nelson Mandela. He had no idea what the purpose of the trip was or where they would be going, but he was not going to turn down a chance to spend time with the great man. At the time, Nando's had about fifteen stores.

Brozin and a group of other business leaders were treated like VIPs. They got to sit on the podium in Chatsworth outside Durban with Mandela, who told the gathered crowd that he had brought with him high-powered business leaders who were aware of the need in that area for a new multi-million-rand hall. He promptly called up Brozin as the first of several guests to make a public commitment to pay for it.

Brozin is seldom lost for words, but he knew that he did not have the money to make good on the request. Mandela knew precisely what he was doing – he had turned extricating money for good causes from business people in public into an art form.

Brozin tried to tap-dance his way out of it. There was no way he was going to flatly refuse, so he fudged an offer with a commitment to look seriously at the president's proposal. Mandela had overestimated the scale of Nando's. It had no budget at that stage for doing the sort of work Mandela envisaged. Its focus was on pouring as much capital as it could into growing the business. But Brozin was not about to embarrass the great man. Mandela eventually managed to get R3 million from Nando's as part of a wide range of donations to get the hall built.

Its presence in the market had made Nando's appear far bigger and more successful at that stage than it actually was. While that cheeky approach was great for getting customers and breaking into new markets with lots of fanfare, it had a downside because the attention meant that they were being asked for money they simply did not have.

The business model went through multiple iterations. Long before the use of the term 'shared value' became a thing, Nando's ensured its operators were incentivised to drive the performance of their respective businesses and gave them a 49% stake in the stores. It worked operationally, but each outlet was its own legal entity. Those that were profitable paid high rates of tax, while others were slower to get off the ground. In a corporate structure, one would offset the other and capital could be sent to where it was most needed. It was an inefficient structure. They listed the company on the JSE and operators were able to switch their stakes for shares in the public company.

It was a mess. Operators stopped focusing on their own outlets and instead became obsessed with the share price. When the economy took a hit in the Asian crisis of 1997, it forced another rethink and the creation of a traditional franchising business – sometimes the old ideas do work best.

In the early 2000s, empowerment shareholders Brimstone decided to sell their stake, and it triggered an offer to minorities to delist the company. It went private, and, from a Nando's perspective, it was the best thing they could have done because it reduced the regulatory and administrative burden and allowed a focus on operations.

By the time of the global financial crisis, Brozin wanted out of operations. He became concerned about his ability to run the global business despite the fact that he had overseen an extraordinarily rapid growth and spread of the business. He had worked hard and knew that his children, who by now had careers of their own, would not be joining the company. It needed professional management. It was generating about $1 billion in sales from 1 000 stores worldwide. It had been a remarkable run, but it was time for a handover. In typical Brozin style, he described it as a need for 'adult supervision'.

Brozin stepped aside but continued to play to his strengths as an ambassador and brand custodian. He also served as an adviser on key projects, including marketing. But it was the philanthropic work that saw him regain his enthusiasm and sense of purpose, most notably with a campaign focused on eradicating malaria across Africa. He became the standard-bearer for the culture of the organisation. It was focused strongly on inclusion, respect and treating others as you would expect them to treat you. That ethos fed through into growing the business in new markets.

To what does Brozin ascribe his success in taking a small idea global and doing it in leaps and bounds ahead of rivals? It was down to taking a single brand, with a strong identity, and sticking to the founding principles of the organisation, while adapting those to new markets and always ensuring it remained relevant to people in those countries in which it operated.

Most stores are company-owned: those in the US, Canada, the UK and India are owned by the group, whereas in South Africa and Australia about half are franchised. It operates a pure franchise model in all other countries.

Unlike the global cookie-cutter approach of one of the many highly successful international franchises familiar to consumers across the globe, Nando's has a brand ethos that ensures if you entered a store in New York or New South Wales, you would be in no doubt about where you were. Nando's restaurants across the globe have similarities, and some elements are tailored to fit specific markets. The consistency is seen in the design elements: there are strong Afro-Portuguese cues, such as the music and food style, plus every outlet has artworks that are one-of-a-kind pieces made by southern African artists and are preserved as a private collection, making it the largest of its kind in the world.

Nando's has been investing in art and artist development since 2001. Today, the Nando's Art Initiative includes five different artist development programmes and supports more than 350 artists on a regular basis. The works range from oils and sculptures to beadwork and weaving, making the company the single biggest buyer of South African contemporary art in the world. The company today spends upwards of R50 million a year on South African art as part of its corporate social responsibility programme, but that has another purpose, which is to keep it true to its values and brand identity.

Despite the fact that only a quarter of its outlets are in South Africa, Nando's remains true to its roots, with a rigorous focus on showcasing southern African creativity through art, design and music. Each market implements the creative platforms and programmes in ways that suit the respective countries, but the collaboration with the home base is strong.

The core food product of flame-grilled PERi-PERi chicken, side order of chips and PERi-Spinach are the same in every market, but there are some localisations in each geography. Just as you will not find beef at a McDonald's in India, Nando's plays to local tastes, often with a twist. The preference, particularly in the north of England, to serve mushy peas with fish and chips sees Nando's in the UK serve Macho Peas, PERi-Samp in Zambia, and a Chicken Paella in New Zealand.

While many in South Africa believe the concept of the rainbow nation is dead and buried, Nando's keeps that spirit alive in all of its markets. It encourages a sense of diversity and inclusivity as being at the core of success for all societies, not only its home market – whether that is in terms of race, gender or any other categorisation of humanity. It strives to demonstrate the power of tolerance and inclusivity rather than the polarisation of nationalist debates that increasingly dominate social media.

While Nando's harbours big but unspecified growth ambitions

in the US and India, it opened in Saudi Arabia in 2016 and, thanks to some of the early lessons learned in Dubai, made promising inroads in that country despite the adverse impact of the pandemic slowing down the pace of its expansion.

It is neither a fast food nor a formal restaurant, slotting rather into a category called 'fast-casual'. There is an element of takeaway convenience coupled with a friendly environment, in which it is good to spend time and socialise. There is none of the freneticism of the American quick-service restaurant (QSR) concepts. With its proper fetch-it-yourself utensils and table service crockery, there is an easy informality that appeals to a wide cross-section of people in diverse communities. There is an exoticism to it, but it is intimately familiar. While each branch is distinct from any other, they are all clearly Nando's.

It helps when your brand plugs into the zeitgeist and you have a pop star such as Ed Sheeran doing a free-style rap song about you. A decade after extolling the joys of Nando's in a behind-the-scenes video with rapper Example, Sheeran told the *Table Manners* podcast that he had Nando's served at his 2019 wedding at home in Suffolk.

Comedian Jack Whitehall on *Live at the Apollo* made dating at Nando's into a cultural phenomenon. Its UK cult following assisted its expansion to other markets by virtue of the fact that Britain is at the epicentre of many young people's travel adventures and the popularity of the brand in the UK has made it easier for it to be transported to new markets. In Australia, with its big South African emigrant population, coupled with Antipodean wanderlust, opening Down Under was a natural extension of the brand as it already had a band of devoted customers.

Its ethos is encapsulated in how it sources its key ingredient – the one thing that makes its offering unique. It would be considerably cheaper and easier for Nando's to source the bird's eye chillies it uses in its sauces and marinades on the open market rather than carry the risk of creating and maintaining its own supply chain. Instead, it contracts out supply to about 1 400 small-scale farmers in Mozambique, Malawi, Zimbabwe and South Africa for all of its global operations. Its customers would not know the difference, but it goes to the centre of the Nando's brand ethos. Before each season begins, prices are negotiated upfront on fair trade principles, and the projects are managed locally by farming organisations to ensure that the farmers are trained and have proper financing, equipment and exactly the correct seedlings to ensure the best-quality product.

In each market it enters, it looks to create a stir. In Australia, it was a stunt about a massive disappearing mango – the three-storey, 10-tonne fruit statue that went missing from the front of the tourist information centre in the north Queensland town of Bowen. It created hype, interest and excitement and all roads led to Nando's.

It had been in the US for nearly a decade when it launched a new store in Washington, DC during Donald Trump's divisive presidency. Trump's America was the antithesis of what Nando's sought to represent. As Trump promised to build his much-vaunted wall along the Mexican border to keep foreigners out of the US, Nando's hit just the right note at the right time and had

America's content-hungry, much-watched breakfast TV shows eating out of the palm of its hand.

It took its South African sense of positivity and optimism and inserted that into a politically fraught and fractious US capital city with the message: 'Everyone is welcome.'

'The campaign shared exactly who we are; we are an equal opportunity company – if you don't like it, tough shit,' says Brozin in the documentary. Signs were put up: 'We are an immigrant employing, gay loving, racism opposing, Muslim respecting, equal paying, multi-cultural restaurant.'

Nando's had learned from the Zimbabwe lesson and took security precautions amidst concerns of a backlash from the powerful Christian right wing and were ready with counter PR measures should there be any public comeback at all. They controlled what they could, knowing that once they put the content in the public domain they would have no control over how the narrative would land in a fractured US political environment.

The bet paid off. The response in public and at the restaurants themselves was overwhelmingly positive. The campaign set the tone and drew the market Nando's wanted to attract. Its focus on diversity and inclusion rang true, especially in Trump's America.

Following the Arab Spring that swept through North Africa and the Middle East in the aftermath of the global financial crisis, Nando's launched its 'Last Dictator Standing' campaign, spoofing what it suggested might be the last 'big men' of Africa, including P.W. Botha, Muammar Gaddafi and Robert Mugabe. The ad hit home, but had to be withdrawn in Zimbabwe as operators received death threats and felt there was a real risk they could be killed by Mugabe supporters. Thanks to the wonders of the internet and social media platforms such as YouTube, the content remains publicly available to anyone searching for it.

Nando's entered the UAE in 2002, becoming the first of several chains to do so in Dubai, Abu Dhabi, Ras Al Khaimah, Sharjah and Al Ain. Ahead of a new store opening in 2016, two weeks before the holy month of Ramadan, it needed a stand-out campaign. Again, it was the lessons gleaned from skating close to the edge of human sensibilities in South Africa that saw the group's slightly risqué campaign hit all the right notes. It was barely a year after the furore around the cartoons of the prophet Muhammad ignited a furious response in France, leading to a gun attack on satirical magazine *Charlie Hebdo* in Paris, which left twelve people dead and eleven injured. There were other incidents of extreme violence that followed in Europe.

The marketing team was apprehensive about how to strike the right note. The ad, produced in Dubai by a local agency, showed a young man sitting on a deck at a Nando's, overlooking the ocean, with the Dubai skyline behind him, holding a piece of chicken to his mouth and waiting for the sun to set. Islamic law requires fasting during the holy month of Ramadan and would demand that he wait until sunset before eating. It was a high-risk strategy. Most multinationals in Dubai spend the largest proportion of their marketing budgets in the region around the holy month when more people are likely to be at home watching TV. The ads are usually filled with clichés of starry skies and lots of night-time scenes – anything to draw attention away from the discomfort of the fast – but there is seldom anything risky or innovative in the marketing drives.

This is precisely why the Nando's advert struck a chord. It amplified the discipline of those who observed the fast and acknowledged how hard it was to follow the rules, but, in doing so, it was entirely relatable to those waiting for the sun to set so that they could finally assuage their hunger.

Nando's is without doubt South Africa's stand-out global success. No South African restaurant concept is likely to match the international reach of McDonald's or Burger King, but a growing number are making impressive inroads as they find new markets beyond South African borders.

As 2021 ended, a team of restaurateurs from Bromley, south-east of London, came to South Africa to be trained in the 'Ocean Basket way'. It was the South African restaurant concept's first foray into the UK, but not its first international venture.

Fats Lazarides opened the first Ocean Basket in Pretoria in 1995. It measured just 60 square metres and had only six tables. The menu offered a handful of dishes, including fish and chips, prawns, hake, calamari and kingklip. There was only one wine on offer and a few soft drink options. In those days, customers could bring their own wine and even their own salads.

The international expansion started just as the global financial crisis was taking hold when the first store opened on the Mediterranean island of Cyprus. Yes, a South African Mediterranean-styled, casual-dining seafood chain founded in

Pretoria opened up in the Med and has been trading strongly for more than a decade.

It now has 44 stores, with active plans for 76 more in 19 countries outside South Africa, including other African markets (Kenya and Nigeria) as well as Dubai, Oman, Qatar, Saudi Arabia, Kazakhstan and Russia. The group indirectly provides jobs for about 9 000 people across the globe.

Ocean Basket claims to be the sixth biggest seafood-focused restaurant group in the world, with its international restaurants doing more than $150 million in turnover in 2021 and growing annually.

Grace Harding took over running the business in 2012 and has driven its international expansion. 'We are creating an international brand. Going global is very different to having an international brand,' she says. The process is slow and steady. There are no sudden decisions and the focus to enter a new market is not taken lightly. The value proposition in South Africa has been transferred globally. Most consumers wanting a seafood fix either go to a corner fish and chips shop or a high-end white tablecloth and crystal glass restaurant. Ocean Basket has deliberately positioned itself in the centre of that global demographic, and it is finding growing appeal in markets around the world.

It has managed to develop a complex global supply chain to make good on its guarantee to franchisees that they will never be out of stock of key menu items. It means it needs scale in markets, and it will not enter a territory unless its key partner in that country has the capacity to help it build a strong brand presence. Cyprus, the third biggest island in the Mediterranean, has nine

Ocean Basket outlets and is a distribution hub for the raw sea-food for Europe and the Middle East. All the group's restaurants get their seafood from similar places. Prawns are farmed and can be sourced nearly anywhere with the correct coastal conditions, but its calamari comes from the Falklands and its kingklip from the fisheries of Namibia and New Zealand.

'Detail is everything,' says Harding. 'And always guard against ego,' she warns.

Famous Brands reads the global trend towards convenience and the willingness of consumers to part with disposable income for the luxury of not having to cook and wash up at home. The model was well adapted to South Africa under the leadership of former CEO Kevin Hedderwick, whose ambitious growth plans took it from a R60-million chain of Steers burger outlets to a R14-billion market darling. Highly acquisitive in the domestic market and with ambitions to take the much-loved Steers brand to expatriate communities worldwide, it made a strategic misstep with the failed R2-billion acquisition of Gourmet Burger Kitchen in 2016 in the UK, and was eventually forced to shut down opera-tions and write off the investment. But Hedderwick's foresight and hunger for growth helped at least one entrepreneur fast-track her global ambitions.

Natasha Sideris grew up in the restaurant trade and oper-ated front of house for her father at the Fishmonger in Rivonia. Ambitious and never shy of doing a hard day's work, she later ran her own Nino's franchise, where Hedderwick ate breakfast most

Saturday mornings. One day, he called her over: 'I like the way you operate. You are going to start your own thing one day and when you do and you need money, give me a call.' The Nino's experience showed her that there was a gap for a restaurant that served proper food in a less stuffy atmosphere than many others offered.

Armed with a BA in psychology – a great asset in the restaurant trade – and with no formal business training, Sideris relied purely on her gut and the experience she had garnered working at the Fishmonger and Nino's before going out on her own with Tashas. The Famous Brands tie-up, in which the firm bought a 51% stake in Tashas for an undisclosed sum, gave her the lift and systems back-up she needed to grow in South Africa. As the wheels came off during the global financial crisis, the new management team at Famous Brands decided to refocus on its core and allowed, again for an undisclosed amount, Sideris to buy back the business she had built in partnership with her brother Savva.

It would have been easy for her to go back to her Greek roots and open a high-end taverna, but she wanted a place where you could go for breakfast, lunch or supper or anything in between several times a week and not be restricted by a particular theme. So Sideris set about creating high-quality, restaurant-grade food you might opt for at home if you were bothered to make the effort.

She got to eighteen stores and then set about her global expansion. Sideris is not one to wait on the sidelines. She relocated to Dubai and set up six restaurants in the UAE, with her eyes on UK and US expansion next. But she is cautious of too much growth too fast. Because of the enormous personal input she has in en-suring that every store is unique but distinctly Tashas, Sideris will not outsource the expansion to anyone else, choosing to be pre-sent for every store opening. Critical to her success in Dubai was the decision to choose a strong local partner and ensure that she was on hand to oversee the development and growth of the stores from scratch, leaving her brother to manage the South African market. Start-up costs at the first store in Dubai, about R30 mil-lion, were higher than at any store because she took 30 South Africans to oversee the project. The second store cost about half that to launch, but she had the traction she needed to get the rest off the ground.

When, and not if, the brand expands to the US, California is likely to be the first port of call. Sideris was offered a site in New York at the early stage of Tashas's move beyond South Africa, but she turned it down. It was simply too soon for her to contem-plate a move of that scale and intensity.

Wilhelm Liebenberg has no such concerns. Of all the places in the world to find a young Afrikaner setting up a swish Parisian-inspired coffee shop, Union Square in Manhattan would probably not be your first bet. As New York was emerging from one of the world's worst urban waves of the pandemic, he secured a prime position just off 5th Avenue on Union Square as part of what he says is the first phase of his global expansion. He opened his first outlet of Coco Safar in Cape Town's Cavendish Mall and later moved to trendy Sea Point.

'We decided more than seven years ago to make Cape Town our innovation hub and the place where we would plant our global flagship, allowing us to fine-tune our brand away from the noise and large style capitals of the world,' says Liebenberg.

The first two international destinations will be Qatar and New York City. Paris, the home of café culture and the inspiration of Coco Safar since Liebenberg experienced the city on his travels as a youngster, is on the list. Taking a swish café concept to Paris may be the equivalent of taking coal to Newcastle, but you cannot fault the ambition. Unlike Starbucks, inspired by Italian coffee bars and deliberately designed for large-scale replication and roll-out, Coco Safar will be a niche offering in high-profile locations in fewer urban markets and featuring custom-made designer espresso machines.

That makes marketing and brand recognition tough, but, in a world of endless duplication, the idea is to create the impression of an independent, stand-alone store rather than a chain. So, developing the brand takes some creative thinking. This is where social media strategy is key. If you take the time to trawl through Coco Safar's Instagram feed, in between the remarkable confectionaries, sumptuous breakfasts and images of classic café fare, including the obligatory steak frite, you will see a carefully curated assortment of images positioning the brand in high-end locations all over the world.

Some of it is downright opportunistic. In among images of diners on plush banquette-style seating taking high tea, a perfect piece of confectionary or a light meal with a glass of wine, there is the imagery of a global destination. Discreetly tucked between the gourmet food is a well-presented copy of the *FT Weekend*. While there may never be a Coco Safar in Paris's Galeries Lafayette, there is an image of a laptop open to the company website with the glorious stained-glass dome creating a cathedral-like backdrop. In between are classic old pictures of real cafés in Paris or Audrey Hepburn from a scene of the movie *Breakfast at Tiffany's*. You get the picture.

Then there are the prizes for 'best croissant in the world' and talk of the 'best coffee pods in the world' – the focus is on making you believe the brand is, if not already in a lot of places, going to those places.

Coco Safar will target those prepared to pay a little extra for a more artisanal experience. That scarcity and exclusivity of the experience is amplified via social media platforms. Making the business stand out is a key route to market, and the company has spent the past five years building a social presence in preparation for its expansion to new markets. Nothing is being left to chance.

Every place in New York needs a schtick. Gone are the days of the *Friends* gang being satisfied with whatever it was Gunther served them at Central Perk. Coco Safar is billing itself to be a 'Pâtisserie & Bakery Lab with a luxury Sidewalk Café, Bakery and Espresso Bar'. Should it fly, more stores in New York will follow.

This is not a fly-by-night decision. Liebenberg has been plotting this move for years. Opening in New York carries high risk. If it bombs, it will set him back significantly, but if it succeeds, it will be the first step towards building a global clientele and getting the gossip columnists chattering. It is about as far away from Starbucks as you can get. Coco Safar has an active, carefully choreographed social media presence positioning it as an extraordinary place to visit.

'After the brand's official debut in the Big Apple, the world will be our oyster,' says Liebenberg.


The official history of South African fast-casual restaurant chain Kauai goes something like this. California college friends John Berry and brothers Carl and Brett Harwin were living on the Hawaiian island of Kauai, surrounded by a tropical paradise and its bounty of fresh fruit. They decided that they should create a food concept that would introduce a tastier, healthier way of life to the world. A bit like the Silicon Valley hustle stories of Bill Gates starting Microsoft in his childhood bedroom and Jobs and Wozniak working out of a garage, the first Kauai juice bar had only one juicer but later grew and went on to supply major hotels, restaurants and health food stores.

They travelled to Cape Town for Carl's marriage to a South African in 1996 and fell in love with the city and its surfing spots, but they realised there were few healthy-eating options open to them. Kauai as a restaurant chain was born. Fast-forward to 2015 and the business had grown to 130 outlets, but it was in trouble. Whereas the burger and chips fast-food joints had long queues and loudly ringing tills, the only thing going for a Kauai was that it was a great place to hang out if you suffered from agoraphobia. It was the one place where you were unlikely to be jostled by other customers. It was trying to compete as a healthier alternative to traditional fast food but was missing the mark and beginning to adapt its menu rather than having the courage to stand out.

Enter Dean Kowarski: his wavy blonde hair protrudes from under the rim of the Kauai-branded, snap-back-style American cap he wears everywhere. He carries a broad smile on his angular face and looks like he hardly has an ounce of body fat. He is highly energised, focused and driven to revolutionise healthy food. He started Real Foods in 2013, and in 2015 he bought Kauai. If Kauai had had a glory day, it had long faded, along with the pastel island floral tones of its dated corporate identity.

Kowarski has turned the fortunes of the brand around, gone back to basics, refreshed its identity and has begun a gradual expansion into new markets. Unlike the heavy footprint of a Starbucks in New York City, where you can have stores trading almost across the street from one another as a result of high footfall in densely populated environments, or the fact that you can have a McDonald's or a KFC dotted at regular intervals in ever-expanding international cities and still make a killing, the market for healthy QSR is more limited.

But food habits are gradually changing as a growing number of consumers become more conscious of the environmental consequences of large-scale farming and the food they ingest. Like Nando's, Kauai is not for everyone but has still grown to more than 150 outlets in South Africa, Namibia, Botswana, the Netherlands, Scotland and Thailand. During the severe lockdowns through the pandemic, Kowarski, ever the innovator, was one of the few in the sector to adapt his business model to the new environment.

While the restaurants were closed to customers in the first hard lockdown, the entrepreneur knew he needed to keep his suppliers going and turned his businesses' food-delivery operation into a fresh fruit and vegetable home service, which meant it complied with the rules of the lockdowns, plus ensured the farmers who supplied him stayed solvent. Not one to sit still for long however, Kowarski tied up with Brait-controlled Virgin Active, selling his food businesses into the gym group and joining the company as its new CEO. Virgin Active in the UK has global reach, and Kowarski's dream of expansion of the food business can be more easily realised if it follows the post-pandemic recovery of the fitness industry. The deal sees Kowarski lose control of the healthy foods business that he built, but if you take with other investors an 8% stake in the global business of Virgin Active, it certainly looks in its earliest of stages that it qualifies for a 'genius' label.

# CHAPTER 10

# Banking in the Big Leagues

*Given a 10% chance of a 100 times payoff,*
*you should take that bet every time.* — Jeff Bezos

Making a scruffy meerkat your brand mascot in the UK might not seem like the smartest idea. Giving him a Russian name, an aristocratic title, a dodgy accent and an implausible backstory would be insane. Yet, that is precisely what former Eskom quantity surveyor-turned-insurance magnate Douw Steyn did with the price comparison site he built called Comparethemarket.

The firm is based in Peterborough, north of London, and is part of a complex global structure that houses more than twenty businesses in seven countries. It is owned by the BGL Group, which in turn is owned by a Guernsey company that is part of BHL.

BHL is South Africa's biggest insurance export and operates businesses under multiple brands in South Africa, the UK, Australia, Thailand, Singapore, France and Turkey. But, it is in the UK that it has the highest profile outside of its home country, thanks to an aristocratic billionaire meerkat called Aleksandr Orlov, who, with a thick faux-Russian accent, captured the hearts and minds of the British public and made Comparethemarket one of the UK's biggest price comparison websites.

Steyn rose to prominence in the early 1990s when he gave Nelson Mandela the space at the plush Saxon Hotel in Johannesburg to work on his memoir *Long Walk to Freedom*, but his entrepreneurial journey started twenty years previously when he founded Steyn's Insurance Brokers from his father's real-estate business premises. After more than a decade of selling other firms' products, he obtained an insurance licence in 1985 and created Auto & General. It claims to have been the first insurance company in the world to employ paperless, computerised and scientific risk-rating underwriting, conducting business over the telephone using voice-recording systems during the sales, policy-amendments and claims-handling processes – common enough today but revolutionary in its time.

Some 80% of the BHL Group's profits are generated outside of South Africa, and the group's 10 000 staff worldwide serve about 10 million customers.

Its first venture outside of South Africa was in the UK. Budget Insurance later became a brokerage and today is known as the BGL Group, which is a leading provider of white-labelled insurance products to major consumer brands in that market. It also owns Comparethemarket. It launched Auto & General and later Budget Direct and a price comparison site in Australia, while its South African interests are held in Telesure Investment Holdings (TIH). A total of 350 of the 4 100 people employed by TIH in South Africa service Auto & General Australia's after-hours call centre from Johannesburg.

While Steyn's ability to build global businesses is remarkable, the meerkat story is one of the more extraordinary brand-building exercises in a foreign market by a South African company. It gained traction in 2012 through a three-year deal to sponsor one of Britain's most watched soap operas, *Coronation Street*. The meerkat developed a cult following, but the British obsession with the creatures predates Orlov. Comparethemarket was simply capitalising on something that already had resonance in the British psyche.

A columnist in *The Independent*, Simon Usborne, summed it up in 2009: 'Britain has gone mad for these upstanding citizens of the Kalahari desert. Meerkats have burrowed into the public consciousness, colonising our billboards, cinemas and television screens. Their adorable faces, quizzical disposition and trademark posture make them seriously cute (and seriously attractive to marketing men) but the diminutive diggers' biggest fans say meerkat mania is about more than charm and charisma. They are the little guys with big hearts whose struggle for survival and fierce sense of family loyalty not only fascinates scientists and seduces film-makers, but also offers a model of duty and fortitude for us all. The mammals' greatest champions go further. They believe – and read on if this sounds crazy – that, in gloomy times, meerkats have a unique power to make us happy. In Germany, they call them *erdmännchen*, or "little earth people".'

The fascination with the creature started with a David Attenborough documentary called *Meerkats United* twenty years earlier, but it was plugging into that zeitgeist that gave the South African company a considerable boost in a new market, as

Usborne explains: 'Aleksandr Orlov is the world's most unlikely insurance salesman. The computer-generated Russian aristocrat with a thick accent and a smoking jacket appears in a series of TV ads for a price comparison website, Comparethemarket.com. The bonkers premise: Orlov is so fed up with careless policy hunters swamping his website, Comparethemeerkat.com, he films his own explanatory ads with the sign-off "seemples". "Cheap carinsuuurance, meeerkats – two veeery different things".'

It contributed to making Steyn a hard-currency billionaire and one of only three South Africans on the prestigious *Times* newspaper list of richest Britons. It includes on that list diamond scion Nicky Oppenheimer in 31st place, with a family fortune built over three generations of nearly £6 billion, followed by Natie Kirsh at more than £4 billion. His fortune originated in wholesaling in South Africa. He built Jetro Cash & Carry in New York State and has business interests in Australia, the UK and Israel. Steyn is in 79th position and is worth £2 billion, twice as much as a year previously and in no small part due to his firms' ability to perform in highly competitive markets.

BHL is a stand-out performer in the insurance market. Other short-term insurance players have dabbled more cautiously in new markets; nearly 20% of Santam's income is from other African countries and small businesses in parts of the Middle East, Southeast Asia and India, while FirstRand's Outsurance has found a small but profitable niche via a company called Youi in the highly contested Australian and New Zealand markets, as well as an investment in the tech-based UK insurer Hastings.

Until the global financial crisis of 2008, South African banks were deeply committed to developing global businesses. The most ambitious of these was Standard Bank, which sought to emulate the success of SABMiller's global expansion and at one point owned stakes in financial institutions in Argentina, London, Russia and across several African countries. Investec invested in and subsequently withdrew from Israel, the US and Australia, and since its demerger with the asset management business of Ninety One, it has shown promising signs of a turnaround in its UK business, underpinned by a solid South African operation. But the global financial sector meltdown led to a new, tough regulatory regime and onerous capital requirements for banks with foreign operations, bringing the focus back to opportunities on the African continent.

In 2020, the long-anticipated split between Investec and its asset management division transpired. As unlikely a mascot as a meerkat might be for a price comparison website in the UK, so too was the use of a zebra as Investec's brand identity, and, surprisingly, the group first used the animal in Britain. Unlike so many other South African global businesses, Investec was eager to demonstrate its African roots and never shied away from its origins as it built its brand off the back of prestigious sporting events, including an early sponsorship of the Epsom Derby and later of international cricket and rugby fixtures. It may have been purely coincidental, but there was also a long-running sponsorship of former CEO Stephen Koseff's favourite football team, Tottenham Hotspur, and a range of cultural events too, from symphonies to open garden festivals. It immersed its brand and highly recognisable zebra into the leisure time of Britain's elite. It also plastered itself for a period all over the London Underground and the city's famous black cabs. It had a massive, visible and unmistakable presence. And it worked, giving the impression that it was far bigger than it was, in a fiercely competitive banking and investment sector.

In any split, no matter how amicable, any shared assets have to be divided and the asset management business, now branded Ninety One, gave up both the Investec name and the zebra on which it had been built, confident it would be able to stand on its own based on the reputation it had built in the City of London.

Ninety One now manages more than R3 trillion in assets for clients around the world. It is impressive but tiny by global standards. Considering at current exchange rates it amounts to only £140 billion, the firm makes up a fraction of the £100-trillion global asset management pie.

Ninety One was founded in 1991 when 29-year-old Hendrik du Toit was headhunted from Old Mutual Asset Managers by one of the bank's early directors, Bernard Kantor. It took a year to lure the asset manager across, and Kantor, on visits to Cape Town, would find himself on the beach at Muizenberg after hours, waiting for Du Toit to emerge from a late-afternoon surfing session. Although another legend puts Kantor on the side of a football pitch as the young fund manager perfected the art of playing hard to get. Eventually they came to an agreement. The asset management company could be in Cape Town and there would be no interference by the bank in how it was run. It started with two desks and approximately R225 million under management, consisting of two pension funds, one insurance fund and a few trust and private client accounts.

'It was daunting in those early days,' says Du Toit. 'We were up against the big established insurers and banks, and investors had become very set in their ways.' The status quo in the early 1990s investment environment played a significant role in the early success of the company. It was a time of great change in the investment industry and teams of asset managers were breaking away from the insurance companies to start their own businesses. Allan Gray was already in business, and firms such as Coronation started around this time too.

There was no obvious gap for another asset manager at the time. Asset management was the preserve of the four big insurance companies, as well as a handful of blue-chip investment banks, such as UAL and Standard Merchant Bank, along with Allan Gray and the long-established 'trust' companies, Syfrets and Board of Executors.

'We decided to give it a go anyway,' remembers Du Toit. 'In one of our early pension fund report backs, we came out after presenting and saw our competitors lined up ready to go in after us. They were led by one of the more respected leaders in the industry at the time, Roy McAlpine, CEO of Liberty Life Asset Management. As they went in, we knew that they would tell the trustees that we were too young to be managing money, that we had never experienced a bull or a bear market, and they were probably right.'

But they were unencumbered by any notion of self-doubt and

set about hiring equally ambitious talent, with a hunger to operate globally.

Its strategy was always global. Du Toit knew there was a ceiling on the amount of available money in the South African market. If the firm was going to be a significant player, it needed a base in an international financial centre.

The early 1990s was a period of significant global and local socio-political change. Investors were disillusioned by the poor performance of their money. The newly formed Investec Asset Management did not have any residual baggage, legacy systems or any infuriating bureaucracy to hold it back. By 1994, Investec Asset Management had successfully broken into the South African pension fund and retail markets, and assets under management doubled every year between 1992 and 1997. It was only then that the international expansion happened, with the acquisition of Guinness Flight Hambro providing it with a UK foothold, even though the team was appalled by the fact that they had to pay R8 to the pound to do the deal.

Du Toit moved to London in 1998. He established a formidable physical presence in the city and set about offering its global money management services from there. Global investors were far more likely to entrust their savings to a London company than a Cape Town start-up. Its biggest market remains South Africa, where it manages some £50 billion in assets for investors across the continent. That is followed by the UK, and there is a further £17 billion managed for clients in the US and Europe. In total, it has clients in some 30 countries globally.

The timing of Ninety One's founding in 1991 could not have

been better. South Africa was shedding its pariah status. The collapse of communism triggered the massive globalisation phase that was sparked by the free market ideology best demonstrated by Nobel prize-winning economist Milton Friedman and practised by world leaders such as Margaret Thatcher in Britain and Ronald Reagan in the US. The opportunities were there for the taking; even the ANC saw the benefits of a free market.

'From those early days we would travel, meet international peers, spend time with them and learn from them,' says Du Toit. 'You learn from your competitors. That is probably the best advice I can give to anyone – do not just talk to your clients. Clients are very important and, obviously, come first in your business, but understand and learn from what your competitors are doing. Good competitors can teach you so much.'

Right from the start, and long before management guru Peter Drucker coined the memorable 2006 phrase, 'Culture eats strategy for breakfast', Du Toit was alert to the fact that building a competitive asset manager was far more than strategy and plans, financial strength, skills or capability. It was about getting the right people into the right teams to work together for the benefit of the organisation. Culture and collective ambition, he knew instinctively, were key.

'This is a merciless industry. We get measured. Your lawyer, your doctor, even your restaurant is probably measured, but many firms with which an individual would engage are not measured as ruthlessly or as brutally as investment managers. We have a benchmark. We have to beat it within risk tolerances, whatever the world throws at us in terms of macro instability or market shocks,' Du Toit says. 'This is a business where you really have to apply yourself to achieve because you also have really, really good competitors.'

Thirty years on, an initial investment by Investec of about $1 million has resulted in approximately a $2-billion dividend flowback to shareholders and $3 billion of value remaining. It is safe to say the bet on the determined young Cape Town surfer paid off.

'I don't think it has ever been as easy to take a small idea or an idea from a small country global and succeed. We see it every day. If you are a good artist, if you have a business idea, if you have something that appeals to humanity – whether it is a thought or belief – it is easy to spread it with current technological means. The opportunities for people who come from small countries, or for that matter small towns in small countries, to fulfil their potential are so much higher. Therefore, we can say we live in a better world for most people on this planet than ever before,' Du Toit concludes.

One of the problems with being a big fish in a small pond is that you worry about running out of oxygen. You can also become overconfident elsewhere in your ability to replicate what you do in your home market. It leads to very expensive mistakes being made.

On balance, there has been more value added than destroyed in deals offshore – most notably the Naspers acquisition of 46% of Tencent for $32 million in 2001, and the globalisation of South African resources businesses, which has yielded massive returns for domestic investors. Other success stories include MTN, despite regular headaches in places such as Nigeria and some Middle Eastern markets, as well as Sibanye, which has morphed from a South African gold miner into a platinum major, thanks in part to its US acquisition of Stillwater. Plus there is Mondi, not to mention Spar, the country's most successful retail dealmaker – which now controls businesses that serve Ireland and parts of the south-east of England, Switzerland and Poland – NEPI Rockcastle, food services player Bidcorp, and the Super Group.

A research report published by Anchor Capital in July 2020 estimates South African companies' overseas forays destroyed more than R300 billion in value.

'For many of these businesses, it started a long time ago as corporate South Africa went on a global diversification spending spree over the past decade, with mainly very poor, and often disastrous, outcomes,' according to Peter Armitage, CEO of Anchor Capital. The report claimed it was impossible to quantify exactly how much value had been destroyed in a bid to find new markets, but the researchers labelled the biggest culprits as Sasol, with its over-time and over-budget Lake Charles project in Louisiana in the US; Woolworths, with its overpayment for David Jones in Australia; and Brait, with its catastrophic investment in British retail chain New Look. Famous Brands burned its fingers on Gourmet Burger Kitchen, hospital groups Mediclinic and Netcare were scorched in their efforts to globalise, while Truworths and Foschini did a range of value-destructive deals in the UK.

Anchor Capital found several similarities when it came to these foreign investments. These included a propensity to overpay in markets where their domestic success has given them an inflated sense of their ability to turn around moribund businesses, and a false sense of security provided by the lower cost of capital in many markets. In numerous cases, companies deployed B-grade management to run new operations, leaving their stars at home to keep those businesses performing optimally, and failing to acknowledge that the local conditions and competitive environments were simply different to what they were used to.

If you go back a little further than a decade, you can add the R100-billion-plus failed Old Mutual globalisation to the collapse of Sage as it overextended in the US, and a R1-billion write-off in the US that Discovery would rather not remember.

Probably South Africa's most ambitious financial services company, Discovery, sought to take its world-leading business model into the most competitive health insurance market in the world via Destiny Health. Its domestic rivals saw it coming and acted fast to prevent it from getting the initial traction it needed to succeed.

'When we started Discovery in the early 1990s,' says co-founder and CEO of Vitality Group Barry Swartzberg, 'South Africa was transitioning out of apartheid and the medical aid market was facing considerable challenges. Medical schemes were under pressure; the country had a high disease burden and a shortage of doctors; and legislation had changed, meaning private health insurers moved to an egalitarian system of community rating without mandatory enrolment. These factors created high potential for adverse selection and medical inflation. There was a clear need for a sustainable approach that integrated traditional medical aids and health insurance. We were forced to focus on the demand of healthcare, encouraging people to limit use of healthcare as opposed to other countries' health insurance markets that mainly focus on managing supply and the cost of supply.'

That led to a dramatic rethink on how to make medical insurance sustainable, available to those who really needed it, and to discourage customers seeking medical attention for minor ailments. It hired the best behavioural economists and focused on how to incentivise its customers to live healthier lives and reduce the risk of serious illness. Its genius was to work out that most people over-consume healthcare but under-consume measures that might prevent serious illnesses in the first place. Humanity's inbuilt bias towards instant gratification means that when you see a doctor and get prescribed medication, the benefits are immediate, as opposed to the long-term benefits of healthy diet and exercise.

Vitality is currently in 31 markets across six continents and impacts on 20 million lives. Today, 90% of Vitality members are outside South Africa, in places such as China, Canada, Ecuador, the US, the UK, France, Germany, Austria, Singapore, Australia, Hong Kong, Macau, the Philippines, Thailand, Malaysia, Sri Lanka, Vietnam, South Korea, New Zealand, Japan and Pakistan.

Discovery has steadily evolved its business model from that of a South African health insurer to that of a domestically and increasingly globally diversified financial services player. Its latest venture was the establishment of a new health-centred insurance technology, Asia-focused business Amplify Health, in partnership with the AIA Group. The start-up, Amplify Health, will operate as a joint venture in Asia (excluding China, Hong Kong and Macau) and plans to become the 'leading digital health technology' business across the region. It is putting serious skills behind the project, appointing the former Discovery Health CEO, Dr Jonathan Broomberg, as its CEO. Discovery says the new business will provide a range of state-of-the-art, production-tested health technology, intellectual property and expertise to AIA's rapidly growing health insurance businesses across the region.

Discovery's genius has been in partnerships. It is how it has grown the Vitality rewards programme and is expanding its influence in China with its stake in Ping An Health. It now hopes to do so in other parts of the East through building on what has already proven to be a successful partnership between Discovery and AIA.

AIA provides what Discovery does not have in its region, which is an established market-leading business, a strong reputable brand in the area and a solid distribution platform across Asia. Discovery has taken a 25% stake in Amplify Health but will earn additional income for its intellectual property ownership and transfer of expertise. It needs to be mindful of the occasional capital requirements a fast-growing business like this might need. Its shareholders expressed trepidation when it raised money from shareholders to fund the growth of Ping An Health in China.

Eagle-eyed football fans would have noticed the appearance of the Vitality brand on pitch-side billboards. The UK is part of Discovery's three-pronged growth strategy: Asia through Ping An and AIA, and the UK via Vitality. The UK is an interesting market and the firm has been quietly setting about replicating parts of its South African business model through VitalityHealth, VitalityLife and VitalityCar. It cut its teeth in all these businesses in South Africa and is applying those lessons to the UK. It will also understand the ferocity of real competition for the first time since it was forced to retreat from its loss-making US business more than a decade previously.

The group has a goal of reaching over 100 million people by 2025. It is reaching those customers directly through its own platforms and then through an innovative partnership model whereby other insurance companies integrate Vitality into their insurance offerings. It made sense to attach Vitality to other insurers rather than start their own competitor businesses in new markets.

It has the data to prove that the programme works and has tracked improvements in health outcomes for participants who have, on average, 10% fewer hospital admissions, 27% fewer chronic conditions and in whom the prevalence of cancer is 19% lower than for those not integrated on the platform. It has achieved strong take-up with the use of short-term incentives as a means of sustainably shifting behaviour and has applied the lessons across its short-term investment and banking businesses.

Vitality is a unique product offering developed, tested and implemented in South Africa, and the lessons learned in its home market are being applied globally. The value of the model is being noticed, and, in the same way that Discovery has been a disruptor, it faces the risk of disruption from a host of fintech start-ups also seeking to capitalise on the shared-value concept.

'Our greatest challenge is to try to stay ahead of the competition. This requires continual investment in capabilities. My biggest worry is managing this investment in the most optimal way,' says Swartzberg.

Discovery has a potential uplift in the form of a 25% stake in Ping An Health, a subsidiary of the world's biggest insurance company Ping An in China. It made its first $29-million investment in the firm in 2010, and five years later increased that stake by 5% and, in September 2021, undertook to raise R6 billion from shareholders to follow its rights as the firm announced plans to raise capital for expansion. Could Ping An Health become Discovery's Tencent? Discovery founder Adrian Gore hopes so; otherwise he would not be pouring further capital into the business, which in 2019 grew revenues by 74% to $1.26 billion, and saw new business premium growth up by 67% to about $717 million. Discovery's share of the after-tax profit was a more modest $7.5 million.

Old-school traders miss the days of open outcry on the stock exchange floors of the world. There was a camaraderie that simply cannot be replicated in the digital world, complains David Shapiro, deputy chairperson of Sasfin Securities, who started his career in his dad's brokerage firm more than five decades ago. Those were the days when your bid was your bond, and somehow, between offers scribbled on a piece of paper based on a price chalked up on a board that required eagle eyes to be seen clearly, buyers and sellers exchanged money for shares.

The JSE floor closed on 7 June 1996 and traders were forced into a digital world. The transition to high-speed, low-cost platforms that have revolutionised the industry was torturous as the industry simply took its high-fee model and its existing clients and put them online. More recently, however, the digital revolution has taken hold and has dramatically reduced the cost of trades, which has served to democratise access to stock markets in a way that was inconceivable two decades ago.

Charles Savage was on his annual family holiday in Mozambique in December 2013 when he had his Eureka moment. The early days of online trading had failed to deliver the cost savings an electronic market should have done, so he decided it was time to disrupt the stockbroking industry once and for all.

Share ownership was the preserve of an elite. The language was intimidating and exclusionary and there was a real fear of complex online trading systems. The financial services industry had long held the view that the problem was with the ordinary person who was unwilling to invest in shares. What Savage realised on that holiday, as he quizzed family members and friends as to their own investing habits, was that the problem was actually in the financial sector itself. They had made it complicated and inaccessible for ordinary people.

He built EasyEquities, with the view of simplifying the way people could invest directly in markets. EasyEquities's journey has been typical of the experience of many start-ups. It costs a lot of money to build the platforms you need to do the business you envisage, but it takes much longer than you expect for users to utilise your offering. Once they do and word gets out, growth can be exponential, and that is precisely what happened with the firm. In 2021, the business was growing at an average of 60 000 new accounts a month, thanks in part to an innovative deal with the equally fast-growing and increasingly upmarket Capitec. While the average customer balance was below R40 000, the rate of growth was boosted with deals with both Discovery and Bidvest Bank, which also encourage their clients onto the platform.

Its genius was allowing small transactions and letting customers buy fractions of shares, enabling users to get experience in investing and to understand the value of diversification at a fraction of the cost of what it would have done via a traditional broker.

At present, just 10% of transactions on the EasyEquities platform are outside South Africa, and Savage plans to increase that fivefold to 50% by 2027. He has a two-pronged strategy: the first is through using EasyEquities's own digital platforms to spread the word about the offering; and, the second is to partner with like-minded companies that are keen to encourage an investing culture in societies across the globe. The firm has an early-mover advantage as it has built systems from scratch.

EasyEquities has gone beyond share investing and has used the same principles to launch a property investment arm, as well as a rapidly growing crypto division. Whereas it took EasyEquities four years to hit 100 000 customers, EasyCrypto did it in two years, as a result of the hype in the market over offerings such as bitcoin and Ethereum. EasyFX enables the seamless movement

of foreign exchange to wherever customers see investment opportunities, while EasyVentures gives exposure to the fast-growing
world of venture capital. It is renewing its focus on EasyEquities
Australia, which it launched before global lockdowns, but growth
slowed amid the uncertainty Covid-19 created. That is now a major focal point for the group, with the creation of its first platform
specifically outside South Africa.

TymeBank is the brainchild of Singapore-based South African
human rights lawyer Coenraad Jonker, who co-founded the bank
with colleague Tjaart van der Walt while working for Deloitte. It
was spun off as a separate entity in 2012, with its main mission
to solve the developing market problem of a lack of financial inclusion. It was bought by the Commonwealth Bank of Australia
(CBA) in 2015, and Jonker moved to Asia to oversee the parent
firm's Asia initiatives. Two years later, the stake was back on
the market as Australian banks found themselves before a Royal
Commission investigating the ethics of the country's banking
practices. CBA was forced to put its global plans on hold and the
shares in the fledgling bank were put on the market.

Tyme would have gone bust had it not been for a timely investment by Patrice Motsepe's African Rainbow Capital, run by
ex-Sanlam CEO Johan van Zyl, and the ex-head of its investments business, Johan van der Merwe. It was touch and go for a
while as the bank struggled to find its niche in the South African
environment. The breakthrough came when it managed to get
Pick n Pay to carry its kiosks in-store and integrate their tills into

their payment systems, allowing for deposits and withdrawals to be made through the retail channel. It signed up three million domestic customers in two years. More recently, it tied up with the Foschini Group, allowing customers in-store to buy on credit immediately, focusing on small, short-term loans that require less capital than longer-term debt.

Tyme raised $180 million in 2021, allowing African Rainbow Capital to reduce its stake from 90% to around 57%. Not that it was easy. The appetite for investing in African fintechs evaporated overnight as the pandemic struck, and it was only the promise that the business would go beyond its home continent to new markets in Asia that piqued investor interest. Apis Capital has an 18% stake in TymeBank, with management and staff the next big block of investors. A further $70 billion came from a funding round led by Tencent founder Pony Ma, who was eager to see the business expand into Asia. Its first stop, the Philippines, is in partnership with the high-profile, local Gokongwei Group, which owns and operates the largest and best-known conglomerate in the Philippines, JG Summit Holdings.

Partnerships are critical for the model to succeed, says Jonker, and there must be mutual benefit to doing business. He will only go into environments with strong local partners and innovative regulators that are tolerant of its cloud-based business model. Being a digital-only bank, it does not need to own its servers and is able to utilise the growing number of global players providing the service rather than investing in its own hardware. While that has a dramatic cost benefit, it scares the living daylights out of traditional regulators, who prefer to have financial businesses physically present in the markets they serve.

It was the deeply unequal South African environment that proved to be a perfect testing ground for the business model of making cheap, understandable and accessible banking services available to an underserved market.

Before Tyme broke into retail, it was providing white label services for mobile operators, with the goal always being to start a bank of its own. It has operating expenses at one-tenth of legacy banks, because it operates using the infrastructure of others, but it is adamant that for the model to work, partners have to be well remunerated. It also understood that despite the big shift to digital banking channels in recent years, most transactions still happen in a branch and thus it was important to get the offering just right and not only for digital natives, to whom the idea of carrying out financial transactions on a phone or other device comes as second nature.

In order to avoid the massive capital requirements of providing credit to millions of customers, Tyme instead focuses on what it calls 'high frequency shorter dated credit' – in other words, allowing customers to borrow small amounts of money for short periods of time. It lowers the risk of default if customers know they need to pay loans back before fresh credit can be extended, and Tyme makes its money from a merchant discount at the point of sale.

Its model is typical of modern-day fintechs – it is hard to tell whether they are more fin than tech. The ability to integrate into retail partners' systems, coupled with an ever-improving data analytics capability, puts it at the forefront of a new generation of digital banks, free of the legacy systems and processes that restrict traditional banks' abilities to innovate.

It is not just the heavyweights leveraging the South African base for hard currency income.

Transaction Capital, based on Jan Smuts Avenue in Dunkeld, Johannesburg, is starting to spread its wings globally, using its domestic base and cost structure to generate foreign exchange without taking on any real additional capital risk. It is doing it tentatively and leveraging its domestic business to do so.

It is the country's biggest second-hand car dealer by virtue of the fact that it has bought control of WeBuyCars; it is the single biggest funder of the country's mini-bus industry; and it provides finance for about 15% of the country's most used public transport system. But the opportunity for foreign exchange earnings comes from a substantial debt collection business. It not only collects for third parties but will also buy up the books of bad debts for cents in the rand to collect for its own account. It operates a significant call centre infrastructure, and has begun experimenting with collecting debts in Australia, using its South African team and infrastructure to do so.

So far so good, and it is also looking to collect debts for clients in the US, allowing it to span three time zones daily.

South Africa's financial sector is remarkable in its ability to fight outside of its weight category. Retrospectively, in the early 2000s, banks may have been too ambitious in their efforts to grow in the same way as SAB had done, and certainly the hopes and aspirations of a firm like Standard Bank, in particular, were crushed by factors outside of its control. The global financial crisis and the resultant crackdown by regulators internationally meant that banks needed far higher levels of capital than ever before to cover the risk of their global businesses. It necessitated a pullback to home markets. However, smaller, nimbler players have shown what is possible with incremental growth rather than the swashbuckling style of buying others' legacy operations.

# CHAPTER 11

# Medtech at the Cutting Edge

*The unprepared mind cannot see the outstretched hand of opportunity.* — Alexander Fleming

The chief of surgery at Grey-Sloan Memorial Hospital, Dr Owen Hunt, leads his clinical team into the trauma unit: 'Now, what you've all been waiting for – the Lodox low-dose X-ray Statscanner, which provides full body, anterior and lateral views at low radiation and makes imaging safer for children and pregnant women. It is our most cutting-edge tool in diagnostic technology.'

If it sounds like a script from an American hospital drama, that is because it is. Dr Hunt is played by actor Kevin McKidd, one of the stars of the ABC television show *Grey's Anatomy*.

For all of *Grey's Anatomy's* soap-opera qualities, its producers were fastidious about ensuring the medical credibility of the show, and the appearance of Lodox on the programme was a major early boost for the device, which had its origins, as so many local innovations do, in the South African mining industry.

Lodox was commercialised as a separate company in 2002 to

focus explicitly on trauma applications. The same year, it obtained regulatory approval from the US Food and Drug Administration (FDA) and began to market its X-ray scanner system in the US and elsewhere. The television appearance of the device was a significant coup for Lodox, which has the South African government as its controlling shareholder via the Industrial Development Corporation.

The show's researchers had visited the emergency room at Los Angeles County Hospital and had seen the machine working. The company happened to have a spare machine in the US and lent it to the fictional hospital for the entire Season 9 of the long-running show. It was exposure that would have cost millions in product placement costs, but because the producers were keen to be seen at the cutting edge of medicine, they were happy simply to incorporate it into the story.

At the time, it was the only X-ray imaging system in the world that could take a full-body X-ray image in a fraction of the time and with minimal fuss. The Lodox scanner takes only thirteen seconds to produce an accurate full-body overview of any injuries and foreign bodies in a patient and can be kept in an emergency room to quickly assess internal injuries to the patient, rather than the half hour it took and the various individual X-rays that were needed to get a composite image from the traditional process.

Designed and manufactured in South Africa, the scanner uses a patented, specialised method of linear slot scanning radiography to produce large-format images with a single sweep of the X-ray source and detector. It has the advantage of speed and convenience, while emitting less potentially harmful radiation.

Critics decried it as less accurate than X-rays, but it was shown to be a breakthrough in making speedy, life-saving diagnoses, the logic being that a patient requiring further examination could always be sent to radiology for more specific checks if necessary after an initial assessment.

The device also found a more morbid but equally critical application in the mortuary and forensic science laboratories of several US pathology facilities, allowing for bodies to be scanned for potentially harmful infections, such as TB and other conditions, thus improving working conditions in stressful environments.

A 2020 insert on CBS News noted a wide acceptance of the machine as a key device for post-mortems among religions opposed to dissection as a means of investigating a patient's cause of death. 'The Lodox will demonstrate trauma, foreign objects in the body, like bullets, and it gives doctors a piece of information to help them decide if an autopsy is necessary, and the family does not have to be subjected to even higher levels of stress,' reported CBS. 'Among the faith leaders attending the ribbon-cutting ceremony were Doug Good Feather of Standing Rock Indian Reservation, Imam Muhammad Kolila of the Downtown Denver Islamic Center and Rabbi Tzvi Steinberg of the Coalition of Synagogue Rabbis of Denver.'

At last count, the company had machines in emergency rooms and pathology labs in the US, South Africa, Taiwan, Venezuela, Switzerland, Lithuania, the UAE and Saudi Arabia – more than 130 customers, half of whom are in the US and most in pathology units.

All of that was the result of a mining industry anti-theft device, which was developed by diamond miner De Beers as a security machine to ensure its miners were not ingesting diamonds to smuggle them off site to expel and sell on the black market later.

South Africa imports up to 90% of all the medical equipment used in its healthcare facilities, mostly from the US, and pays for it in dollars, which goes some way to explaining the high levels of healthcare inflation in the country.

The local industry produces most low-tech medical appliances, such as bandages and other commodities, but does have a few firms working in medium- to high-technology devices, predominantly in medical imaging.

Nothing happens in isolation. The Lodox actually has its origins in another South African discovery that saves tens of thousands of lives globally each year. A South African doctor, Allan MacLeod Cormack, discovered computerised axial tomography, the ubiquitous CAT or computed tomography (CT) scan. It was a landmark discovery that allowed clinicians to view the interior of the human body in three dimensions without using invasive means. His work saw him share the Nobel Prize for Physiology or Medicine in 1979 with Godfrey Hounsfield, who built the first commercially available CT scanner in the UK.

Cormack's discovery came after he served as a resident medical physicist in the radiology department at Cape Town's Groote Schuur Hospital, which was later to become famous for being the site of the world's first successful heart transplant under Chris Barnard. He supervised the use of radioisotopes, as well as the calibration of film badges used to monitor hospital workers' exposure to radiation. He also witnessed how radiation was used in the diagnosis and treatment of cancer. While Cormack's primary interest was particle physics, he became fascinated by imaging technology and its deficiencies, and began a series of experiments that formed the foundational theoretical basis for CT scanning.

The Industrial Development Corporation is also a big investor in CapeRay Medical (Pty) Ltd, which has played on this legacy and developed novel and leading-edge breast-imaging technology through its Aceso system. The tech claims to be able to achieve earlier diagnosis of breast cancer, giving greater potential for saving lives, and doing so in a more comfortable fashion for women, with reduced breast compression and lower doses of radiation.

Earlier, in the quiz in Chapter 2, I promised a compelling story about molybdenum. Well, here it is. South Africa is a minor producer of the mineral, but a state-owned company transforms imported product into something critical in the field of diagnostics.

Molybdenum, described by a mining industry friend as the 'Toyota Corolla of metals', is mined as a principal ore, but it is also recovered as a by-product of copper and tungsten mining, which, when extruded, produces a silvery-white metal that is a good conductor and highly resistant to corrosion. That makes it valuable for use in high-strength alloys. It also has one of the highest melting points of all pure elements. Only tantalum and tungsten have higher melting points, making it useful in mechanical lubricants.

When there were tungsten shortages in the First World War, it was used to strengthen the steel that went into making tanks and armoured vehicles. In addition, it is used in pigments and fertilisers, and it is also a micronutrient essential for life. You will find it in rice, potatoes and leafy vegetables, as well as listed in the ingredients in many health supplements available on the shelves.

China produces nearly a third of the world's 250 000 tonnes a year, followed by the US, Chile, Peru and Mexico. We may not produce much of it, but the South African Nuclear Energy Corporation (Necsa) at Pelindaba is a leading global supplier of industrial and medical isotopes and is one of the world's leading producers of Molybdenum-99 (Mo-99), a manufactured medical radioactive isotope extracted from enriched uranium.

Pelindaba, near the picturesque Hartbeespoort Dam, is in a nature reserve and, if you know where to look as you drive by, it looms ominously out of the North West Province bushveld. The facility was built by the National Party government as part of its top-secret nuclear programme. The enrichment plants were decommissioned in 1991 when the Cold War was ending and as part of the global non-proliferation treaty.

NTP Radioisotopes is a subsidiary of Necsa and is also headquartered at Pelindaba. It offers a uniquely integrated production, processing, packaging and delivery service of radiopharmaceuticals to users around the world.

The NTP website explains: 'When a low-enriched uranium (LEU) or a highly enriched uranium (HEU) target is inserted into the core of the high-flux SAFARI-1 nuclear reactor, the target is bombarded with neutrons emitted from the reactor core. This neutron bombardment splits some of the heavy U-245 atoms – a process known as fission – into several smaller atoms known as fission fragments. Around 400 different isotopes are formed in this process, including radioactive isotopes Mo-99 and I-131. After being irradiated for between 100 and 200 hours in SAFARI-1, the targets are removed from the reactor core and safely transported to NTP's adjacent hot cell complex, also located at the Pelindaba site. Here the targets are dissolved and commercially valuable isotopes like Mo-99 and I-131 are separated and extracted from the solution and purified to medical grade.'

Mo-99 is used in medical diagnostic imaging and is pivotal in the global fight against cancer, heart disease and other illnesses worldwide. The US alone carries out some 40 000 tests a day using the technologies enabled by it. The 20-megawatt SAFARI-1 research reactor has been in operation since 1965. The reactor runs 24-hour shifts about 300 days a year, and Mo-99 is processed on site all through the year. It supplies some of the biggest nuclear medicine, medical imaging and radiopharmaceutical companies in 50 countries with the life-saving medical radioisotope. It has a short shelf life and cannot be stockpiled, which means it requires reliable production and on-time delivery, something that had to be navigated carefully during the pandemic.

South African-born and -educated ophthalmologist Dr Percy Amoils became known as the man who 'made Nelson Mandela weep'.

Mandela suffered from chronic dry eyes as a result of the damage done to them in the unprotected glare of the Robben Island quarry, where he spent much of his incarceration as political prisoner 46664. Among Amoils's many inventions was the 'rotary epithelial scrubber' – an adaptation of an ordinary electric toothbrush used in corrective laser surgery. It works in a circular motion, scrubbing away cells for a smoother surface for laser procedures. Before Amoils's innovation, a scalpel was used, but it left an uneven surface. The scrubber was used in preparation for Mandela's cataract surgery.

Amoils studied mechanical engineering before becoming a medical doctor. He coupled his passions into a third direction – developing medical innovations in his backyard workshop, most often dressed in pyjamas covered with a lab coat at the end of his regular workday. A voracious reader, Amoils adapted the Alexander Fleming quote: 'Invention always comes to the prepared mind.' He patented several inventions in his specialist field, including those that made it safer to detach retinas and improve cataract surgery. The Amoils Cryo Pencil, invented in 1965, was able to save the eyesight of former British Prime Minister Margaret Thatcher, who had a detached retina. One of his inventions, the Amoils Ophthalmic Cryo Unit, is in the Science Museum in Kensington, next to the first CT scan machine, which also has its roots in South Africa, as described above.

According to the UN Comtrade Database on international trade, South African imports of pharmaceutical products was $2.41 billion during 2020, mostly from the US, China and India. It is a number that local manufacturers want to see reduced.

Covid-19 exposed many serious shortcomings in the global

medical supply chain and showed just how vulnerable the planet is to future outbreaks of infectious diseases. It has led to a renewed focus on homegrown vaccine production due to the fact that Africa was left at the back of the vaccine queue during the pandemic. Just a handful of African countries manufacture vaccines and a few carry out the end-stage production process, known as 'fill and finish', where the product is processed, put into vials and shipped. Only Egypt is producing a Covid-19 vaccine from scratch.

South Africa and Algeria are the only African countries so far to announce plans to produce the pharmaceutical ingredients to make Covid-19 vaccines from scratch. The World Health Organization (WHO) hired South African start-up Afrigen Biologics and Vaccines to reverse-engineer an mRNA vaccine against Covid as close as possible to the version produced by Moderna. The African Union aims to grow vaccine production on the continent from 1% of its vaccine requirements to 60% in the next two decades.

South African scientists were regularly at the forefront of research in Covid-19 variants, showing the high levels of expertise and capability in the domestic industry – even though that expertise had negative consequences in terms of the country being labelled as the source of new outbreaks rather than as a centre of excellence.

As Reuters reported: 'On Friday Nov. 19, Raquel Viana, Head of Science at one of South Africa's biggest private testing labs, sequenced the genes on eight coronavirus samples – and got the shock of her life. The samples, tested in the Lancet laboratory, all bore a large number of mutations, especially on the spike protein that the virus uses to enter human cells. "I was quite shocked at what I was seeing. I questioned whether something had gone wrong in the process," she told Reuters, a thought that quickly gave way to "a sinking feeling that the samples were going to have huge ramifications".'

Viana quickly phoned one of her colleagues at the National Institute for Communicable Diseases in Johannesburg, gene sequencer Daniel Amoako. 'I didn't quite know how to break it to them,' she recalls. She told Amoako, 'To me, it looks like a new lineage.'

The discovery of the Omicron variant in southern Africa caused global alarm, with countries limiting travel from the region and imposing other restrictions for fear it could spread quickly, even in vaccinated populations.

A single decision by Aspen Pharmacare CEO Stephen Saad two decades ago to ignore the advice of his bankers may very well prove to have been the catalyst for the creation of a substantial new export sector for South Africa.

Aspen Pharmacare is South Africa's most global company, with businesses in more than 50 countries. It bought SA Druggists in a R2.4-billion hostile takeover in 1999. It was a shape-shifting deal that not only provided the base for global expansion but again served to change its destiny more than twenty years later.

Saad recalls how angry his bankers, Investec, were when he reneged on an agreement with them to sell the group's manufacturing facilities.

'When I walked into the facility, I realised this was the heart and lungs of the operation,' Saad said in a 2018 interview. 'You should have heard the bankers! Oh, the chaos. No one wanted to buy shares anyway and that was a problem for them, and then although we had an agreed position on the factories, I refused to sell.'

That decision, at age 34 and with a capital-intensive global expansion programme in his sights, was pivotal. The bankers regarded the factories as a distraction from the bigger goal, but the decision to defy his funders not only put Saad in a position to play a significant role in the development of vaccines in the Covid-19 pandemic but also to gear up to be a substantial exporter of medicines from South Africa in the future.

One of the major vulnerabilities of global medicines manufacture was exposed by the pandemic. The high concentration of factories making active ingredients in countries such as India, for example, meant that when one country saw Covid-related disruption, the supply network failed – ports were affected or governments simply put protectionist measures in place to guard their own interests. The problem had been building for some time. According to the EU, 40% of its finished medicines were made in China and India, while 80% of active ingredients, critical in drugs manufacture, came from there too. There were already concerns about shortages before the pandemic, but those were amplified at the height of the crisis, leading to a substantial rethink of how the industry will operate with greater degrees of localisation into the future.

In October 2021, Aspen opened the southern hemisphere's largest general anaesthetics manufacturing line at Gqeberha in the Eastern Cape, adding production at the plant where it already filled and packaged the Johnson & Johnson Covid-19 vaccine. It was a big move for Aspen, which had previously manufactured those products in Europe. It made other products at the plant for export, including drugs for late-stage cancer, Parkinson's disease and some autoimmune illnesses.

Saad ascribed the ability to ramp up production of other medicines to the fact that the J&J relationship had enabled it to scale its plant in the Eastern Cape more effectively. Previously, its Durban factory had been a mass producer of low-value generic medicines, but it had also switched that facility to higher-margin anaesthetics.

'We never want Africa to be at the back of the vaccine queue again,' Saad said. The factories showed their value early on. Recent developments have simply amplified why the choice had long-term benefits. By 2003, Aspen's Unit 1 facility at Gqeberha had US FDA approval to make certain generic anti-retroviral drugs at the height of the AIDS pandemic, and, by 2006, it was the biggest supplier of ARVs in Africa. It has also made TB drugs there and through the pandemic made doses of dexamethasone, a steroid found to be useful in treating some Covid patients.

The decision to keep the SA Druggists's factories, while maddening for the bankers at the time, turns out to have been the right one, even though few believed Saad would pull it off: 'It was the mouse swallowing the elephant, and, even if you chopped it into pieces, everyone thought the mouse would simply end up regurgitating it,' he remembered. That is ancient history now.

By far the most successful skincare product to emerge from South Africa since the turn of the century is one called Bio-Oil. Chartered accountant brothers David and Justin Letschert bought Union Swiss in 2000. They were running their own mergers and acquisitions consultancy when the 50-year-old company, with a portfolio of about 120 mostly loss-making businesses, came up for sale. The owner wanted to sell the whole lot as a going concern and was unwilling to allow anyone to cherry-pick its most attractive assets. That turned out to be an opportunity for the brothers, who eventually bought the whole firm out of sheer frustration and set about restructuring it to focus on the core Bio-Oil product. At the time, it shifted about R5 million in products annually. That amount has rocketed to over R1 billion, most of it due to a single stand-out oil used to treat scarring, which is now sold in more than 50 countries.

'Start with one country at a time, make sure you have lots of cash and a good distribution partnership,' CEO Justin Letschert told students at Stellenbosch University Business School. The business is run from Cape Town, and getting the product known in each of its new markets has had to happen one country at a time.

Letschert told the students that product owners often get attached to what they are selling and lose perspective on its value in the global market. Unless what they produce is markedly superior and is in a new category, then the odds of international success are limited. There are no quick wins and profits can take a long time to manifest. It can take five years to break even as new markets require plenty of spending. When the firm launched Bio-Oil in the US, nearly 1 800 other skincare companies launched products in the same year. For many South African companies under the impression that they face a competitive environment in their home market, they are in for a surprise when they hit the global stage. Many developed markets also enforce and police their regulations far more rigorously than the founders of local start-ups are used to.

The brothers created a system to identify new markets using criteria such as GDP per capita as a first means to identify whether a country has a population with high enough incomes to afford their offering. It is important to know where not to bother going. While the US remains the world's most attractive market in terms of disposable income, it is a ferociously competitive one, and mistakes and poor decisions are punished quickly and severely.

A key factor many exporters fail to recognise is around duties, and many markets protect their domestic manufacturers with crippling import tariffs. A country such as Brazil, for example, has a big market for skincare products, but 40% of the local price tag is made up of duties.

Finding good distributors is key in every country. Because you are competing with potentially 194 other countries in the world for attention in different markets, it is up to you to find distributors, not the other way around, and you cannot simply leave the business to your partners to run. You require a presence in a market and must be prepared to make several trips a year to inspect progress or a lack thereof and identify ways of working better. It is a slog, especially in the beginning when budgets are tight and travel is mostly in economy class. The Covid-era switch to Zoom has its advantages but will not replace experiencing the markets.

As the late former Tiger Brands CEO Peter Matlare once told me when he was considering expanding operations into Nigeria, none of his board had been to the markets of West Africa, smelled the dust in the air or properly understood what it was to have made a positive impact there.

The Letschert brothers had no experience in manufacturing and all they intended at the start was to do what accountants do, and that is to create a sustainable financial structure, fix the business and sell it at a profit. They understood the need to focus on three key areas: supplier relationships, logistics and distribution, while outsourcing the manufacturing of the actual product. The decision to focus on a single product was pivotal to the success of the business, which was free of cumbersome distractions, and they decided early on that they would position the business for global growth.

It was also a time when there was a far greater focus than ever before on the scientific process of formulating skincare products, and of repositioning Bio-Oil from being a beauty product to a cosmeceutical one.

They occupied a unique market position.

At the time, no other brands were specifically targeting the scar market because commercial products to treat scars did not exist then. The skincare industry seemed to think that scars belonged in the medical field, and the pharmaceutical industry did not think scars were a big enough medical problem or market to focus on. In a shrewd move, the Letscherts repositioned Bio-Oil from being a tissue oil that was used for special occasions to a scar and stretchmark product that could be used for a variety of conditions, and it proved to be popular.

They launched Bio-Oil in the UK in 2002. This also proved to be their first big test as the rand collapsed, meaning they had to almost double their investment. To make matters worse, the UK's biggest pharmacy group was refusing to carry the product unless they changed the packaging and removed the word 'scars' from it. So they launched without Boots and were the top-selling body-care product in the UK within three years.

Plastic surgeon Dr Des Fernandes started his research into how to protect his patients from melanoma in the 1970s, just as aware-ness about the destructive power of UV rays to human skin was being properly understood.

'When I was a medical student, the average doctor saw maybe four melanomas in their time practising. Today one sees at least four melanomas a year. I was driven by the concept that "preven-tion is better than cure", and that is why I spent all that time going through medical journals and the *Index Medicus* [a biblio-graphic index of medical articles going back to 1879],' he says.

Fernandes discovered a 1959 paper written in German that ref-erenced the use of vitamin A to reduce the size of simple basal cell cancers. Because so much research in the aftermath of the Second World War was in English, it had received little attention.

He began treating scars with Airol, which is a vitamin A acid, and discovered over time that it helped unsightly acne scarring to heal and that it was also useful in reducing the signs of ageing. His earliest kitchen-made creams had a shelf life of about a month. Fernandes brought in an analytical chemist to stabilise the formulations, which he then offered free of charge in his plastic surgery practice. His waiting list grew from four to eight months as word spread and patients were visiting him not for surgical consultations but to acquire the cream he was producing.

He put his sister in charge of the Environ business and set about doing the science and developing new products globally via agents in their markets. It now sells considerably more of its product globally than locally. Environ is a private business and likes to keep its successes close to its chest. It sells 140 products via agency arrangements in 70 countries.

Environ got a head start on rivals, says CEO Val Carstens, as they were the first in the world to utilise a 'full brigade' of antioxidants. Regulatory issues vary from country to country, and the firm has appointed consultants in each territory to ensure that local requirements are met, while a strong discipline in trademarking is required to ensure that all product innovations can be protected as much as possible. The biggest challenge the firm faces in its home market is that many of its potential customers believe imports are better quality at higher price points than the local product.

# CHAPTER 12

# Bling, Rings and Shiny Things

*Luxury goods are the only area in which it is possible*
*to make luxury margins.* — Bernard Arnault

The world's second biggest luxury goods group, Richemont, is Swiss. It is the finest example of how to build one of the world's 200 most valuable companies from a South African base.

It all started with an investment in a Pretoria dry-cleaner, moved on to the acquisition of a bankrupt cigarette maker and then the first listing of an Afrikaner-controlled drinks producer on the JSE in 1945.

Although he trained in chemistry, Anton Rupert's real genius was in marketing. He chose his industries carefully, convinced that booze and tobacco would never go out of fashion and would do well in good times as well as be resilient in recessionary times. He made his first cigarettes on a single machine in his garage in Stellenbosch, having sold the dry-cleaners to fund the buyout of a bankrupt tobacco producer called Voorbrand in 1939.

From that emerged the Rembrandt Group, which won the right to market Rothmans of Pall Mall in South Africa and, in less than a decade, buy that company with money borrowed from Volkskas and Sanlam. From his Stellenbosch base, Rupert built that company into Britain's biggest exporter of cigarettes. In 1945, he listed drinks maker Distillers Corporation on the JSE, making it the first Afrikaner-controlled company on the market. The firm, later rebranded Distell, was sold to Heineken in 2021.

But it was tobacco that created the global empire. Rupert's biographer, Ebbe Dommisse, recalled how on an international trip in the early days of building the conglomerate, Rupert phoned his office in Stellenbosch to instruct his team to work on the branding of a new cigarette he wanted to name after the one-legged former governor of New York (then New Amsterdam), Peter Stuyvesant. He arrived home to find the team had discarded his idea and created 'General Custer' – it was a short conversation.

Peter Stuyvesant, 'your international passport to smoking pleasure', became one of the world's most recognised tobacco brands, thanks to its image of healthy, wealthy, young people living the high life, sailing, skiing and enjoying the best of everything the world had to offer. Lexington's 'after action satisfaction' played on similar themes.

In 1988, the Rembrandt Group founded the Swiss luxury goods company, Richemont. It bought Rembrandt's shares in Rothmans and incorporated that with luxury brands, such as jewellers Cartier, designer clothing makers Alfred Dunhill and Sulka, the now defunct men's haberdashery that once counted the Duke of Windsor, Winston Churchill, Henry Ford and Clark Gable among its customers, leather bags specialists Seeger, watch makers Piaget, Baume & Mercier and Vacheron Constantin, as well as pen makers, I beg your pardon, writing instrument makers, Montblanc.

Rembrandt and Richemont later consolidated their respective tobacco interests into Rothmans International, and four years later with British American Tobacco, making it the world's second biggest cigarette producer.

Today, Compagnie Financière Richemont, more commonly known as Richemont, is the world's second largest luxury group in terms of turnover, just behind LVMH.

Rupert's entry into luxury also came via a connection to a man who made fancy cigarette lighters. Robert Hocq was the owner of a leading lighter manufacturing company called Silver Match.

Cartier began life in 1847 as an upmarket jeweller and gained a global following – expanding its influence around the world with three Cartier brothers each assuming control of their own operations in Paris, London and New York. By the mid-twentieth century, there was no unifying brand ethos. According to *Time* magazine in 1976, 'Some world-travelling Cartier customers came to regard the New York store as shamefully déclassé,' and quoted a customer who said Cartier New York was 'trying to appeal to the American secretary'. It was not a compliment. The heirs further diluted the value of the family name and sold to disparate investors, which did nothing to resuscitate the firm's fortunes.

Hocq made the world's first gas cigarette lighter in 1953 and his Silver Match company became a world leader. He wanted to make a gold version of his lighter and was turned down by luxury goods makers until becoming the official licensee for the first

Cartier lighter, described as having a 'sleek and fluted' design. It injected life into a dying brand and Hocq put together a consortium of investors that included Anton Rupert and they bought Cartier Paris in 1972, followed by the London business two years later and Cartier New York in 1979 – reuniting them under one umbrella, Cartier Monde. The lighter became the first in a range of more affordable luxury products that made the dream of luxury more attainable, and was followed by a range of status symbols from pens to watches and sunglasses.

Hocq was hit by a car and died outside his offices in Paris. Rupert, who by now had built a portfolio of brands including Piaget, Chloé, Hackett and Alfred Dunhill, bought out the rest of the shareholders to create the Vendôme Luxury Group – the basis of Richemont.

By the time Anton Rupert died in 2006, the group was a globally dominant player run by his son Johann. The journey has been far from trouble-free; the group survived the slump in luxury spending in the recession that followed the global financial crisis, a collapse in China in 2012 when a clampdown on bribery using Swiss watches was shut down, and a crisis in the Swiss franc in 2015. Despite the massive disruptions brought about by restrictions on global travel during the Covid-19 pandemic, duty-free sales went more online, paving a way for opportunity for the firm via its online platform Net-a-Porter.

According to New World Wealth, the demand for luxury goods generates about $2 billion a year in South Africa and much of that is a result of shoppers from other parts of the African continent visiting the stores of global brands in Cape Town and

Johannesburg. Foreign brands, like those created by Richemont and rival LVMH, dominate spend, thanks to the enormous international appeal of the offerings, but South Africa has a growing array of luxury offerings of its own gaining greater global appeal.

In as much as tourism is a local product and unique to every market, it is an export, as it is a significant generator of foreign exchange. In 2018, tourism contributed 9% or 1.5 million jobs and earned the economy R425.8 billion, representing 8.6% of all economic activity in South Africa, according to the World Travel & Tourism Council's 2021 annual review of the economic impact and social importance of the sector. Some 42% of that income came from international travellers.

By 2021, the contribution to global GDP by tourism had halved. From being a creator of one in four new jobs in the world in 2019, there were 62 million job losses as a result of a collapse in travel volumes due to the pandemic. In South Africa, the effect was equally devastating. The 2021 report noted the contribution of travel and tourism to GDP had fallen to 3.7%, with a 66% drop in international spending and 43% in domestic travel expenditure. The sector lost 473 000 jobs as a result of the dramatic slowdown.

Tourism, however, is one industry that can recover quickly from a crisis because of the massive, vested interests of the global industry, which has high fixed costs and needs to get paying customers utilising its facilities. South Africa's luxury lodges and unique game experiences, while they happen in situ, are exports of a different kind in that they are big foreign exchange earners.

The New World Wealth report points to the value of game lodges as a significant earner of foreign exchange in the South African luxury sector, which is dominated by high-end safari lodges. South Africa is home to some of the best safari lodges in Africa, and most of those are located in Sabi Sands, adjacent to the Greater Kruger National Park. The dream of the luxury experience offered by the lodges has drawn global investment by the likes of Richard Branson, whose Virgin Group investment in Ulusaba sees it as one of the world's most desirable big-game destinations, alongside the likes of Mala Mala, Londolozi, Sabi Sabi and a host of others. It is an industry leading South Africa's much-needed tourism recovery because of its ability to draw wealthy travellers from around the globe. While out of reach to the vast majority of South Africans, the sector is a critical cog in the South African industry of luxury experiences.

South Africa's highest profile luxury export can be found in London's most sought-after shopping district, Mayfair.

Turn left onto Piccadilly out of the Green Park tube station, and about halfway up towards Piccadilly Circus turn left into Old Bond Street. On the corner is the De Beers flagship diamond store. You could be in Dickens's London. The street will just allow two cars to pass, the stone facades rise three to four storeys on either side and any direct natural sunlight it receives is fleeting. The Artful Dodger would have loved it here. Two shops away from De Beers is Roger Dubois, then Cartier, Valentino and further down is Prada, Rolex, Tiffany and Ferragamo. At number 28 on the site of the old Clarendon Hotel is the quaint Royal Arcade, built in 1879, the year of Imperial Britain's most humiliating defeat at Isandlwana and a day later its most vaunted victory at Rorke's Drift. The arcade is home to boot makers and shirt makers, even an umbrella maker. There is also a hairdresser where a cut and blow will cost … well, if you have to ask … you are probably in the wrong place.

De Beers opened its brand-new, 250-square-metre flagship store at the end of 2021, adjacent to its first site on the same street in 2002. Its focus on natural diamonds (none of the lab-manufactured stuff, please) plays on the themes it created during the years when it dominated more than 80% of the world's sales. In a world of high fashion, it will have you believe a diamond is not a diamond unless it comes from De Beers and carries the Forevermark. The engraving is invisible to the naked eye, but includes the De Beers Forevermark icon and the diamond's own unique number. The inscription is 1/20th of a micron deep – 1/5000th the depth of a human hair.

And, of course, smaller diamonds cannot accommodate the inscription, naturally pressuring the buyer to acquire a stone big enough to carry the mark – it is very clever indeed. A special proprietary viewer is required to see the inscription, which can be registered via the website 'providing reassurance that your diamond is uniquely yours'. The relaunch was timed to coincide with a new global advertising campaign reinforcing its messaging that only a diamond symbolises an enduring commitment between a loving couple. Proof, if it was needed, that if diamonds are indeed a girl's best friend, then the best friend to the diamond is an extraordinary marketing machine.

You might not think of architecture as a prime export opportunity. But Stefan Antoni has proven that it can be. His unique design ethic is visible along Cape Town's Atlantic seaboard and the distinctive projects he has driven in Mauritius and other havens of the wealthy.

In 2012, he became painfully aware of the limitations in the local market. Most customers in for a R50-million to R100-million home are likely only to invest once, so, accepting his business model would be unlikely to conjure up the annuity income and the repeat business everyone desires, so he needed to create new markets.

Today, the Cape Town-based studio SAOTA employs 300 staff in that city, delivering architectural projects in multiple markets on six continents. Not only that, but it also owns an in-house interior design studio that employs nearly as many people. It consults directly to SAOTA clients around the world and also does work for other architectural firms that do not have the expertise themselves. Like the architectural firm from which it originates, ARRCC trades off the idea of delivering a design ethic that defines twenty-first-century laid-back luxury and works across residences, offices and hospitality. In 2020, it won Design Firm of the Year in the Luxury Travel Guide Global Awards.

Among the designs are the Longcheer Yacht Club in China delivered in 2020, homes on Lake Huron in Canada in the same year, several homes in California, including 8408 Hillside in Los Angeles in 2019, and Uluwatu in Indonesia in the same year, Le Pine in France in 2018, and one in Double Bay, Australia.

But there have been bigger projects too. In 2015, SAOTA designed Epique Island, a 75-villa residential estate located on the 2.6-hectare peninsula jutting into the Aegean Sea at Bodrum in Turkey. The firm designed an entire residential estate, reflecting the barefoot luxury style for which the architect became famous in South Africa, and delivered ten variations of three types of villas. It was the third Turkish project in two years. It has completed mixed-use developments in places such as Dubai and even Azerbaijan. SAOTA has designed multi-residential developments, mainly apartment blocks, hotels and resorts, and several corporate headquarters in African cities, including in Nigeria, Côte D'Ivoire and Senegal. Its reach has included the UK, Switzerland, Spain, the US, Mauritius, Thailand and India.

All generate global revenues in hard currency with a South African cost base.

Staff working in Cape Town on projects in the US, for example, will arrive at work during American office hours and that will be staggered, according to which time zone the particular project is in. Staff on an LA project would arrive later in the Cape Town day, for example, than a team working for a client in Florida. The same goes for projects in other parts of the world; this is aimed at ensuring that the teams and their clients' diaries are properly aligned.

Not to be outdone in the luxury stakes by her dad, Hanneli Rupert launched her own range of curated, luxury handcrafted products sourced only from the African continent. This includes her own handbag range, Okapi, which she started in 2008. She began her drive for ethically sourced, curated products in 2010, carrying everything from organic perfumed soaps by Tammy Frazer, to accessories from Ethiopian brand LemLem and sneakers from Cameroon-based SAWA.

South Africa is also home to scores of accomplished small jewellery makers beneficiating raw materials found in South Africa and delivering products with a global aesthetic.

Kirsten Goss, for example, completed a Fine Arts in jewellery design degree at Stellenbosch University. The daughter of Pat Goss, a founding member of the company that would become FirstRand, was determined to head to London and make her own mark.

She worked for 'a very famous fashion jewellery company', tried her hand at banking for a while in an effort to fund an expensive London lifestyle, but eventually went back to her passion and started making jewellery under her own name in London in 2002. She even had her own flagship store bearing the moniker: Kirsten Goss London.

'My dad gave me priceless advice – to get an address and not work from home as it would provide for greater commitment to the cause. This was excellent advice, as I immediately had rental debt and we all know what that does – gets you out of bed, dressed and determined to clear it. The rest is history.'

She began making jewellery in London, but wanted to live in

South Africa where she now has three stores – one each in Cape Town, Durban and a new outlet in Johannesburg in the plush Hyde Park shopping centre. Thanks to the marvels of the internet and the brand equity developed during her London years, about 20% of sales are outside of South Africa. The surge in e-commerce has opened up the world to South African producers, and there is a strong emphasis in her business to drive more global sales.

'I believe in producing something unique and authentic. I don't believe in being a slave to fads and fashion,' says Goss. 'We want our clients to buy into something a lot more classic and considered that will transcend time and be loved by any generation to come. Like little pieces of art that are handmade by in-house goldsmiths.'

Jewellery making is a great beneficiator of local commodities. The independent players source all the materials, do the design and manufacturing in-house and market and retail through their own stores and online channels, making it unique in South Africa. The industry is awash with quality designers, all of whom need a return to higher levels of tourism to capitalise on a global market hungry for unique design.

To step into Jenna Clifford's Morningside design studio is to step into a treasure trove of global celebrity visitors to South Africa – there was hardly a celebrity who would arrive in Mandela's South Africa who would escape the photo op. She started the business in 1992, delivering strong, bold, eye-catching and distinctive designs. She employs 60 people, including artisans and craftspeople. While many younger designers cannot afford the cost of carrying stock of precious metals and high-end stones in their early days – that is the stuff that Clifford trades on.

Katherine-Mary Pichulik started her design business after inspiring travels around India in 2012 and returned home to create something fundamentally different from what other start-up studios were doing. She shunned the precious metals and stones and instead went shopping at a local specialist rope store, combining the woven materials with items such as Ghanaian agate stones, fossilised forms from Niger, West African brass parts and Ethiopian recycled glass.

There is a new generation of luxury designers and producers drawing on African heritage in a fundamentally different way.

Laduma Ngxokolo is betting that tourists will return in their droves to South Africa's most popular shopping centre, the V&A Waterfront, and took advantage of the fact that owners Growthpoint needed tenants as gaps appeared even in prime real estate during the pandemic. The pricey prime position is an opportunity to showcase his wares, which are inspired by generations of Xhosa bead-working. He founded MaXhosa in 2012, with a knitwear range inspired by Xhosa aesthetics. His clothing got a welcome boost with a showcase on American comedian Eddie Murphy's *Coming to America 2* and generated a positive response to his work, which has been showcased in the fashion capitals and biggest annual fashion weeks in the world. His design work has been displayed and archived in the Smithsonian Museum and the Museum of Modern Art in New York, as well as in museums in Hamburg, Switzerland and Berlin, as examples of the evolution in African design. If imitation is the sincerest form of flattery, then MaXhosa is on the right track. In 2018, Zara was forced to withdraw one of its designs after it emerged it had copied one of Ngxokolo's signature patterns.

In September 2019, Amanda Laird Cherry was honoured at the World Fashion Awards in London, taking home the Fashion Designer of the Year award. The Durban-born designer now lives in Charlotte, North Carolina.

David Tlale, too, has received international recognition and was the first South African fashion designer to showcase solo at the Mercedes-Benz Fashion Week in New York in September 2012. He started out studying accounting and was destined to become an auditor. During the pandemic, his focus turned to home and he set up four stores in the lockdowns in different parts of the country, aiming at local consumers but looking forward to the return of the foreign visitor.

While ostrich feathers were all the rage at the turn of the previous century, thanks to hat fashions of the day, today they are more useful in feather dusters than high fashion. While the low-cholesterol meat they produce has a solid market, volumes are not big enough for exports of any great significance. Ostrich leather is pricey and some manufacturers use it in belts, wallets, shoes and bags. Firms such as Cape Cobra Leathercraft make products in South Africa using locally sourced raw materials for global brands, including Calvin Klein and others.

But the most innovative use of things to do with ostriches comes from broken eggshells. When Cape Town design company Avoova installed eggshell-inlaid tables on Russian billionaire Roman Abramovich's yacht, the firm found itself leapfrogged into the international luxury goods arena.

It is ironic that many of the raw materials used in luxury goods can be found in South Africa, from platinum to gold and diamonds, but Avoova decided to use something that ordinarily would be discarded to make its product. The firm focuses on small luxury items that it sells online and through retail stores. It started in 2005, opened its first shop in Cape Town for the FIFA World Cup in 2010 and, like all luxury groups, ensures it has price points that allow accessibility and those that allow for vanity to prevail – like that which provides for an inlaid table for a yacht, for example.

Robertson and Caine have been building catamarans in Cape Town since 1991 and the firm has launched more than 2 000 vessels for the global market. John Robertson started his first boat-building business in 1980, in a garage on Zeekoevlei in the unpretentious southern suburbs of Cape Town. He later teamed up with Jerry Caine to start a new enterprise, which has grown to be one of the top three catamaran builders in the world and the main supplier of catamarans in the North American and Caribbean markets.

They had no cash in the early days so they adopted a high-end, bakkie-builder approach of creating custom-built yachts and drawing cash from the client at different stages of completion. The big break came three years after they started, and a yacht charter company was looking for a reliable boatbuilder to manufacture ten catamarans. The CEO of The Moorings had seen one of their early craft at a boat show and had been impressed by their craftsmanship and put in an order. They delivered and became the company's exclusive supplier.

Because of the extreme climatic conditions of its coastline, South Africa was associated with good sturdy boats. The country's more challenging waters are better suited to single-hull boats than the luxury twin-hulled boats that have ready markets in places like the East Coast of the US, the Caribbean, the Seychelles, the Mediterranean, Asia and the South Pacific.

Robertson and Caine has offices in Tampa, Florida, to get closer to a wealthy client base, and uses it as a purchasing department for the high-end components required for its high-spec craft. Its 1 800 staff produce a new boat every second day from a range of six models, all from a 60 000-square metre facility in Cape Town. The company has a local design team as well as one in Florida constantly seeking feedback from customers on what improvements can be made to the development of future models. Customer feedback led to the development of its most recent model, a twin-hulled powerboat, which was showcased for sale at the Miami International Boat Show.

In the old days, the boats would be delivered by sailing them from the factory to wherever they were needed, but the increase in sales means that this is no longer viable, although owners are perfectly entitled to pick them up personally and sail them wherever they like. Today, the completed boats are driven to the Royal Cape Yacht Club, ready to sail and launch to a dedicated berth. From there they go for loading around the corner at the Cape Town harbour, where as many as sixteen at a time are loaded onto a freighter and delivered to customers around the world.

When Jeff Bezos's new 417-foot, three-masted, $485-million yacht readied to leave the boatbuilding yard in Rotterdam where it had been constructed, it provoked fury from locals, as it would require the city's newly reconstructed and renovated Koningshaven Bridge to be dismantled again to let the giant boat out.

It did not matter that Bezos was going to pay for the operation; it was more a protest against the ostentatious nature of his purchase.

What the world missed was that the company that built the boat has its roots in South Africa. Today, Oceanco yacht builder is a Netherlands- and Monaco-registered business. Founded in Durban in 1987, it is currently strictly a mega-yacht builder, developing nothing smaller than boats 80-foot long. Founder and CEO Richard Hein built the company's first hulls in Durban and then moved them to the great Dutch shipbuilding yards for completion. It later consolidated the business in Rotterdam before being taken over by Greek steel magnate Theodore Angelopoulos in 2002 and has changed owners at least once since then. Hein still runs the company but out of the small Mediterranean principality of Monaco.

Probably the oldest known African craft is making pots. The earliest examples were purely utilitarian and the oldest known piece of African pottery dates back to 9400 BC in Mali. Zimbabwean-born artist Fée Halsted has brought a modern twist to African ceramic artworks. The Ardmore studio in the Caversham Valley in the KwaZulu-Natal Midlands has up to 60 local artists working at any one time, producing a wide range of freehand, sculpted ceramics that have truly gone global. It uses common whimsical themes of gloriously bright African animals adorning a range of vessels. Halsted started the studio in 1985 with her first student, Bonnie Ntshalintshali. The area was bitingly poor and she wanted to create jobs. The early offerings were fairly basic, but, as time has passed, Ardmore has developed a strong brand identity. Even though each piece is painstakingly handmade, it displays its origins.

Works from Ardmore have been sold via the world's great auction houses at Christie's, Sotheby's and Bonhams in London. Since 2010, the studio has begun designing and creating its own distinctive fabric ranges, which are made into soft furnishings and, more recently, it has embarked on a collaboration with the Gqeberha-based leather and canvas luggage maker Melvill and Moon to incorporate those materials into some of its ranges.

President Cyril Ramaphosa awarded Halsted with the Order of Ikhamanga in Silver for her contribution to the arts. Ardmore ceramics have been given as state gifts to heads of states, including the Queen of England, and there is at least one piece in the White House. The works have been exhibited in galleries around the world, including the Museum of Arts and Design in New York and the Museum of Cultures in Basel. The largest American collection can be seen at the Wiener Museum of Decorative Arts in Florida.

Sculptor Carrol Boyes obtained a degree in Fine Arts at the University of Pretoria and embarked on a teaching career in Cape Town. At the age of 35, she left teaching to focus on making jewellery, which she sold at the vibrant Greenmarket Square in the centre of Cape Town. She gradually developed a unique design style and, by 1992, had opened her first factory in Limpopo, followed by another in Paarden Eiland, making a unique brand of pewter and stainless steel cutlery and ornate human figures, as well as pottery featuring the distinctive imagery made famous by her homeware. She later went on to create her own fabric range.

At the time of her death at the age of 65 in 2019, Boyes was running 45 outlets across South Africa and her products were being sold in 51 countries. Much of her early global growth came about organically, mostly from expatriates looking for business ideas in their new homes and who approached her for the rights to become international distributors. It was a success story beyond her own wildest dreams. 'I want this business to continue long after I am gone,' she said in one of her final corporate videos placed on the company website. 'It was never my intention for it to grow to the size it is today. I would like the South African public to be proud of the brand we have created that can be sold across the world.'

These are but a few examples of remarkable entrepreneurs who have successfully not only scaled their businesses in South Africa but have transformed them into companies with global reach. There is so much more that can be done, but one sees little evidence of active state engagement to promote the real genius of South African creators globally.

# CHAPTER 13

# Dreamers, Doers and Superachievers

*All good ideas start out as bad ideas,*
*that's why it takes so long.* — Steven Spielberg

America has Hollywood, India Bollywood and Nigeria Nolly-wood. South Africa has a significant, independent production industry that serves global brands and, when pandemics allow, has a thriving world-beating industry making local and interna-tional adverts. Local productions such as *My Octopus Teacher* and *Tsotsi* have hit Oscar pay dirt, but the movie industry is small. The parts that do exist, however, are flourishing and are world-beating exporters of content created in South Africa for global audiences.

The last place on earth you might expect to find an anima-tion powerhouse producing blockbuster Netflix movies is on an old farm on the edge of suburban Tokai in one of the last bits of what was once rural Constantia. Global lockdowns and a switch by moviegoers to streaming services played neatly into the strengths of Triggerfish. What started life as a tiny animation studio on Dreyersdal farm in 1996, is now a multinational venture that has collaborated with the likes of Disney and Netflix and has an expanding trophy cabinet, showing the growing respect it has among its international peers. It has been described as Africa's answer to Pixar.

The first big break for Triggerfish came when it was commissioned to produce animation for the South African version of the American children's TV show *Sesame Street*, *Takalani Sesame*, in 1998, in what became a first-of-its-kind collaboration in the local film industry. So happy were the American owners of *Sesame Street* that Triggerfish started doing work for the US version of the show too. The projects have grown in scale, budget and international reach since then.

The opportunity to grow came in the early 2000s with the emergence of digital CGI technology, which replaced the labour-intensive and time-consuming stop-frame drawing process. Suddenly, the world started to open up. Triggerfish began producing its own work rather than only doing third-party contract work, and their first full-length movie, which was about a falcon that learns critical life lessons travelling to a fabled city called Zambezia, earned $34 million at the box office. With money from a private investor, owner Stuart Forrest created a pilot of the film and found a Los Angeles agent to take it to market. With presales of the film under its belt, it raised further funding in the US and cash from the National Film and Video Foundation of South Africa and the Industrial Development Corporation. The company was on its way. As soon as that money was in place and production was underway, Forrest started punting his next project, and the state-owned Industrial Development Corporation was all too willing to back it. That led to the story of an adventurous Zebra that does not quite have the same number of stripes as his friends and has to go on a big journey to gain the respect of the herd.

The movies were distributed to 150 countries and were translated into nearly 30 languages.

In 2015, with support from Disney, Triggerfish expanded its reach in the search for new animation talent on the African continent and launched Triggerfish Story Lab, with an eye on telling more African stories using animation for global distribution. Nothing happens in isolation, but the success of Marvel's *Black Panther* triggered demand for content from the African continent, and Triggerfish had a supply ready to go, and found demand strong.

Its success has come from international collaborations with the world's biggest animation producers and ensuring that its work stands up against the best. It was nominated for an Oscar for its 2016 adaptation of Roald Dahl's *Revolting Rhymes*, and has won multiple awards, including for a series of BBC adaptations of the popular Julia Donaldson stories, *The Gruffalo* and *Stick Man*.

Triggerfish opened a studio in Galway in Ireland in 2019, just ahead of the pandemic. Fortunately, animation lends itself to remote work and the team had been outsourcing to that country for years, so it carried on with the support of the Irish government on the basis that it expected to create 60 jobs over three years.

Triggerfish is also playing a critical developmental role in the

African animation industry, using international funding sources to create the Pan-African Triggerfish Story Lab, supported by the Walt Disney Company; the all-women Mama K's Team 4 Writers Lab with Netflix; and the free Triggerfish Academy digital learning platform, supported by the German Federal Ministry of Economic Cooperation and Development and the Goethe-Institut.

In 2021, the fightback story of a seal named Quinn became one of the most-watched movies on Netflix and was in the top ten downloaded in 27 countries. Triggerfish is about 5 kilometres, as the crow flies, from the False Bay coastline, home to one of the world's biggest great white shark populations, themselves the subject of countless documentaries over the years. Without giving away the plot, Quinn is fed up with being terrorised by great white sharks and gathers a 'seal team' to push back against tyranny.

Travel about 45 kilometres from Dreyersdal along the picturesque False Bay coastline, past a pungent sewage works, and, as you cross the bridge over the N2 highway towards Stellenbosch, you will notice the masts and rigging of a nineteenth-century sailing ship. There were two, but one was destroyed in a fire. This is the home of Cape Town Film Studios, which describes itself as 'the most successful film studio in the developing world'. It is a custom-built, Hollywood-style film studio complex that has been integral to some of the past decades' most popular series and a growing number of films. It has five sound stages, water tanks for ocean scenes, even a tropical beach location, as well as a number of ready-built existing backdrops from a prison set, a 1950s American motel scene, an eighteenth-century American town scene and an African town set.

It is a public–private partnership and its shareholders include Videovision Entertainment, eMedia Investments and the investment arm of the Western Cape government, Wesgro.

Among the global hits produced there, at least in part, are seasons one, two, three and four of the successful *Black Sails* franchise, the evocative *Outlander* series about time travel and love across the centuries, as well as *Homeland*. There have also been a wide range of movies, most of which you will never see, but include the latest from the *Mad Max* franchise starring Charlize Theron.

Zak Calisto created Cartrack in South Africa in 2004 in response to the dramatic rise in vehicle crimes and to tackle that problem for owners and insurers alike. Fewer than twenty years later, Cartrack is owned by Karooooo, a firm that still earns 70% of its revenues in South Africa but is headquartered in Singapore and has its primary listing on the Nasdaq and a secondary one on the JSE. Karooooo, with five 'o's' is deliberate.

Calisto loves the place, but Karoo.com was taken and its US owner wanted too much for it – so Calisto registered seven names, from Karoo with one extra 'o' all the way to Karoo with nine 'o's', so it does not matter how many 'o's' you add, you will end up at the same place.

The firm has 1.5 million subscribers across 23 countries and counts 78 000 businesses in those territories as its clients. It uses data collected from devices installed on vehicles to give owners real-time analytics about their vehicles and fleets. To do so, it has thousands of employees globally. The reason to move to Singapore was multifaceted: 'It is a triple-A country,' Calisto says, pointing to the fact that companies in countries with high sovereign rates generally find it cheaper to raise capital, 'and it is well located for growth in Southeast Asia.'

Calisto, an actuarial science dropout from Wits University, says it is easier to find the right talent in Singapore and outsources much of his research and development work for the evolving fleet management business to Europe.

It is a warning to South Africa to get its act together. Entrepreneurs with audacious goals are not specific about where they live and work. They will go to the most supportive environment that helps them to grow.

South Africa's Western Cape region is actively pursuing investors via Wesgro, the provincial government's tourism promotion and investment arm. It is pushing the region and Cape Town as the best place from which to work remotely – inspired by the global work-from-home phenomenon that the world was obliged to adopt because of the Covid-19 pandemic.

It has turned that into an opportunity to attract skilled workers as it aims to position the city of Cape Town and the rest of the province as a remote-working destination. Its campaign focused on the concept of semigration – encouraging South Africans to base themselves in the Western Cape – but it also made a concerted push to attract foreign nationals to move and work remotely as countries across the globe sought to compete for longer-stay tourists who could work from anywhere.

The region is home to half of the country's emerging tech companies, with 550 of them employing 40 000 people.

Ten years ago, a farmer needed sturdy boots, a flask of cool water and a broad-brimmed hat to walk the fields to get a sense of looming problems around soil conditions, plant health and the likely yield of the crop. Now they need a decent digital device, a piece of software and their favourite beverage and can do it from the comfort of their own office thanks to (nearly) ten-year-old South African drone-mapping business Aerobotics, which is drawing more capital than it needs as it talks to global funders about its worldwide ambitions.

Founders James Paterson and Benji Meltzer started the business in 2014 and were initially focused on building diagnostic abilities for fruit and tree farmers. If you have ever flown over the extensive rolling corn and wheat fields of the American Midwest, it is easy to see additional applications for the tech, which uses artificial intelligence, drones and other robotics to track and assess the health of farming operations. That includes identifying when plants are sick, tracking pests and diseases, and providing analytics for farmers to better manage yields.

Also useful is the capability to improve forecasts through

reliable yield estimates and helping farmers to plan their annual harvesting and packing schedules, which gives them cutting-edge information they can use to manage customer expectations on delivery and quality of produce.

Like all tech enterprises nowadays, one of its most valuable assets is data, and the company is building up the largest proprietary dataset of trees and citrus fruit in the world, having mapped 81 million trees to date. It has offices in the US, Australia and Portugal and operates in eighteen countries across Africa, the Americas, Europe and Australia.

The US is the firm's main target for expansion, says CEO Paterson. 'We are committed to providing intelligent tools to optimise automation, minimise inputs and maximise production.'

You have heard of tech, fintech, healthtech – now agritech. Large-scale modern agriculture requires ever-increasing levels of technological advancement to be competitive in an era of growing climate unpredictability and heightened competition. Agriculture has advanced in leaps and bounds over the past 100 years. The first steam-powered tractor was used in the UK in 1798. For the next 130 years, the machines were cumbersome, expensive, unwieldy and unreliable. They did not gain, um, traction until after the First World War.

It was all a bit hit-and-miss in the early days. One of the first tractors made by Herbert Saunderson's company in Bedford, more famous as the centre for military trucks, broke down during a demonstration at the 1898 Royal Show. But he was determined to prove the usefulness of the vehicle. Eight years later, during a far more successful demonstration of his Tractor One that was held in a wheat field, he blew spectators away. The programme, according to Britain's *Farmer's Weekly*, started with the tractor pulling a binder to harvest some of the crop, and the sheaves were then carried on the tractor's rear-load platform to a threshing machine on the headland. The tractor's belt pulley was used to power the thresher, and it was used again to mill the grain. While the flour was rushed off to a nearby bakery to be turned into bread, the tractor ploughed and cultivated the stubble and then pulled a drill to sow the next year's wheat crop, while visitors enjoyed a picnic tea that included the freshly baked bread. Entrepreneurs have always liked to show off the genius.

Nowadays, farming without tractors is akin to going to war with a wooden club. And agritech companies such as Aerobotics are at the forefront of an information revolution that aims to help farmers lift their game with better and faster access to information than ever before.

'We're also bullish about the opportunity to launch our technology platform in several more countries over time, especially in markets where we feel the available range of financing options is narrow or cumbersome to navigate for consumers,' says Paterson. As the global agricultural industry stretches to meet expected population growth and food demand, and food security becomes more of a pressing issue with global warming, a start-up from South Africa is using artificial intelligence to help farmers manage their farms, trees and fruit.

Unless you are a competitive motocross or mountain bike rider, odds are you have not heard of Leatt Corporation, which sold $22.1-million worth of protective gear into that segment in 2021. Its biggest seller, making up more than a quarter of its sales, comes from the body armour riders wear to protect them from serious falls, followed by neck braces and world-leading helmets. The company, headquartered in Cape Town, has a state-of-the-art design studio, manufactures in China and sells 98% of its products in the lucrative US market from a recently acquired distribution centre in Nevada.

It all started in 2001. The weekend after Dr Chris Leatt's son started riding motocross bikes, the entrepreneur saw a friend by the name of Alan Selby die in a crash. He immediately set about designing a neck brace that would provide protection against the sorts of injuries from which his friend succumbed but would also be practical enough for competitive riders to wear without it becoming onerous. By 2004, he had sold his first Leatt-branded neck brace in South Africa. BMW made an offer to buy the patent on his neck brace early on. He declined and has sold more than a million of the devices and counting.

Following the launch in South Africa, the braces were on sale in the US within two years and quickly gained popularity, boosted by being featured in leading industry publications. Demand spiked after a video endorsement by the paralysed former US motocross champion, David Bailey, who encouraged the use of the neck brace for all riders. It was a powerful statement and set the firm on a strong growth trajectory.

From neck braces, the firm expanded into chest and other body protection ranges after that, developing products for highly competitive adults and children, making it one of the foremost producers of protective gear in the world.

Leatt trades on the OTCQB venture market board in the US, which is used by companies that are not quite ready for the rigours of a Nasdaq listing. But it is building up a highly credible and enviable financial track record, teeing it up for a possible public listing at some point in the future. With a return on equity of around 45%, the business is highly profitable. Should its founder be looking for an exit, it would not be hard to achieve.

Imagine if transport systems worked better. They could be more efficient and therefore cheaper to run, with less downtime and wastage, which ultimately would make them less harmful to the environment. GoMetro helps its customers do exactly that. It is a cloud-based software-as-a-service offering, which means it can service any customer in any geography. It all began as a result of a collapsing domestic consumer rail service and went global, due to the inability of the South African government to deliver on its commitments to improve public transport.

Civil engineer Justin Coetzee used to catch the train into work from Platform 2 at the Bellville station every day, but he became increasingly frustrated at how erratic the service was and how poorly information was communicated to passengers. This is clearly not a solution for the Swiss or Japanese public transport networks, but there are enough people in less efficiently run jurisdictions who could do with help in making the best of what they have, while their governments figure out how to improve them.

Most rail commuters would tut in dismay and wait for the next service to appear and, as it deteriorated, would seek new ways of getting to work or simply look for a job closer to home. The inability of the public transport network to communicate with its travelling public made no sense to Coetzee, who set about addressing the problem. He figured out that the rail operator had to know where each train was on its network. Why could the same information not be available on the phones of normal passengers?

Today, the GoMetro mobility management platform supports all types of public transport systems, including rail networks, bus operations, minibus taxis, metered taxis, long-distance freight, on-demand response services and distribution services.

Coetzee's first partner was the Passenger Rail Agency of South Africa, and he was able to provide real-time information to rail users.

Two years later, in 2014, GoMetro launched Gauteng on the Move and developed data on all bus operations across the province to integrate them with Metrorail and what was then the ambitious Rea Vaya Bus Rapid Transit system, as well as the Gautrain. This was the country's first multimodal journey planner.

By 2015, Coetzee had mapped the entire minibus taxi network that connected at Bellville station. For the first time in South Africa, the minibus taxi network was visible and could be engaged digitally, which provided the base from which to digitise minibus taxi operations in more than twenty cities around Africa and Latin America.

There has also been a useful data-mining opportunity because the information gathered from each vehicle has enabled owners to better understand utilisation, distances covered and exactly how much earning time the vehicles were operating for. In one experiment in 2017, operators could reduce vehicle requirements by 30%.

'I want us to build transport systems that use the power of data to ensure that they work and succeed,' says Coetzee. 'These systems are designed for, right-fitted and responsive to the ever-changing needs of their users. Better management, more efficiency, less idling and less dead mileage will have a tangible impact on decarbonisation and sustainability.'

The initial goal was to help travellers better navigate the often hard-to-understand intricacies of informal or dysfunctional public transport systems, but the new opportunity has been for transport operators to better design services that bring their network closer to their customers. And as public transport disproportionately benefits and helps the poor in developing markets, the technology is directly helping the most vulnerable access transport services and opportunities.

South Africa was an early adopter of GoMetro's service. In 2018, 90% of the company's sales were local, with just two projects outside the country. In 2019, public expenditure in South Africa fell off a cliff, ironically as the country's anti-corruption drive froze budgets, programmes and expenditure as officials became paralysed into inaction for fear of being seen to waste public funds or spend money on programmes that may or may not be seen to be priorities for the administration. It led to a brake on progress. For all of the government speeches and platitudes about high-speed train networks and future projects, it has not been put into action. As a result, investment in new projects, like most of the rail network, ground to a halt.

GoMetro learned a quick and important lesson in being too heavily dependent on a single client, in this case the South African government, or on the fortunes of one jurisdiction, so Coetzee focused domestically on helping private-sector players, the ever-nimble taxi industry, improve its offering, while he went on a frantic search for international customers. The most important of these is the UK-based bus company Ascendal Group. Over three years, GoMetro went from an almost total dependence on South Africa to more than 80% of its sales being outside the country, with equal distribution in the US, Latin America and the UK.

'I would like that to grow to more than 90% of global revenues over the next five years. The markets are significant in the US, Latin America and the UK. More importantly, right now GoMetro is focused on growing international licensing and subscription revenues to build a strong recurring revenue stream in multiple countries,' Coetzee says.

You would hardly put South Africa's education system in a world leadership position, but entrepreneurs have seized the opportunity to build world-class schools in the country for a small market that can afford the fees. About 5% of children in South Africa are privately educated and it has led to a growth industry inside the country, with some interesting global opportunities too.

Graeme Crawford, the founder of Crawford College, later sold to ADvTECH, went on to create Reddam House and expanded it first into Australia, before being bought out by Middle Eastern education providers Inspired Schools, as a first step towards building a global network of educational institutions. Reddam now owns more than 70 schools on five continents.

When it comes to building global education businesses in South Africa from scratch, few can match Robert Paddock, the founder of the University of Cape Town (UCT) online school, the Valenture Institute. Long before that, he and his brother Sam created GetSmarter. It started in 2008 as the online offering for UCT and sold in 2017 for $103 million to listed US education provider 2U. It now runs global short courses for the likes of the Saïd Business School in Oxford, and Harvard in Boston, from its Woodstock offices in Cape Town. (Disclaimer: I have a business relationship with GetSmarter and have built global courses that are hosted on the platform.)

The 2U CEO, Christopher Paucek, came across a Facebook advert for an MIT course GetSmarter was offering. They connected and after years of discussions came to a sale agreement. At the time, 2U was offering fully fledged degrees, while GetSmarter was providing short courses. They were targeting the same working professional market but were not in direct competition. Edtech companies are ten-a-penny and universities such as Harvard are approached weekly by start-ups claiming to be the new best thing. GetSmarter had earned its stripes as the UCT online platform. But it was not easy getting the attention of the global heavyweights. Rob Paddock travelled to Boston nineteen times in eighteen months, building relationships with MIT, until, finally in February 2016, GetSmarter launched its first international course in collaboration with the institute. That was followed by courses with Harvard, Oxford, the London School of Economics and Cambridge. Most of their students are from outside South Africa but are serviced out of Woodstock.

Following the sale of GetSmarter, Paddock paused to catch his breath and launched the Valenture Institute, with offices in South Africa, Boston and London, aimed at giving young people between Grades 9 and 12 access to global education virtually. It is priced at $5 000 a year, and the goal is to educate 100 000 students from around the world by 2030.

Online education increased dramatically in popularity in privileged schools during the pandemic, where children had access to digital devices that enabled them to log into classroom teaching from home. Full-blown online education is a different proposition to teaching using online as a delivery mechanism.

The Valenture Institute offers teaching based on 'self-discipline', allowing young people to pace their learning and get high-quality tutoring from staff.

The problem, argues Paddock, is that the traditional education system cannot be built fast enough to meet the educational needs of the country. Despite the annoyance of trade unions that the model allows for a scaling up of teaching without much additional staff input, demand has been strong.

In the early days of the pandemic, the Valenture Institute initially opened as an online-only offering, but it quickly learned it needed to have some physical presence, as children wanted a collegial environment in which to learn, so it offered micro-schools.

While all academic activities take place online, pupils still come to a physical school every day. The campus provides internet connectivity, laptops and a mentor from the community who ensures that they are supervised.

Where better to test the strength of security gate systems than in South Africa, a place notorious for the destructive, persistent ingenuity of its burgeoning criminal class? It has given birth to a range of global security industry leaders – among them Trellidor, which has become an exporter of its security gates to some of the world's more challenging environments, including the high-traffic London Underground system.

Made in the group's Durban factory, Trellidor designed a large sliding gate for the bigger-than-average apertures at many London Underground stations. It spent eighteen months and R3 million researching the problem of securing stations on the network and developed the Trellidor Trojan 3 EMESC T3000 gate, weighing in at 50 kilograms per square metre but able to be operated by a person with below-average strength, which means it required a superlative mechanism and easy locking capability. It is rated by the demanding UK standards body as being the most secure in the world. The company has sent more than a dozen of the heavyweight gates around the world as authorities increasingly seek to combat issues such as bomb threats, violent crowds and the ever-present threat of global terrorism.

Initially called L&L Metal Finishing, the firm was started in 1976 by Leon Pallace and was inspired by the old-fashioned lift cages still in use in some old buildings at the time. In the 1980s, he designed a trellis-style security gate and called it the Trellidor. It was so successful that he changed the name of the company. By 1996, the firm was expanding beyond South Africa's borders and found markets in Australia, Israel, the UK, Portugal, Swaziland, Zimbabwe, Malawi, Mauritius and Namibia. Now, in addition to 70 franchisees in South Africa, there are 17 outside the country.

There is a common thread that runs through this group of business builders who have started to crack the global big league. Their genius has been self-sufficient thinking and innovation, independent of state programmes, backing and support.

# CHAPTER 14

# Start-ups Lead the Way

*The next two decades will see even more start-ups become huge than the last two decades.* — Michael Jordaan

South African home services platform SweepSouth has big ambitions. In December 2021, it made its first acquisition, buying Egyptian rival FilKhedma for an undisclosed amount. In addition to home cleaning and DIY services, FilKhedma also provided home beauty treatments, something SweepSouth has now introduced into its other markets. Although they were founded a year apart, they used different technologies, and the biggest challenge was incorporating the Egyptian firm's web-based business onto the SweepSouth digital platform.

The deal came eighteen months after SweepSouth launched in Kenya under its own brand, shortly after expanding into Nigeria. Founded in Cape Town in 2013, the company now has a presence in Africa's major markets: north, east, west and south, but getting there was by no means guaranteed.

When co-founder Aisha Pandor gave up her day job after years of study that culminated in her being awarded her PhD in human genetics from the University of Cape Town in the morning and her MBA from the Graduate School of Business later on the same day, her parents worried she had lost the plot. Her father, Sharif, a business person, and mother, Naledi, a long-serving government minister, had not banked on their daughter moving back home with her Swedish-born husband, Alen Ribic, and two small children. But that is precisely what they did to pursue the agony and occasional ecstasy of a start-up.

The pair had been inspired by the business models of the ride-hailing services they had seen operating in the US. They bootstrapped everything they had in the belief that a similar smartphone-driven business model, at the time shaking up everything from transport to accommodation to content distribution, could change the dynamic of the often-abusive relationship endured by many domestic workers in South Africa.

They created SweepSouth as a platform to democratise the relationship between service provider and customer for women who wanted to do domestic work when and where it suited them at a rate higher than the minimum wage. They also figured, correctly, that there was a pool of potential employers who did not want to enter into the traditional, full-time, employer–employee relationships.

If, for a moment, you have a romantic idea that the twenty-first-century start-up scene is all about people in elasticated loungewear busily coding, while sipping dreamily on regular cappuccinos, think again. There was serious grind involved. The extraordinary technological advancements of the past twenty years mean you can build ideas more efficiently than ever before and better communication means you can get all the help you need and can afford from anywhere on the planet; but the actual slog is very much real.

Despite the noble efforts of many in the South African technology environment, Silicon Valley remains the global epicentre of best practice and access to funding.

'An idea is not necessarily good because it is old, or necessarily bad because it is new,' said taskmaster Henry Ford, inventor of the modern-day production line and founder of the car company that still carries the family name. 'Ideas are of themselves extraordinarily valuable, but an idea is just an idea. Anyone can think up an idea. The thing that counts is developing it into a practical product.'

Quite so, but getting others to a point where they will invest their money in it is quite another.

After winning a pitching competition at SiMODiSA, a South African private-sector-led industry association aimed at helping great ideas get off the ground, SweepSouth entered the hustle of the competition circuit. Many small companies go from competition to competition, gleaning not only useful pitching experience but also the publicity they bring and, if you win, some prize money to help fund growth. A few even find investors this way.

In 2014, barely out of the starting blocks, SweepSouth was named one of Africa's top-ten start-ups to pitch at the Dublin Web Summit. In 2015, it became the only South African start-up to crack the nod to secure a place on the Silicon Valley-based accelerator programme, 500 Startups. It secured $125 000 in seed funding and a place on a four-month mentorship programme in California.

The funding ecosystem is a complex, interconnected web. Angel investor Dave McClure founded 500 Startups to back start-ups from over 50 countries. He has supported the likes of the jobs marketplace TaskRabbit, cloud communications company Twilio, and digital gift-card service Gyft, in their early stages. It so happens that Gyft was created by California-based South African Vinny Lingham. And Lingham was not McClure's first South African connection. He had been marketing director of PayPal in the early days and worked closely with South African co-founder Elon Musk, and Roelof Botha. Lingham, in turn, was an early backer of SweepSouth, along with his investment partner Llew Claasen, as well as Pule Taukobong's Africa Angels Network and Polo Leteka Radebe's Identity Development Fund.

After seven years of slog, just as SweepSouth was beginning to gain real traction, it all stopped. Dead. South Africa's decision to impose one of the world's hardest lockdowns in its immediate first response to the Covid-19 outbreak meant that freedom of movement was severely curtailed. There was a moment when Pandor thought the pandemic would destroy not only what they had built but also remove a jobs lifeline for more than 20 000 people. All of the services on the platform required users to go into other people's homes, and it was not possible to do so through multiple lockdowns.

However, just months before the start of the pandemic, SweepSouth raised more than R50 million from an assortment of investors, including Naspers Foundry, the Michael & Susan Dell Foundation, and the musician Black Coffee, who has made investments in a number of local start-ups.

Had SweepSouth not had a capital buffer, the business model might very well have been broken. And even once the lockdowns were eased, recovery was slow as employers and employees needed to find new ways of working together amid the fear of vaccinations. Besides the pressure on the business and the people dependent on it, real life had to continue, and gradually SweepSouth managed to regain not just the confidence of those booking help via the platform, but the workers themselves who were naturally apprehensive about going into strangers' homes and breathing in the same air. Some careful coaching on safety and rigorous attention to detail meant that the pre-pandemic trust was quickly recovered.

Naspers Foundry is very selective about what it backs. In addition to SweepSouth, it has invested in Aerobotics, a firm that uses AI-driven software and drone technology to help farmers monitor everything from disease outbreaks to estimated crop yields. In addition, their service helps insurers measure and price their risk and, in the event of a claim, assess the real damage and their actual liability rather than a broad estimate.

It has also invested in Food Supply Network, a Stellenbosch-based software company helping restaurants manage their supply chains better through creating an independent marketplace, and The Student Hub, which helps young people up their skills and complete accredited online courses. Naspers Foundry has helped WhereIsMyTransport get off the ground. The firm provides data to users to understand transport systems and mobility in emerging market cities. It has, for example, mapped out the complex transport network in a congested city such as Mexico City to help businesses and institutions understand the logistical complexity of moving around a particular region.

Naspers Foundry has also invested in two new insurance players: Ctrl helps users compare simple insurance products on a single platform, making the purchasing decision easier; while Naked Insurance was started by two former EY consultants, who were fed up at having their industry clients ignore their advice, and so they built and applied their knowledge themselves in a brand new fintech environment.

In the early 2000s, Naspers, then a traditional media company, saw the potential of the internet as a business game changer and set about buying Chinese technology companies. One by one, the investments failed. Humbled by having lost billions, Naspers was preparing to return home when one of the best venture capital investment opportunities in history presented itself on a plate – not that it knew that then. It was the last throw of the dice for Naspers in China, where its investors had become fed up with it throwing good money after bad. That was until a young entrepreneur named Pony Ma turned up with a proposal that for $32 million, Naspers could have 46.5% of the company he was building. The company had been founded just three years earlier and was unknown but for a popular instant messaging platform called QQ.

Over the years, Naspers has reduced its single-stock exposure to Tencent to around 30% – that stake is worth about $120 billion. Then CEO and now chairperson Koos Bekker has said it was the luckiest deal in history and that it has become a useful source of cash for the group's global diversification into food delivery services, gaming and classifieds investments. Now a small share of that is being used to find the genius in a new generation of South African start-ups.

Getting paid is the biggest obstacle for any new business. Countless studies show that businesses that make it easy for customers to pay grow faster than those that do not. Market traders, for example, that allow only cash transactions do less turnover than those that can facilitate a digital payment. Customers with a limited amount of cash in their pockets are more likely to second-guess a purchase decision than those with a digital payment option. If you are building a platform business where your only interaction with the customer is virtual, it has to be easy otherwise they simply go elsewhere. Airbnb co-founder Brian Chesky said the most critical factor in setting up the home-sharing platform was getting payments resolved. Once that happened, he said, the rest was 'fairly easy'.

It explains why so many African fintech start-ups are all about trying to facilitate payments.

Much of the world operates on the same set of rules. You can swipe your credit card in Boston, Beijing, Bloemfontein or Bangkok and can rest assured that the world's biggest payments businesses, such as Visa, Mastercard or American Express, will verify within a moment that you are good for the payment, facilitate the transaction and ensure you are able to leave a shop with your purchases.

It is not that simple everywhere. SweepSouth has seen differently evolved levels of payment services in each of its markets and has had to find ways of tapping into those. South Africa's banking system is famously world class and payments move quickly through an established, globally connected payments system. The payments challenge was one of the biggest shocks for SweepSouth, which suddenly faced a host of cultural and business obstacles they had not anticipated and had to find ways around.

Legal frameworks and wage levels also vary considerably: 'Our government is far from perfect, but in some other countries you can have government shut down a business without any notice as a result of a random decision, and that can cause chaos,' Pandor says. Cultural and legislative differences across geographies mean progress is slower than she would like. Nevertheless, South America is next.

Making sure that businesses can be paid, and doing it digitally, is the reason Katlego Maphai and three cellphone industry colleagues, Carl Wazen, Bradley Wattrus and Lungisa Matshoba, established Yoco Technologies. In 2021, Yoco raised R1.2 billion from investors – a record amount for a South African fintech and the highest ever for a small-business-focused payments platform in the Middle East and Africa. The amount brought the total raised to R1.5 billion since it was founded in 2015, suggesting serious plans are afoot for growth.

Among early investors was Twitter co-founder Jack Dorsey's

Square, later rebranded Block. Yoco was the first investment on the African continent for Dragoneer, a San Francisco-based investment firm that allocates money on behalf of a range of family offices, foundations, endowments and sovereign wealth funds.

Most investors in Yoco hail from the San Francisco area, suggesting a strong appetite for the high-growth potential African exposure brings. Among them are Breyer Capital, which usually focuses on American and Chinese investment opportunities, and HOF Capital, which has more than $1 billion in 1 250 investments under management and is constantly seeking visionary entrepreneurs.

Apple co-founder Steve Jobs once explained his firm's decision to create not only its own devices but also its own operating system by quoting Alan Kay: 'People who are really serious about software should make their own hardware.' From the start, that is what Yoco has done. Using cellphone principles, Yoco disrupted the South African payments environment by ensuring quick and seamless over-the-counter access to its payment machines, which allow merchants immediate access to the national payments system.

'Yoco has big plans for seizing this opportunity by continuing to deepen its market presence in South Africa and expanding into Africa and the Middle East region,' says Wazen. At the time of writing, it was piloting new technologies in Mauritius, with plans to enter at least one other new country in 2022.


The Stellenbosch-based Alphawave Group's initial success was in niche radio frequency and antenna technology in the late 1990s and early 2000s, when wireless communication was exploding. In 2014, it revised its focus to invest in electronics, data and software. The business is the creation of Stellenbosch maths graduates in the early 1990s and has evolved into a builder of complex business systems designed to improve workflow using a new wave of emerging technologies. It employs more than 350 people, with around 170 of those in engineering, computer and data science or technical development roles.

In addition to the impressive work it has done in creating the algorithms necessary to develop the most sensitive radio telescope in the world as part of the MeerKAT space telescope for the Square Kilometre Array project in the Karoo, it has also become a leader in new technologies via its subsidiary Skynamo. This is the group's first emerging technology business to scale internationally, following a $30-million cash injection from US investment firm Five Elms in early 2020. It has created an innovative sales platform that enables teams to remain in the field longer, with reporting systems back to head office, which minimises the old requirement of a regular, in-person check-in.

Inrange Golf, born out of the original antenna business, is fast becoming a leader in smart driving ranges, with a footprint of 50 installations in the UK, the US and the rest of the world expected by 2023. The firm places multiple radar sensors around driving ranges, and each sensor is able to track the flight of every ball within its field of view. The sensors are placed to create an overlapping radar field array, providing multiple data points on each ball's flight so that it can identify which bay the ball has been hit from, instantly relaying the data to that bay's logged-in device. It is all done by the time the golfer lowers their club.

Both Skynamo and Inrange Golf are getting serious traction and scaling fast internationally. Such has been the advance in technology that they have the potential to be ten times bigger than the niche antenna companies launched by Alphawave in the previous decade. The Alphawave Group has also invested in a strong pipeline of new technology innovations that could follow in the scaling footsteps of Skynamo and Inrange, fuelled by the more established profitable businesses in the portfolio.

Jeremy Ord co-founded Dimension Data in 1983 with a group of old school friends, Keith McLachlan, Werner Sievers, Peter Neale and Kevin Hamilton. The company went on to list on the JSE in 1987 and expanded to the Asia-Pacific region, Europe and the UK, when it bought UK telecommunications company Plessey in 1998. It listed in London in July 2000, raising $1.25 billion. Its valuation spiked as investors piled into shares on the promise of a looming technological revolution, but as the dotcom bubble burst and valuations plummeted so did its popularity as an investment. The company's shares peaked in a buying frenzy at R70, but they bottomed out three years later below R2 a share. Ten years on, it was acquired by Nippon Telegraph and Telephone for £2.1 billion and soon delisted from both the JSE and the London Stock Exchange.

By the time CEO Brett Dawson, who succeeded Ord as CEO, stepped down in 2016, the firm employed 31 000 staff in

58 countries, had annual revenues of $7.5 billion, and had a presence on what it calls 'all six inhabited continents'. In 2019, TechCentral speculated the firm might make a return to the JSE. If there had been plans, they were no doubt impacted by the pandemic, and there is no clarity on whether the one-time market darling will make its comeback or not.

Another technology company from that time, Datatec, founded in 1986, drew far less attention, but the Johannesburg-based international ICT solutions and services group operates in more than 50 countries across North America, Latin America, Europe and Africa. It too went on a global acquisition spree and was bruised by the fallout of the dotcom bubble bursting. Today, it counts several of those early deals among its main divisions, including Westcon-Comstor, Logicalis, Datatec Financial Services and Analysys Mason. Its founding CEO Jens Montanana remains at the helm of the firm, which has a low media profile but continues to perform well with annual revenues of more than $2.3 billion, strong underlying earnings and a special dividend to investors of more than R1 billion.


Car ownership is expensive. South African start-up FlexClub offers a car subscription service focusing, for now, on a significant opportunity in emerging markets: people who do not qualify for finance in the traditional process of buying, insuring and financing cars. The founders met while working for Uber. Marlon Gallardo is Mexican, while Rudolf Vavruch and CEO Tinashe Ruzane are South Africans.

'On the scale of consumer experiences that suck, buying a car is right up there and carries much longer-lasting financial consequences than calling a taxi. Any market where customer value could be higher is one ripe for change,' says Ruzane. 'What companies like Tesla, Amazon and Netflix all have in common is an unrelenting focus on building better experiences for customers.'

The global motor industry is almost wholly dependent on vehicle financing. If you do not have cash and banks will not provide finance, then cars do not get sold. Banks have a low-risk tolerance and will not finance if they think risk is high. FlexClub started in South Africa as a means to enable Uber drivers to get access to vehicles and enable them to make a living. They subsequently expanded the model to Mexico and have worked in both countries with Uber to give drivers the tools of the trade.

'We wanted to help a community of ride-hailing drivers who had been excluded from accessing cars. But right now, we've built the product to work for anyone and not just ride-hailing drivers,' says Ruzane.

The principle of FlexClub follows the trend of music streaming versus ownership of the album or renting versus owning a house. What these models reveal is that there is a significant market for people who would rather rent than own products, and they will pay, relatively speaking, a premium to do so.

As the name suggests, the FlexClub model is flexible and allows for subscribers to opt for short- or long-term leases, or even a hybrid of both, depending on their needs. They pay a single monthly fee and can cancel at any point. They can opt to buy the car outright, but if the vehicle they are leasing no longer suits their needs, they can switch it for another.

Ruzane pioneered a leasing system within Uber after managing to convince WesBank, along with Kia and BMW, as well as several car rental companies, to make vehicles available to drivers via a leasing mechanism. It worked well and the firm asked him to relocate to the Netherlands in 2016 to roll out a similar programme in its more than 40 markets.

Ruzane did that and quickly realised there was a big opportunity outside of the corporate structure, so he took the idea private with his former employer as his first client.

'The more global auto executives I engaged with, the clearer it became that this would become the future of mobility financing globally,' says Ruzane, 'but the auto industry was not ready to build the necessary technology for the transition to subscriptions. The opportunity was ripe for a company that could quickly build the right technology to close this gap for the auto industry.' By 2019, its earliest investors provided $1.2 million and included the reclusive start-up funder Jonathan Beare's Buffet Consortium and Michael Jordaan's Montegray Capital.

In the beginning, they sourced vehicles from individual car owners in South Africa, who could either put a car they already owned on the platform or buy one, all with the goal of earning revenue from it in much the same way a car rental or leasing company would earn revenue from their fleet. FlexClub would then offer these to Uber drivers.

From the start, the goal was to build technology that would power a new way of buying vehicles that did not include transferring the risks or responsibilities of traditional ownership to customers and did not rely on customers being locked in for years to provide affordable access to a vehicle. It took two years, but Avis and later Europcar put their subscription offers on FlexClub, becoming the first global firms to partner with the start-up.

FlexClub's expansion to Mexico as a second market after South Africa is not only because Gallardo is Mexican, but also since the market is suited to the model. It has twice the number of new passenger vehicle sales than South Africa every year, and the needs of its entrepreneurs are not wildly different from those in South Africa. It launched there just before the pandemic, yet the country currently delivers 10% of group revenue. Ruzane anticipates an uplift as the pandemic recedes. The timing of the launch was terrible and the business, which relies on human mobility, found itself constrained by global lockdowns, but the firm flexed and many of its users then switched to deliveries of goods and packages rather than people.

South African IT engineer Justin Trent was working in London at the dawn of the new century. His first job in IT was for an American company that shut down soon after it began its UK expansion drive, leaving twenty customers in need of IT support. It was not Trent's problem. He could have packed up his things and easily found another job, or he could offer his services to clients left high and dry by his former employer. Twelve of those companies signed up and he began servicing those customers from their own premises, keeping his own costs to a bare minimum.

Within ten years, Trent and fellow South African and business partner Oliver Potgieter were running a leading IT support company, focusing on about 300 financial services customers, mostly hedge funds and in the alternative investment sector. By the time they sold in 2010, they had more than 100 staff and offices in London, New York, Hong Kong and Singapore.

They returned to South Africa with money in their pockets but no plan to speak of.

'Towards the end of our London tenure, cloud computing started to make some serious inroads into the IT space. South Africa was still, however, very behind in its cloud adoption and this presented a perfect opportunity to get ahead of the market, or so we thought,' says Trent. 'Olly and I then started a cloud computing company that was aimed at aggregating the best-of-breed public cloud solutions and reselling them to IT companies to on-sell to their clients. The reality of the situation, however, was that connectivity was poor and expensive, and hardly anyone knew what cloud computing was.'

Cloudbox was way ahead of the market. While they might have been among the first to promote the idea of cloud computing, it was a laborious and painful process of educating companies on the benefits of cloud computing and trying to recruit resellers who did not know how to shift from a support model, heavily propped up with hardware sales, to an annuity revenue business supporting cloud services and hardly any hardware.

In 2014, Trent received a call from Nick Watkins, who was one of his London clients. Watkins had successfully launched a hedge fund called Tenax Capital in 2004 and exited in 2013 after growing it to a billion-dollar fund.

Trent and Potgieter had set up Tenax's IT systems from scratch and supported and maintained its IT infrastructure. They had built up a solid relationship of mutual admiration and trust. Watkins had moved to South Africa with his eye on starting something in cloud computing. He joined the pair as a shareholder and brought with him a set of structuring and finance skills that helped shape Cloudbox into an investible asset. They set about raising capital for growth. From 2015 to 2019, the company grew at a compound rate of 30% a year.

In 2018, they hired the ex-CEO of one of their suppliers from their London days, Nick Goodenough, as CEO of the newly created UK business. 'We felt that with the difference in resource costs we would be able to compete at a much lower price point than UK companies and make better margins than selling to South African businesses,' Trent says. They made the announcement of the development on LinkedIn and one of Trent's old hedge fund clients made contact, offering to help shape the cloud offering for the hedge fund industry and also assist in re-introducing them to the tight networks in which that industry operates.

One of the reasons they had exited their first UK businesses was to have a more relaxed lifestyle and not have to put up with the pressures of traders and hedge fund managers, but the pull was strong and they took the leap. Within eighteen months, they had sixteen companies in the financial services market, including one of the world's largest hedge fund start-ups, on their books.

'We set up the majority of these from scratch with 95% of the work effort being carried out in South Africa. We were suddenly supporting users in nine different countries, all while Covid was wreaking havoc around the world.'

It was not all a work-from-home utopia, though. They found they needed a presence in markets where their customers operated, so they also set one up in Singapore, where one of their UK clients, who is backed by Temasek, has a branch office. Again, it would seem as if they were in the right place at the right time. Until recently, Singapore has tightly regulated cloud computing, but it has become more open-minded in recent times, which has led to a boom in the industry.

They had hoped to create a business that required little of them after set-up and that would simply generate an annuity income stream and would not need much in the way of resources, and only little customer interaction. They got the annuity part right, but every customer needs someone to talk to – at least for now.

The international operations of the business were only two years old at the time of writing, but the UK already generates 50% of revenues. With Singapore coming on stream towards the end of 2021, the firm hopes to have 80% of its revenues from outside the South African home base by 2025.

This is a business built on deep networks, long working relationships and trust created over twenty years of slog, but it does mean that referrals have been by far the best form of marketing. The realisation that its biggest clients are in a small, closely held hedge fund industry is also a reminder that reputation is everything.

Some of South Africa's earlier high-tech enterprises still exist.

Today owned by Shoprite, Computicket launched in 1971 and became the first of its kind in the world to operate a centralised computerised system that changed the way bookings could be made for entertainment, sport and even travel tickets. Founder Percy Tucker was lauded as a visionary and received multiple accolades domestically. It took a decade for other countries to introduce similar systems. Tucker's aversion to standing in box-office queues and his frustration at queuing for opera tickets in Commissioner Street in the 1950s made him realise there had to be a better mechanism for selling seats for shows.

He travelled the world looking for automated solutions and finally discovered a failed UK system. He hired key staff on contract to work in South Africa to finish the job they had started. On 11 June 1971, the front page of *The Star* newspaper published: 'The Benoni boy's space age ticket scheme is a world first.' For many users of the system, an upgrade on its underlying tech and ticket delivery mechanisms could do with some work – but its owners tell me a refurbishment is a priority.

Meanwhile, another South African start-up created by old schoolmates Jamie Hedley and Mike Kennedy enabled event organisers to manage the ticket sales process themselves when they created Quicket, which today operates in 35 countries. It can have as many as 2 500 events listed at any one time.

South Africans are used to the vision of a khaki-clad law enforcement officer hurtling with an apparent death wish across multiple lanes of traffic, hand raised, delivering the dreaded: 'Do you know how fast you were going?' A stupid question, really. Even if you did know, you are unlikely to share the incriminating evidence with someone hell-bent on separating you from your money.

The odds are that the officer in question used a radar gun to determine your speed and knows precisely how fast you were travelling, and is simply assessing just how obnoxious you are about to become, before writing out the ticket.

That technology has also been used to get more precise rulings in sport. It is thanks to South African engineer Henri Johnson, who in 1992 perfected the first radar gun to measure the speed and angle of fast-flying balls, using radio waves reflected back to a device of any object in its path and applying something called the Doppler Shift principle. It allows for not only measuring the extraordinary speeds at which a cricket ball is delivered down the pitch, but also whether it was likely to have hit the stumps in a contentious call on LBW, for example, ending countless arguments and ultimately one day completely eliminating the job of the umpire. Howzat!

# CHAPTER 15

# People You Don't Want to Export

*A great emigration implies unhappiness of some kind in the country that is deserted.* — Thomas Malthus

Elon Musk is a local who has gone global – and even off-world – but he is not one to hark back to his South African heritage. In 2021, Musk became the richest person on earth, thanks mostly to a surge in the value of shares in the electric car company Tesla. It was also the year *Time* magazine named him Person of the Year. For many, it was an odd choice in a year a small group of scientists helped alleviate the worst impacts of the most serious pandemic to afflict humanity in a century through creating vaccines in record time, but the editors' choice, as they say, is final.

Making it to the cover of *Time* as Person of the Year is a rare accolade for a business leader but not unprecedented. Car maker Walter Chrysler was the second person awarded the accolade in 1928, a year after Charles Lindbergh was named for being the first person to fly across the Atlantic. More recently, Facebook co-founder Mark Zuckerberg made it in 2010, and Bill Gates, co-founder of Microsoft, in 2005, but for his charitable work rather than business accomplishments. Musk's rival for the global super-rich stakes, Amazon founder Jeff Bezos, cracked the nod back in 1999, and Andy Grove, the founder of Intel, in 1997. Otherwise, it is largely a list of American political figures, with an occasional nod to the likes of environmentalist Greta Thunberg in 2019, a nomination for veteran David Attenborough in 2022, and others who have done extraordinary things, such as the astronauts of Apollo 11, who became the first humans to go to the moon.

Churchill and Stalin made it twice, and Adolf Hitler once, in 1938.

Musk has spoken about being bullied at school and has no fond memories of his time growing up in South Africa. Seeking to avoid conscription, he packed in his early studies at the University of Pretoria to build a life in the US. Since co-founding and selling PayPal, he has developed a list of audacious projects, including the likes of The Boring Company, which is digging tunnels in California for electric-powered, high-speed trans-port; Tesla, which is revolutionising battery-powered cars; and SpaceX, which among multiple successful satellite launches won a $2.9-billion NASA contract to land astronauts on the moon.

*Huffington Post* and Thrive Global founder Arianna Huffington wrote of the entrepreneur: 'Musk isn't just changing how we transport ourselves; he's augmenting human possibilities. And by doing it all with his relentlessly optimistic, space-half-full showmanship, he's offering a model for how we can solve the big, existential challenges in front of us.'

Investment bank Morgan Stanley dared to forecast Musk would become the world's first dollar trillionaire. Analyst Adam

Jones said there was also significant potential in twenty-year-old SpaceX, which he said was 'challenging any preconceived notion of what was possible and the time frame possible, in terms of rockets, launch vehicles and supporting infrastructure'. Jones said SpaceX's Starship reusable rockets that could take people and cargo to the moon, and possibly even Mars one day, had the potential to transform investor expectations around the space industry. Musk owns about 48% of SpaceX.

Musk made it not only because he is the highest profile global business leader of his generation, but also in recognition of the problems his businesses are seeking to solve: 'Few individuals have had more influence than Musk on life on Earth, and potentially life off Earth too,' *Time* said in an article explaining its choice. Musk is without doubt an extraordinary visionary who has succeeded in building multiple, groundbreaking businesses that would not ever have gained the traction had he launched them in South Africa. 'He sees his mission as solving the globe's most intractable challenges, along the way disrupting multiple industries,' wrote *Time* editor-in-chief Edward Felsenthal.

Mark Shuttleworth remains regarded as South Africa's most successful tech entrepreneur who made it big in South Africa. He was born and raised in Cape Town and went to the University of Cape Town. Soon after graduating, he started Thawte Consulting in 1995. The internet was still in its infancy. Thawte soon became one the biggest online providers of digital certificates, which are used to help prove that websites are legitimate and secure. Four

years later, in 1999, Shuttleworth sold Thawte to American internet company VeriSign for $575 million in shares, but he had the
good sense to cash in before the dotcom bubble burst. Bloomberg
says he made more than $700 million by getting out in time.

Shuttleworth formed an Africa-focused technology venture
capital arm, HBD – short for Here Be Dragons, a homage to
ancient maps and their description of unchartered territory. He
relocated to the Isle of Man for tax reasons and has backed a
series of young entrepreneurs. In 2004, he started programming
Ubuntu as an open-source project and formed his firm Canonical
to explore business prospects arising from it. Canonical sees
3 million downloads of its software and 50 million security up-
dates each day. Because it is open source and Ubuntu is free, it
does not require registration. The vision for Canonical is to provide the platform that you see everywhere other than the personal
domain. It makes its money from about 800 paying customers,
including Netflix, Tesla and Deutsche Telekom.

While Musk no doubt would have succeeded at whatever he
turned his hand to in South Africa, the opportunity to scale significant ideas that shape the future is harder in an environment
that is less accommodating, even hostile, to commercial success.
It is one of the reasons why so many capable South Africans seek
their fortunes elsewhere. Musk would not have accomplished
what he has achieved with PayPal, Tesla and SpaceX had he
stayed in South Africa, which lacks the ecosystem to support his
brand of genius.

Societies lose people all the time for a multiplicity of reasons, but dysfunctional societies lose a disproportionate number of skills and fail to replace them through either immigration or training. In fact, they become hostile to immigration and see it as a threat to domestic jobs rather than as an opportunity for growth. That skills shortage is increasingly apparent in South Africa and worsened as the global economy reopened following successive waves of Covid-19, offering new opportunities to skilled workers to transfer their skills to where they are sought after.

At some point, a loss of skills reaches a tipping point. The former US President Barack Obama, himself the son of a Kenyan immigrant to the US, said in 2018 that talented young Africans should drive change at home rather than emigrating. He urged African governments to do more to curb a brain drain. 'If we have African leaders, governments and institutions which are creating a platform for success and opportunity, then you will increasingly get more talent wanting to stay,' Obama said.

In 2021, Musk revealed he would be paying $11 billion in taxes in the US. Imagine for a moment he was liable for that amount in South Africa. Not only would the corporate entities he started pay tax on their profits, but the people they employed would also be making a PAYE contribution and paying other taxes, including VAT, fuel levies and a range of local rates and taxes. His personal tax bill in the US translates to R165 billion, which is about a third of the value of all of the R528-billion personal income taxes collected in South Africa in 2021, half of all the R346 billion in VAT payments and just shy of the R214 billion all South African companies paid in tax. If Musk was a South African taxpayer, he would be the single biggest contributor and the fifth biggest line item in the domestic tax arena. It is a moot point as he left the country long before becoming economically active and has made his (very successful) life elsewhere to the benefit of that society. But it is interesting to contemplate.

Added to the list of those who left South Africa is the owner of the *LA Times* and San Diego *Tribune* newspapers. The Gqeberha-born Dr Patrick Soon-Shiong is estimated by *Forbes* magazine to be worth more than $7.5 billion. The transplant surgeon made his fortune from the creation of a blockbuster cancer drug called Abraxane and the sales of his companies American Pharmaceutical Partners in 2008 and Abraxis BioScience in 2010 for a total of $9.1 billion. He has registered more than 230 patents worldwide and is the founder of NantWorks, which is a network of healthcare, biotech and AI start-ups. He took his latest cancer drug maker NantKwest public in 2015 and biotech start-up NantHealth in 2016. Soon-Shiong, who also teaches at the University of California and Imperial College of London, has published more than 100 scientific papers during his medical career.

Unlike most emigrants who become so busy immersing themselves in their new geography and looking to survive in often tougher, more competitive environments than they are used to, Soon-Shiong has been talking about investing in medical technologies in South Africa. In late 2021, NantWorks signed a collaboration agreement with the CSIR and the South African Medical Research Council to transfer biologic manufacturing technology for Covid-19 and cancer vaccines and next-generation, cell-based immunotherapies to South Africa.

The aim is to enable the rapid clinical development of next-generation vaccines for infectious diseases and cancer at centres of excellence across the country so that South Africa can serve as a scientific hub for the continent. NantWorks has said it will invest in large-scale manufacturing facilities and a biologics manufacturing campus in the Western Cape and begin the transfer of technology, know-how and materials for DNA, RNA, adjuvant vaccine platforms and cell therapy.

In early 2022, Soon-Shiong was in South Africa to open a Centre for Epidemic Response and Innovation at Stellenbosch University, in addition to supporting the establishment of institutes for infectious disease and cancer centres of excellence at UCT and his alma mater, Wits University.


Long before Musk made the journey across the Atlantic, theoretical physicist Emanuel Derman had left South Africa and was establishing himself in America in the late 1960s. He became well known as an author when he wrote about the connections between physics and finance in *My Life as a Quant*. He developed groundbreaking models on interest rate modelling and ended up at Columbia University in New York, where he became the director of its programme on financial engineering. He would not have attained the same level of global recognition had he not joined the Goldman Sachs fixed-income division in 1985, where he became one of the co-developers of the Black–Derman–Toy interest-rate model. He rose through the ranks and today still teaches at Columbia University.

Ron Dembo graduated with a BSc in chemical engineering from Wits University in 1969 and went on to achieve his PhD in the US. He taught at Yale University and became visiting professor at MIT, in addition to creating Algorithmics, a Toronto-based risk management software business advising financial institutions. It employed more than 850 people in 23 offices worldwide and served scores of clients, including 25 of the 30 biggest banks in the world. Dembo sold to the Fitch Group for $175 million, and six years later IBM snapped it up for nearly twice that. Dembo's latest venture, Riskthinking.AI, is a Toronto-based firm tackling one of the biggest hurdles facing companies today: measuring climate-related financial risk.

No amount of domestic incentive would have held these individuals back from pursuing their global ambitions. Those sorts of skills are highly sought after and are in demand worldwide, especially in North America.

In April 2022, Sequoia Capital, one of the oldest and most successful venture capital firms in Silicon Valley, announced it was appointing the head of its US and European Venture Capital operations, South African-born Roelof Botha, as its boss. Botha is the son of economist Roelof Botha and grandson of Pik Botha, also Roelof, a former South African foreign affairs minister under the P.W. Botha government, who also served under Nelson Mandela.

Roelof, the younger, has done well in the US. In 2008, he was ranked 22nd on the Forbes Midas List, an annual ranking of venture capital professionals and, by 2021, he was 9th. He graduated with a BSc in actuarial science, economics and statistics from UCT in 1996 and briefly worked as a business analyst at McKinsey in Johannesburg before moving to the US, where he earned an MBA from Stanford University Graduate School of Business.

At the same time, he teamed up with fellow-Pretorian Elon Musk and became director of corporate development for PayPal. By 2001, he was the CFO. The firm went public in 2002, only to be bought out by Meg Whitman in October that year. She gave Botha the opportunity to stay on as CFO post-acquisition, but he left to join Sequoia Capital in January 2003 and has been part of the team that today counts Apple and Google among its most successful venture capital investments. Its recent successes include home rental platform Airbnb, fintechs Stripe and Square, cyber security specialist Okta and software company Snowflake.

Botha's appointment is a big deal in that it marks just the third transition in Sequoia's leadership since it was founded by venture capital pioneer Don Valentine in 1972.

The *Financial Times* pointed out Sequoia has dropped the global managing partner title that had been given to predecessors, with Botha instead becoming Sequoia's 'senior steward' to set 'the overall tone' for Sequoia, while allowing greater autonomy for its fast-growing investment businesses in China and India.

David Frankel is co-founder of Founder Collective, a seed-stage venture capital fund with offices in New York City and Boston. Chosen by the *Financial Mail* as South African Technology Achiever of the Year in 2000, the Wits University-trained electrical engineer won a Fulbright Scholarship and earned his MBA with distinction from Harvard University. He was an early investor in South Africa's internet connectivity boom as a director and co-founder of Internet Solutions and served on the board of Dimension Data. He remains on the board of Rand Merchant Investment Holdings.

Emigrants have travelled from across the globe for generations and the US economy has created more wealth than anywhere else on earth, consistently, for most of the past century. America's success in drawing talent is summed up by *Financial Times* economics writer Alan Beattie's 2011 book, *False Economy*, which compares the fortunes of America and Argentina, both in the early stages of their development in the nineteenth century, endowed with natural resources and huge potential.

The difference came in the paths they took to shaping their future. Generations of young Europeans, eager to find their fortunes in the new world, made a choice of whether to head to the Pampas or the Prairies. America boomed and Argentina has lurched from crisis to crisis – political, economic and social – for over 200 years. Beattie argues it has something to do with the way in which the respective countries' modern founders chose to set them up: 'On the face of it, the economies of the two countries looked similar: agrarian nations pushing the frontiers of their settlement westwards into a wilderness of temperate grasslands. In both, the frontier rancher – the gaucho and the cowboy – was elevated to a symbol of courage, independence and endurance. But closer up, there were big disparities in the way this happened. America chose a path that parcelled out new land to individuals and families; Argentina delivered it to the hands of a few rich landowners.'

That, argues Beattie, is the big difference in how their respective economies were structured from independence. Argentina sought to replicate and preserve the rigid hierarchies that were imported from Europe, and the US sought to break with those ties, putting greater emphasis on the power of the individual to craft their own destiny. 'America was fortunate enough to have imported many of the farming practices of northern Europe and the aspirations of its people. The farmers of New England, the densely populated states of the north-east, came largely from Britain, Germany and the Netherlands – all countries with a lot of people and not much land. They brought with them a tradition of skilled farmers on small homesteads. Argentina by contrast had a history of a few rich landowners on great estates left by the Spanish and the aristocratic elitism that came with it. America favoured squatters; Argentina backed landlords,' according to Beattie.

Probably the most famous deliberate exporter of human talent was SABMiller, which sent its world-class South African business model, as well as more than 100 of its smartest executives, to new markets for more than a decade and a half to become the second biggest brewer and one of the priciest takeover targets in the world of beer in history. Most of those executives returned home over time. In terms of inculcating a value system and a work ethic into people and giving them a chance at global exposure and getting international experience, SABMiller was a global leader.

It is a model that JSE-listed Spar has emulated after buying troubled businesses in other parts of the world. Spar is headquartered in the Netherlands, but country operations are autonomous and the South African unit that serves independent local retailers has also bought businesses in Europe. Its Irish business, which also operates in parts of the south of England, has been a solid performer, but the operations in Switzerland and Poland needed help. The local group installed senior South African executives in both areas, which has led to a turnaround in the Swiss operations and progress in Poland.

The rise in the brain drain of senior leaders in recent years from top JSE jobs is also testament to the ability of senior executives to relocate on favourable terms. Vikesh Ramsunder, the former CEO at Clicks, left to run a business in Australia, less than a year after members of the Economic Freedom Fighters blockaded and damaged stores in response to a controversial shampoo advert, and after the July 2021 riots that saw damage of approximately R750 million to more than 50 Clicks stores in KwaZulu-Natal.

There have been other senior resignations of executive directors, which firms are required to report on in terms of the law. It is not quite a tsunami but a growing trend. What is more worrying is the anecdotal evidence of younger South Africans looking at options to globalise their future. The country has to find a way to incentivise its brightest and best to stay.

Ralph Wichtmann, a consultant at Sovereign Trust, points to political instability, safety and security, education, a volatile currency and a lack of job opportunities in South Africa as some of the main reasons for emigration. If the South African government is serious about growth and securing long-term sources of income tax, it needs to grow its skills base.

If exports are regarded as a net positive for a country because it encourages companies to grow, invest in new capacity and employ new workers, the constant outflow of talent is one of the most destructive forces in damaging the country's social fabric, the skills base and intellectual capability to tackle some of its most intractable problems.

Had the likes of Adrian Gore, Brian Joffe or Michiel le Roux followed many of their university classmates as part of a long-running brain drain out the country, rather than create Discovery, Bidvest and Capitec, there would be fewer job opportunities and considerably less innovation locally. Imagine, too, if more of those founders' former classmates stayed, and instead of creating value outside of South Africa, what could have been done in the country of their birth.

While the South African government will bend over backwards to avoid answering direct questions on emigration patterns, there is plenty of data, most notably in the South African Revenue Service (SARS) tax statistics, which shows South Africa's skills base is shrinking as a growing number of professionals choose to leave the country. Their departure impacts short-term revenue collection, as they pay their taxes elsewhere, while the drain also means fewer businesses are created, which undermines job creation over time.

The world's most successful countries are those that draw rather than shed skills. South Africa is a net exporter of its most valuable domestic asset – skilled people. Not everyone who leaves is a Musk, but many of those who do choose to take their skills elsewhere would be valuable contributors to society. They are generally well-educated and have skills valued in other economies.

In 2020, a quarter of the 2 500 Professional Provident Society clients who stopped using the company's services stated emigration as the reason for doing so. Official tax statistics showed in 2019 and 2020 that approximately 9 000 income earners in the R750 000-plus tax bracket either saw their wages drop or they left the country. While SARS says it cannot define the numbers of people who leave permanently, the National Treasury is getting worried. Personal income taxes make up around 38% of all taxes collected in the country, and higher income earners are also among the most significant contributors to VAT, via their purchasing habits and property transfer duties. They also contribute the lion's share of local government revenues in the form of paying rates for municipal services, and they are more likely at some point to create a business at scale that employs others.

While the economy bumbled its way through the so-called lost decade of the Zuma years, the tax base grew by about 500 000, while the number of people on grants expanded from 16 million to 18 million. Individuals declaring incomes of at least R750 000 a year make up less than 10% of the total population but pay a third of all personal income tax. Losing them is disastrous for the fiscus.

There is no doubt that the number of people paying the top whack of tax is falling, partly due to a tougher economy, migration and, it would seem, higher levels of evasion. Former High Court Judge Dennis Davis, who formed part of the Katz Commission into tax reforms in the early 1990s, now consults for SARS. He tells the story of how a SARS inspector was having breakfast under the oak trees at the Alphen Hotel in Constantia one recent Saturday morning when the Ferrari Club of South Africa pulled in for a break and to compare notes on whatever they compare notes about. The inspector snapped pictures of all sixteen vehicles and found not one registered to an entity declaring more than R300 000 a year in income. That sparked an investigation, the outcome of which is yet to be publicised. Certainly, the number of people declaring income of over R1.5 million a year, at which the marginal tax rate of 45% kicks in, is under pressure and is expected to shrink, unless the South African economy grows, allowing for personal income increases and facilitating a rise in tax contributions.

The proliferation in private schools offering A-level qualifications, as well as Cambridge-accredited curricula, suggests parents who might be able to afford it are planning to send children outside the country for tertiary education, setting them up for global careers. It shows a demonstrable lack of confidence in the South African education system. The mere fact that emigration advisory firms compete for business and advertise their services in mainstream media suggests it is a thriving sector and provides a clue to the scale of the problem. These companies reported a spike in inquiries following the state failure to contain the July 2021 riots, which cost in excess of R40 billion and did incalculable damage to confidence.

A July 2021 BrandMapp survey reported 27% of tax-paying South Africans said they were definitely planning to emigrate in the next five years. Just 30% of people said they were optimistic about the country's future. Surveys are not perfect but are a useful barometer of sentiment. The biggest reasons for leaving: safety, governance, and their own as well as the country's future prosperity.

A study by New World Wealth and AfrAsia Bank showed a significant reduction in the number of dollar millionaires living in South Africa. Admittedly, it is not all due to emigration. Some of those just cracking the $1-million net worth level would drop out or come into the fold depending on the level of the exchange rate; some would have lost businesses or seen the value of assets depreciate. Between 2017 and 2020, the number of dollar millionaires in South Africa dropped by 8 600 to about 35 000 – a drop of 20%.

The reality is that the country needs to do more to convince its wealthier citizens to stay. In 2015, I wrote in my 'Rants and Sense' column in the *Business Times*: 'Everyone needs to be just a little bit nicer to taxpayers, a little more cognisant of the fact that without their goodwill, we would be in deeper trouble. Goodwill is slowly fading and this runs the risk of eroding a small base of individual and corporate taxpayers unless the state either gets a grip on its spending or does considerably better PR. As public anger at state hubris grows, the South African Revenue Service is finding it harder and harder to extract money from reluctant taxpayers. SARS says it is owed about R100 billion in unpaid taxes and is having to use commercial banks as agents to raid the personal accounts of those who owe it money. Fewer than half of South Africans pay any income tax, according to the National Treasury 2015 Tax Statistics Bulletin. Worryingly, the number of companies that pay tax is declining against a backdrop of falling profits ... The tax stats show that fewer companies are paying tax than in 2013 – in fact, just a quarter of companies pay any tax at all. In all, 45% report zero taxable income and nearly a third make an assessed loss. Most company taxes come from a minuscule 0.1% of corporations. Those companies with a taxable income of R100 million a year contribute 65% of all company tax.'

And things got worse after that.

The local business environment is simply not conducive to supporting ideas on the scale of Musk's imagination. To be fair, only Silicon Valley could have provided the sort of incubation of ideas that had the funding and the investor patience to bring them to fruition. Just as Silicon Valley is an outlier in terms of environments in which ideas can flourish, Musk himself is an outlier, and most entrepreneurs would have crashed and burned in that pressure-cooker environment. In addition, personal success is never the work of only one individual.

Even the world's smartest individuals with the best ideas need a productive ecosystem around them that draws like-minded people together, who share similar goals and aspirations to develop ideas into world-beating businesses. The Silicon Valley environment is precisely that sort of place, and it has not happened by accident.

American entrepreneur Sam Altman described it well in the *Financial Times*, 'The natural state of a start-up is to die; most start-ups require multiple miracles in their early days to escape this fate. But the density and breadth of the Silicon Valley network does sometimes let start-ups cheat death. Silicon Valley works because there is such a high density of people working on start-ups and they are inclined to help each other. Other tech hubs have this as well but this is a case of Metcalfe's law – the utility of a network is proportional to the square of the number of nodes on the network. Silicon Valley has far more nodes in the network than anywhere else,' he wrote, and remarkably does not rely on old school tie or any social connections. 'Silicon Valley is a community of outsiders that have come together. If you build something good, people will help you.'

The entrepreneurial environment of Silicon Valley has evolved over time and is characterised by innovation, collaboration and risk-taking. It is one where many of the start-ups are founded by ex-employees of established tech giants who are drawn to the area and has thus become a highly supportive environment for entrepreneurial ventures.

Many of South Africa's wealthiest families are descendants of immigrants themselves.

German-born Ernest Oppenheimer arrived in South Africa from Britain as a diamond buyer in Kimberley for Dunkelsbuhler and Company at the age of 22 in 1902. It was a heady time and the young Oppenheimer saw plenty of opportunity. He was a serial over-achiever in a generation of high achievers who had descended on South Africa to make their fortunes.

He became mayor of Kimberley a decade after arriving in the town and, by 1917, had started Anglo American in partnership with US-born William Honnold, with funding from J.P. Morgan. He became a member of parliament in 1924 and still ran his business interests, gaining control of De Beers in 1927. He was succeeded by his son Harry and later by his grandson Nicky. The family remained invested in De Beers into the twenty-first century, when it sold its stake to Anglo American for about $5 billion. The Oppenheimers are still domiciled in South Africa and, like many other wealthy families, including the Motsepes and Ruperts, made significant contributions to the Solidarity Fund to help bridge gaps in government efforts to deal with Covid-19.

But capital goes where the opportunities are. In 2021, the family office for Nicky Oppenheimer and his part UK-based son Jonathan set up an outpost in Singapore to boost its Asia exposure and partner with that region's wealthy elite, using professional management headed up by a former chief of staff for Oppenheimer Generations, Edoardo Collevecchio, who told Reuters that the synergies between Africa and Asia would be substantial over the next three decades.

The Oppenheimers followed the likes of Google co-founder Sergey Brin and Dyson founder James Dyson in setting up investment companies in Singapore, where family offices have grown fivefold from 2017 to 2019, thanks to its high levels of governance, tax treaties and political stability. This is precisely what Karooooo's Zak Calisto has done. Money, like water, follows the path of least resistance.

There is also a temporary migration of skills as a result of better opportunities elsewhere.

Among them is classically trained opera singer Pretty Yende, who has graced global stages to critical acclaim. South African comedians are also finding new markets, most notably Trevor Noah, who has become firmly entrenched in the US late-night television scene after taking over *The Daily Show* from the respected Jon Stewart. Noah won the audience over and has become a global star of the comedy scene. When attempting to break into international markets, he shared a London agent with Loyiso Gola and Conrad Koch. Gola has managed to crack the UK comedy scene and has performed at the Hammersmith Apollo, while Koch is increasingly focused on globalising his ventriloquism, most notably with his Chester Missing character.

'Ventriloquism is having a revival worldwide. I've always

suspected that the mix of current affairs, stand-up style writing and uniqueness of being from Africa would be a great sell globally, so taking what I do to the world has always been part of the plan. The biggest hurdle is that my comedy is often very political, which is itself a sell, but to get it to make sense to international audiences it would need an immense amount of time outside of the local market. That process is wildly expensive because it means not earning here while you develop there,' says Koch.

Koch tested the waters at the Just for Laughs Comedy Festival in Montreal, where he rebuilt his entire body of work for the Canadian market, and he then moved on to tour small Canadian fringe festivals. He describes the response as 'explosively good'. He received glowing five-star reviews in Canada and a similar response in Australia. Koch was set to debut at the Edinburgh Festival in 2020, when lockdowns put those plans on ice. Like South Africa's biggest music export, Johnny Clegg, Koch studied anthropology, and he believes it has given him a unique view on the world and the ability to deliver material on contentious subjects like race and a post-colonial world in a way that is globally relatable.

'The South African market is very small, and the money to be made globally is ridiculous. The only other ventriloquist on earth who I know of who does anything close to what I do, combining current affairs with ventriloquism, is Jeff Dunham. Dunham allegedly makes $25 million a year. I would be crazy not to give it a shot,' Koch imparts.

# CHAPTER 16

· · · · · · · · · · · · ·

# Future Imperfect

*The best way to predict the future is to create it.*
— Abraham Lincoln

In *Guns, Germs, and Steel,* author Jared Diamond argues that one of the reasons some countries succeed and others fail has to do with where they are located and how well-endowed they are with natural resources. That is certainly part of the story. South Africa, for the first 200-odd years of its colonial history, had the advantage of geography due to its strategic location along the spice route. It had also been generously endowed with the natural resources upon which its industrial economy was built.

But along the way, its custodians made catastrophic choices, the consequences of which we will live with for generations to come. The biggest of these was the calculated and forced exclusion of black people from the economy. The choices of policy-makers, from the time of Jan van Riebeeck all the way to F.W. de Klerk, set South Africa on a direct course for conflict and catastrophe.

De Klerk's momentous decision to release political prisoners and unban liberation movement parties changed the course of history for the better. What followed a period of great uncertainty to the political transition was nothing short of remarkable as the country saw a decade and a half of unbroken expansion, in which jobs were created, inflation was tamed and growth ran at close to 5%.

It was by no means perfect, but it showed what was possible when sensible choices are made. The country was embraced back into the global community, trade resumed, and its corporations and citizens were no longer regarded as international pariahs. The world loves a comeback story. South Africa was on a sustainable trajectory, only to have that dashed by the lost decade of Jacob Zuma.

There was a great deal of optimism that the country would pull itself back from the brink when Cyril Ramaphosa won leadership of the ANC in December 2017. When he attended the World Economic Forum gathering in Davos in January 2018 as the incoming president, he was greeted with open arms. That goodwill was squandered, however, as the ANC descended into its factional battles within months of Ramaphosa assuming office, and the true extent of state capture was gradually exposed.

Ramaphosa's failure to take control and ensure the speedy prosecution of the perpetrators of state capture was seen as weak and created the impression of a false, rather than a new, dawn. As the ANC once again prepares to elect its leadership for another five-year period in December 2022, there will be attempts by a significantly weakened but no-less-determined faction within the party to unseat him and regain control of the levers of political power.

The world is wondering when exactly Ramaphosa will play his hand and institute the multitude of spoken-about reforms required to get South Africa back on a sustainable growth path. When De Klerk faced down the nationalist hardliners in his own party and chose to release political prisoners in 1990, it was not because he had had some kind of Damascene conversion – he did it because he was out of options. Ramaphosa, too, is out of options. He either reforms his party or he allows the country to be taken further down the path of self-destruction.

University of Chicago scholar James Robinson argues the point that success is not about exogenous factors but rather about the way humans organise themselves in their societies that makes the difference between those who succeed and those who fail.

Ideally, you want plenty of resources and you want to be well-located geographically near rich and peace-loving neighbours who share your values for common prosperity. But it is about the choices we make in how we organise our societies that makes the difference between progress and regression. When there is daily conflict for even the most basic of resources for survival, societies are going to be far less likely to progress than those where most citizens do not have to worry about whether their children will have enough food today or whether their teachers, when they do turn up, will be imparting anything of any real value in the classroom.

Economists understand what generates prosperity. They know that it is about investment in safety, public healthcare and education, property rights and consistent innovation. So, if it is that easy, why can Haiti not get it right, or, for that matter, Lebanon or South Africa?

So much of what defines a successful country is based on a set of common values and how those determine the actions policy-makers take to improve life for citizens as a whole. In his book, *Why Nations Fail*, co-authored with Daron Acemoglu, Robinson looks at a city on the border between the US and Mexico called Nogales.

The only difference between one part of the town and the other is that there is a border fence that runs through the middle of the settlement. It should be fairly similar on both sides of the border – the northern half is American, the southern half is Mexican. North of the fence, in Nogales, Arizona, people invest in businesses and houses with a high degree of certainty that they are unlikely to fall victim to crime or the possibility that the government is going to take away their assets. They have decent incomes and their children go to good schools. The same cannot be said for the people who live on the opposite side of the fence in Mexico, where incomes are a third lower, education standards at a fraction of what they are across town and there is a far higher infant mortality rate.

There is little to separate the city geographically and there are no wild disparities in climate. Yet, living standards on the northern side are considerably higher than those in the south. The reasons are not dissimilar to those spelled out by Alan Beattie in *False Economy*. It is about the choices citizens make about the way in which their countries are governed, who pays tax, how much and how often, and how that money is used in society to shore up services to the population.

Societies that outperform create appropriate incentives to do

so in a conducive environment. South Africans must be incentivised to invest in South Africa. The lack of clarity around policy
and the rise in populist rhetoric as the ANC sees its once enormous popularity wane is devastating to long-term investment.

Decades of underinvestment as a result of widespread corruption and the deployment of political appointees to positions of
considerable political and budgetary influence have seen mounting failures in the delivery of basic services. The private sector
has been left with little choice but to intercede, which is why you
can go to a supermarket to renew the licence disc for your car or
to your bank to renew your passport. These are public–private
sector partnerships that have been created to improve basic delivery of services, which are already funded by tax money and
which should be provided by the state without any third-party assistance at all. The same goes for education, health cover, security
and, increasingly, electricity and water as wealthy South Africans
take themselves off the grid to minimise the risk of service failure
by state entities.

On the one hand, it shows a systemic failure; on the other
hand, it shows the marvels of collaboration and how when state
services do fail there is a willing and capable private sector to
pick up the pieces. It should not be necessary, but it is. Private-
sector companies fill potholes in large metropolitan cities in a
part-public-service/part-marketing campaign/part-survival exercise to limit claims. A charity delivers water to residents when
municipal water infrastructure fails, and drills for water at one
of the country's leading public hospitals because the government
department tasked with doing the job fails to do so.

In *The Upside of Down*, I detailed how that failure of the state has led to considerable opportunity for the private sector to provide alternatives to failed services. Fed up with Eskom? – get off the grid with renewable energy. Worried about crime? – hire as much private security as you feel is necessary. Scared about water security? – drill a borehole/build a massive underground storage tank to reserve rainwater. Need to get a Christmas card to Granny? – send it via courier. But that has come at considerable additional cost to the South African economy, both in terms of taxpayers having to fork out twice for practically everything they need done and in terms of the majority of people living with a dearth of state support.

Entrepreneurs cannot succeed long term if they do not have appropriate infrastructure that helps them do their work. They need a functioning government in order to ensure that the roads and ports work so they can get their product to market; they need to be able to rely on law and order to respond quickly in an emergency; and they need to have a predictable path in terms of economic policy that is accommodative to growth. So much of local businesses' energy is absorbed in finding ways around obsolete processes. Imagine what could happen if safety, energy, water provision and other functions could be relied upon to function.

The world is a frightening enough place without South Africans adding endless variations of self-harm into the mix. From climate change and global inequality in the aftermath of the pandemic to the weaponising of information and the speed with which it moves unchallenged across social media – all affect our thinking as to how we approach the world. It would be helpful if our domestic politics and the contestation it leads to were less destructive.

Don't you admire people who not only make to-do lists but also systematically work through them, tackling one thing at a time? The reason productive people are more effective than the rest of us is because of the ability to prioritise what is important and take action to resolve it, before moving on to less important issues.

Probably the biggest stroke of genius that has protected South Africa from the worst excesses of some of its more vulgar politicians has been the relentless focus on inflation targeting by the Reserve Bank. Monetary policy alone cannot drive an economy, but it can provide a stable base upon which a well-managed economy can thrive.

Over the past two decades, the South African Reserve Bank has avoided the 20%-plus inflation death spirals of the 1970s and 1980s by focusing on one thing only – keeping inflation within a band of 3% to 6%. Inflation targeting is a tool used by central banks to specify an ideal inflation rate or, as in the case of the Reserve Bank, a range. The only way to manage it is through interest rates. If inflation rises, so must rates to remove money from the financial system, thereby discouraging spending, which lessens demand and keeps a lid on prices. Should inflation drop too low, that can stifle growth, so central banks cut rates to make money more plentiful, and that encourages consumer and business spending.

It is technical and really quite boring stuff. What it has achieved, however, is not.

It has delivered a period of relative monetary policy stability. One only needs to look at the chaos that erupted in the Turkish financial system in 2021 when that country's president intervened in the central bank and its policy-making efforts, causing the lira to tumble in value and interest rates to spiral.

In 2018, Lesetja Kganyago was voted Central Banker of the Year by his peers for withstanding considerable pressure to allow the state capture crowd in. Instead, he focused on his job. He did just one thing – manage price stability.

'In South Africa today, we are playing for high stakes. There are things going right and there are things going wrong. We could tip into a bad equilibrium – or into a good one. The recent spate of looting gave us a glimpse of an unacceptable future: a prolonged breakdown in law and order, large numbers of violent deaths, extensive destruction of property, and shortages of even basic goods such as fuel, food and medicine. At the same time, 2021 has brought us good news. Prices for our export commodities have increased strongly. Our terms of trade, which compare the costs of our imports to the prices of our exports, have never been more favourable. Our economic recovery from the Covid-19 shock has proceeded faster than expected, despite disruptions. Although we are learning many horrifying details about state capture, the process of repairing our institutions is clearly moving forward. There is tangible progress on structural reforms,' Kganyago said at a lecture on inflation targeting delivered in Stellenbosch.

In that same speech, Kganyago made another salient point, which speaks to the art of list-making. The Reserve Bank's success at managing the critical backbone of the economy has come down to a relentless focus on just one thing: inflation targeting.

'If everything is a priority, then nothing is a priority,' the governor said.

It is time for a plan that outlines those priorities, one by one by one.

What would your number-one priority be?

Mine would be job creation.

It sounds good and would bring a roar of approval at a political rally; it might even bring hope and, for a while at least, some votes. But it is a non-starter. So scratch it off the list. We do need jobs, but not in the way we have been trying and failing at miserably to achieve so far.

Why is the US short of workers? It has a thriving economy that expands and contracts according to the prevailing economic cycle. People who build businesses need others to help them do the work, so they do the hiring, pay the salaries and ensure that the ensuing tax revenues are paid to the relevant authority, which then disburses the money to where it is needed. And when someone fails at their job, they are fired and have to find a new opportunity better suited to them, leaving the position they messed up open to someone else.

It is brutally efficient. And, as was demonstrated, the system sheds jobs faster than it creates them in a time of crisis to give the businesses a chance at survival, so that when the cycle turns, they can once again invite applications to work.

Focus on this one thing and gradually the rest will start to fall into place.

To his credit, in his sixth State of the Nation Address in February 2022, the president was less about bullet trains and smart cities and more about the practical reality of giving the economy a fighting chance at recovery.

Wearing a locally made suit and shoes stitched in KwaZulu-Natal, the president, more modestly turned out than normal, punted the benefits of localisation.

It was only in partnership with the private sector, Ramaphosa finally acknowledged, that the capital required for investment in failing public infrastructure would be forthcoming and, with that, private money and the skills needed to do the work would follow.

He announced the beginning of the end of Eskom's monopoly on selling electricity, by publishing legislative amendments that enable the trading and reselling of electricity among private players.

Ramaphosa also announced amendments to the Business Act to review obstacles to doing business in South Africa and appointed a private-sector executive to his office to help shred red tape. Former Exxaro CEO Sipho Nkosi became the latest in a series of appointments to his office to tackle a range of issues that should be fixed by departments and the ministers in them, but that have failed to materialise.

The president has several obstacles to success. The biggest is his own party, which recent elections have shown is rapidly losing popularity, leading to desperation among some of its factions that are dependent on the cash cow of the state to fund their livelihoods. Also, Ramaphosa needs to regain credibility, to act on big decisions faster than he does, even relatively simple ones like the appointment of a chief justice. His propensity for consultation leads to the perception, increasingly hard to stifle, that he is indecisive.

There are no quick fixes, but there are actions that can be taken quickly that can show the power of progressive governance in freeing up capital and crowding in productive elements of the private sector. Bear in mind that the likes of the Guptas and their numerous acolytes were private-sector players – so this cannot be a free-for-all, but what it could do is create a culture of confidence in an economy that, if you look at Stellenbosch University's Bureau for Economic Research's Business Confidence Index, has been negative almost consistently since 2008. Confidence provides its own stimulus. Once private-sector players see real action being taken to address their major concerns, they will start to invest. There is no shortage of capital for the rebuilding of South Africa, its infrastructure and its key institutions – it just needs the security to do so.

It is easy to lose hope and dismiss South Africa as a failure waiting to happen.

But it does not have to be that way. Smart policy choices will radically alter the country's economic trajectory. A good place to start would be choices that reduce the regulatory burden and remove barriers to entry for foreign investment eager to see the country succeed, if only as a gateway to the rest of Africa.

Reforms that would lead to job creation by a private sector willing to risk capital because it is encouraged to generate a reasonable return would instil renewed hope that an economic recovery is possible.

Utilising the damning findings of the Zondo Commission report to prosecute those at the centre of the state capture project would go a long way to demonstrating that law and order not only exist but are also applied regardless of social, political or economic status. Putting guilty people in jail would act as a warning amid worrying levels of rising lawlessness that there are consequences for those who break the law.

Not everything has to happen at once. But progress must be visible.

# Acknowledgements

Whatever glory there is in the publication of a book goes to the author, but its creation is the work of an extraordinary group of unsung heroes, without whom none of us would manage to get our work to you.

To Pan Macmillan South Africa, under the leadership of Terry Morris, to the ever-tolerant publisher Andrea Nattrass and the team of great people whose mission in life is to get this and other books into your hands, thank you.

To proofreader Wesley Thompson and editor Sally Hines for panel beating an occasionally chaotic manuscript into its current coherent form, thank you. To Dr Nechama Brodie, whose super-lative research skills lubricated the passage of this book, thank you for wading through the detritus on the internet and finding the data I needed from which to hang the stories in this book.

To 'Team Bruce' at Mojalefa Media: Catherine Goodwin, Brett Walters and Pippa Rowles – your tolerance and support is greatly appreciated.

It takes a special kind of masochism to write a book, but it is also tough on those nearest and dearest, as those who write while holding down a day job and a couple of side hustles become obsessive, reclusive and flick between bouts of euphoria and despair as the manuscript develops.

To my boys, who would prefer it if I never wrote another book, I only hope that you can be as lucky as I am to meet and be inspired by so many brilliant, brave and remarkable individuals as are featured in this book. These are some of the people who are helping to shape the world you are inheriting. It is a privilege to tell their stories and to learn from their courage and determination as they dream up, create, build and expand their ideas and make them relevant to the world.

For as long as there are remarkable people in the world, I have to tell their stories.

# Also by Bruce Whitfield

*The Upside of Down: How Chaos and Uncertainty Breed Opportunity in South Africa* (updated edition 2021)

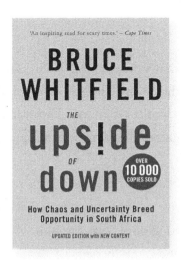

In a world shaped by Covid-19 and characterised by fake news, manipulated feeds of information and divisive social media agendas, it's easy to believe that our time is the most challenging in human history. It's just not true.

It is a time of extraordinary opportunity. But only if you have the right mindset and attitude. Fear of the future breeds inaction and leads to strategic paralysis. Problem solvers thrive in chaotic and uncertain times because they act to change their future. Winners recognise that in a world of growing uncertainty, you need to resort to actions on things you can control.

A robust mindset is the one common characteristic Bruce

Whitfield has identified in two decades of interrogating how South Africa's billionaires and start-up mavericks think differently. They don't ignore risk or hope that problems will go away. They constantly measure, manage, consider and weigh up opportunities in a tumultuous sea of uncertainty and find ways around obstacles.

'With everything that's happening right now, it's easy to get bogged down with doom and gloom. In this book, Bruce Whitfield shares his wealth of financial knowledge and shows how to snap free of negative thinking and adopt a can-do mindset.'
– *YOU* magazine

'Opportunities arrive all the time but, because of an atmosphere of doom and gloom, not enough of us dare to dream. Whitfield understands the power of storytelling in channelling positive energies towards turning those visions into reality.'
– Karina M. Szczurek, *Cape Times*

'If one is tired of the negative headlines, this is the ideal book to help ignite a renewed sense of hope. Packed with stories about ordinary South Africans who rose in times of great difficulty, *The Upside of Down* is testament to its title, and perhaps all that is needed is a shift in perspective.'
– *The Namibian*

**Find out more at**
**www.brucewhitfield.com**